Get the eBook FREE!

(PDF, ePub, Kindle, and liveBook all included)

We believe that once you buy a book from us, you should be able to read it in any format we have available. To get electronic versions of this book at no additional cost to you, purchase and then register this book at the Manning website.

Go to https://www.manning.com/freebook and follow the instructions to complete your pBook registration.

That's it!
Thanks from Manning!

T0386016

Data Science with Python and Dask

JESSE C. DANIEL

MANNING
SHELTER ISLAND

For online information and ordering of this and other Manning books, please visit www.manning.com. The publisher offers discounts on this book when ordered in quantity.

For more information, please contact

Special Sales Department
Manning Publications Co.
20 Baldwin Road
PO Box 761
Shelter Island, NY 11964
Email: orders@manning.com

Manning Publications Co.
20 Baldwin Road
PO Box 761
Shelter Island, NY 11964

Development editor:	Dustin Archibald
Technical development editor:	Mike Shepard
Review editor:	Ivan Martinović
Production editor:	Deirdre S. Hiam
Copyeditor:	Michelle Melani
Proofreader:	Melody Dolab
Technical proofreader:	Karsten Strøbæk
Typesetter:	Happenstance Type-O-Rama
Cover designer:	Marija Tudor

ISBN 9781617295607
Printed and bound by CPI Group (UK) Ltd, Croydon, CR0 4YY

To Clementine

contents

v

CONTENTS

PART 3 EXTENDING AND DEPLOYING DASK 179

9   *Working with Bags and Arrays   181*

9.1   Reading and parsing unstructured data with Bags   183
        *Selecting and viewing data from a Bag   184 • Common
        parsing issues and how to overcome them   185 • Working
        with delimiters   186*

9.2   Transforming, filtering, and folding elements   192
        *Transforming elements with the map method   193 • Filtering Bags
        with the filter method   195 • Calculating descriptive statistics
        on Bags   198 • Creating aggregate functions using the foldby
        method   199*

9.3   Building Arrays and DataFrames from Bags   201

9.4   Using Bags for parallel text analysis with NLTK   203
        *The basics of bigram analysis   203 • Extracting tokens and
        filtering stopwords   204 • Analyzing the bigrams   208*

10   *Machine learning with Dask-ML   211*

10.1   Building linear models with Dask-ML   213
        *Preparing the data with binary vectorization   214 • Building a
        logistic regression model with Dask-ML   220*

10.2   Evaluating and tuning Dask-ML models   222
        *Evaluating Dask-ML models with the score method   222
        Building a naïve Bayes classifier with Dask-ML   223
        Automatically tuning hyperparameters   224*

10.3   Persisting Dask-ML models   227

11   *Scaling and deploying Dask   229*

11.1   Building a Dask cluster on Amazon AWS with
        Docker   230
        *Getting started   232 • Creating a security key   233 • Creating the
        ECS cluster   234 • Configuring the cluster's networking   237
        Creating a shared data drive in Elastic File System   241
        Allocating space for Docker images in Elastic Container
        Repository   246 • Building and deploying images for scheduler,
        worker, and notebook   246 • Connecting to the cluster   253*

11.2   Running and monitoring Dask jobs on a cluster   256

11.3   Cleaning up the Dask cluster on AWS   261

appendix   *Software installation   263*

preface

The data science community is such an interesting, dynamic, and fast-paced place to work. While my journey as a data scientist so far has only been around five years long, it feels as though I've already seen a lifetime of tools, technologies, and trends come and go. One consistent effort has been a focus on continuing to make data science easier. Lowering barriers to entry and developing better libraries have made data science more accessible than ever. That there is such a bright, diverse, and dedicated community of software architects and developers working tirelessly to improve data science for everyone has made my experience writing *Data Science with Python and Dask* an incredibly humbling—and at times intimidating—experience. But, nonetheless, it is a great honor to be able to contribute to this vibrant community by showcasing the truly excellent work that the entire team of Dask maintainers and contributors have produced.

I stumbled across Dask in early 2016 when I encountered my first uncomfortably large dataset at work. After fumbling around for days with Hadoop, Spark, Ambari, ZooKeeper, and the menagerie of Apache "big data" technologies, I, in my exasperation, simply Googled "big data library python." After tabbing through pages of results, I was left with two options: continue banging my head against PySpark or figure out how to use chunking in Pandas. Just about ready to call my search efforts futile, I spotted a StackOverflow question that mentioned a library called Dask. Once I found my way over to where Dask was hosted on GitHub, I started working my way through the documentation. DataFrames for big datasets? An API that mimics Pandas? It can be installed using pip? It seemed too good to be true. But it wasn't. I was incensed—why hadn't I heard of this library before? Why was something this powerful and easy to use flying under the radar at a time when the big data craze was reaching fever pitch?

After having great success using Dask for my work project, I was determined to become an evangelist. I was teaching a Python for Data Science class at the University of Denver at the time, and I immediately began looking for ways to incorporate Dask into the curriculum. I also presented several talks and workshops at my local PyData chapter's meetups in Denver. Finally, when I was approached by the folks at Manning to write a book on Dask, I agreed without hesitation. As you read this book, I hope you also come to see how awesome and useful Dask is to have in your arsenal of data science tools!

acknowledgments

As a new author, one thing I learned very quickly is that there are many, many people involved in producing a book. I absolutely would not have survived without all the wonderful support, feedback, and encouragement I've received over the course of writing the book.

First, I'd like to thank Stephen Soehnlen at Manning for approaching me with the idea to write this book, and Marjan Bace for green-lighting it. They took a chance on me, a first-time author, and for that I am truly appreciative. Next, a huge thanks to my development editor, Dustin Archibald, for patiently guiding me through Manning's writing and revising processes while also pushing me to become a better writer and teacher. Similarly, a big thanks to Mike Shepard, my technical editor, for sanity checking all my code and offering yet another channel of feedback. I'd also like to thank Tammy Coron and Toni Arritola for helping to point me in the right direction early on in the writing process.

Next, thank you to all the reviewers who provided excellent feedback throughout the course of writing this book: Al Krinker, Dan Russell, Francisco Sauceda, George Thomas, Gregory Matuszek, Guilherme Pereira de Freitas, Gustavo Patino, Jeremy Loscheider, Julien Pohie, Kanak Kshetri, Ken W. Alger, Lukasz Tracewski, Martin Czygan, Pauli Sutelainen, Philip Patterson, Raghavan Srinivasan, Rob Koch, Romain Jouin, Ruairi O'Reilly, Steve Atchue, and Suresh Rangarajulu.. Special thanks as well to Ivan Martinović for coordinating the peer review process and organizing all the feedback, and to Karsten Strøbæk for giving my code another pass before handing off to production.

I'd also like to thank Bert Bates, Becky Rinehart, Nichole Beard, Matko Hrvatin and the entire graphics team at Manning, Chris Kaufmann, Ana Romac, Owen Roberts and the folks at Manning's marketing department, Nicole Butterfield, Rejhana Markanovic, and Lori Kehrwald. A big thank-you also goes out to Francesco Bianchi, Mike Stephens, Deirdre Hiam, Michelle Melani, Melody Dolab, Tiffany Taylor, and the countless other individuals who worked behind the scenes to make *Data Science with Python and Dask* a great success!

Finally, I'd like to give a special thanks to my wife, Clementine, for her patient understanding on the many nights and weekends that I holed up in my office to work on the book. I couldn't have done this without your infinite love and support. I also wouldn't have had this opportunity without the inspiration of my dad to pursue a career in technology and the not-so-gentle nudging of my mom to do my English homework. I love you both!

about this book

Who should read this book

Data Science with Python and Dask takes you on a hands-on journey through a typical data science workflow—from data cleaning through deployment—using Dask. The book begins by presenting some foundational knowledge of scalable computing and explains how Dask takes advantage of those concepts to operate on datasets big and small. Building on that foundation, it then turns its focus to preparing, analyzing, visualizing, and modeling various real-world datasets to give you tangible examples of how to use Dask to perform common data science tasks. Finally, the book ends with a step-by-step walkthrough of deploying your very own Dask cluster on AWS to scale out your analysis code.

Data Science with Python and Dask was primarily written with beginner to intermediate data scientists, data engineers, and analysts in mind, specifically those who have not yet mastered working with datasets that push the limits of a single machine. While prior experience with other distributed frameworks (such as PySpark) is not necessary, readers who have such experience can also benefit from this book by being able to compare the capabilities and ergonomics of Dask. There are various articles and documentation available online, but none are focused specifically on using Dask for data science in such a comprehensive manner as this book.

How this book is organized: A roadmap

This book has three sections that cover 11 chapters.

Part 1 lays some foundational knowledge about scalable computing and provides a few simple examples of how Dask uses these concepts to scale out workloads.

- Chapter 1 introduces Dask by building a case for why it's an important tool to have in your data science toolkit. It also introduces and explains *directed acyclic*

xiii

graphs (DAGs), a core concept for scalable computing that's central to Dask's architecture.

- Chapter 2 ties what you learned conceptually about DAGs in chapter 1 to how Dask uses DAGs to distribute work across multiple CPU cores and even physical machines. It goes over how to visualize the DAGs automatically generated by the task scheduler, and how the task scheduler divides up resources to efficiently process data.

Part 2 covers common data cleaning, analysis, and visualization tasks with structured data using the Dask DataFrame construct.

- Chapter 3 describes the conceptual design of Dask DataFrames and how they abstract and parallelize Pandas DataFrames.
- Chapter 4 discusses how to create Dask DataFrames from various data sources and formats, such as text files, databases, S3, and Parquet files.
- Chapter 5 is a deep dive into using DataFrames to clean and transform datasets. It covers sorting, filtering, dealing with missing values, joining datasets, and writing DataFrames in several file formats.
- Chapter 6 covers using built-in aggregate functions (such as sum, mean, and so on), as well as writing your own aggregate and window functions. It also discusses how to produce basic descriptive statistics.
- Chapter 7 steps through creating basic visualizations, such as pairplots and heatmaps.
- Chapter 8 builds on chapter 7 and covers advanced visualizations with interactivity and geographic features.

Part 3 covers advanced topics in Dask, such as unstructured data, machine learning, and building scalable workloads.

- Chapter 9 demonstrates how to parse, clean, and analyze unstructured data using Dask Bags and Arrays.
- Chapter 10 shows how to build machine learning models from Dask data sources, as well as testing and persisting trained models.
- Chapter 11 completes the book by walking through how to set up a Dask cluster on AWS using Docker.

You can either opt to read the book sequentially if you prefer a step-by-step narrative or skip around if you are interested in learning how to perform specific tasks. Regardless, you should read chapters 1 and 2 to form a good understanding of how Dask is able to scale out workloads from multiple CPU cores to multiple machines. You should also reference the appendix for specific information on setting up Dask and some of the other packages used in the text.

About the code

A primary way this book teaches the material is by providing hands-on examples on real-world datasets. As such, there are many numbered code listings throughout the book. While there is no code in line with the rest of the text, at times a variable or method name that appears in a numbered code listing is referenced for explanation. These are differentiated by using `this text style` wherever references are made. Many code listings also contain annotations to further explain what the code means.

All the code is available in Jupyter Notebooks and can be downloaded at www .manning.com/books/data-science-at-scale-with-python-and-dask. Each notebook cell relates to one of the numbered code listings and is presented in order of how the listings appear in the book.

liveBook discussion forum

Purchase of *Data Science with Python and Dask* includes free access to a private web forum run by Manning Publications where you can make comments about the book, ask technical questions, and receive help from the author and from other users. To access the forum, go to https://livebook.manning.com/#!/book/data-science-with-python-and -dask. You can also learn more about Manning's forums and the rules of conduct at https://livebook.manning.com/#!/discussion.

Manning's commitment to our readers is to provide a venue where a meaningful dialogue between individual readers and between readers and the author can take place. It is not a commitment to any specific amount of participation on the part of the author, whose contribution to the forum remains voluntary (and unpaid). We suggest you try asking the author some challenging questions lest his interest stray! The forum and the archives of previous discussions will be accessible from the publisher's website as long as the book is in print.

about the author

Jesse C. Daniel has five years' experience writing applications in Python, including three years working within the PyData stack (Pandas, NumPy, SciPy, scikit-learn). He joined the faculty of the University of Denver in 2016 as an adjunct professor of business information and analytics, where he taught a Python for Data Science course. He currently leads a team of data scientists at a Denver-based ad tech company.

about the cover illustration

The figure on the cover of *Data Science with Python and Dask* is captioned "La Bourbon-nais." The illustration is taken from a collection of works by many artists, edited by Louis Curmer and published in Paris in 1841. The title of the collection is *Les Français peints par eux-mêmes*, which translates as *The French People Painted by Themselves*. Each illustration is finely drawn and colored by hand and the rich variety of drawings in the collection reminds us vividly of how culturally apart the world's regions, towns, villages, and neighborhoods were just 200 years ago. Isolated from each other, people spoke different dialects and languages. In the streets or in the countryside, it was easy to identify where they lived and what their trade or station in life was just by their dress.

Dress codes have changed since then and the diversity by region, so rich at the time, has faded away. It is now hard to tell apart the inhabitants of different continents, let alone different towns or regions. Perhaps we have traded cultural diversity for a more varied personal life—certainly for a more varied and fast-paced technological life.

At a time when it is hard to tell one computer book from another, Manning celebrates the inventiveness and initiative of the computer business with book covers based on the rich diversity of regional life of two centuries ago, brought back to life by pictures from collections such as this one.

Part 1

The building blocks of scalable computing

This part of the book covers some fundamental concepts in scalable computing to give you a good basis for understanding what makes Dask different and how it works "under the hood."

In chapter 1, you'll learn what a *directed acyclic graph* (DAG) is and why it's useful for scaling out workloads across many different workers.

Chapter 2 explains how Dask uses DAGs as an abstraction to enable you to analyze huge datasets and take advantage of scalability and parallelism whether you're running your code on a laptop or a cluster of thousands of machines.

Once you've completed part 1, you'll have a basic understanding of the internals of Dask, and you'll be ready to get some hands-on experience with a real dataset.

Why scalable computing matters

Welcome to *Data Science with Python and Dask*! Since you've decided to pick up this book, no doubt you are interested in data science and machine learning—perhaps you're even a practicing data scientist, analyst, or machine learning engineer. However, I suspect that you're either currently facing a significant challenge, or you've faced it at some point in your career. I'm talking, of course, about the notorious challenges that arise when working with large datasets. The symptoms are easy to spot: painfully long run times—even for the simplest of calculations—unstable code, and unwieldy workflows. But don't despair! These challenges have become commonplace as both the expense and effort to collect and store vast quantities of data have declined significantly. In response, the computer science community has put a great deal of effort into creating better, more accessible programming frameworks to reduce the complexity of working with massive datasets. While many different technologies and frameworks aim to solve these problems, few are as powerful and flexible as Dask. This book aims to take your data science skills to the next level by giving you the tools and techniques you need to analyze and model large datasets using Dask.

Who is this book for? Who is this book not for?

It's worth noting right away that Dask is well suited to solving a wide variety of problems including structured data analysis, large-scale simulations used in scientific computing, and general-purpose distributed computing. Dask's ability to generalize many classes of problems is unique, and if we attempted to cover every possible application in which we could use Dask, this would be quite a large book indeed! Instead, we will keep a narrow focus throughout the book on using Dask for data analysis and machine learning. While we will tangentially cover some of the more general-purpose aspects of Dask throughout the book (such as the Bag and Delayed APIs), they will not be our primary focus.

This book was primarily written with beginner to intermediate data scientists, data engineers, and analysts in mind, specifically those who have not yet mastered working with data sets that push the limits of a single machine. We will broadly cover all areas of a data science project from data preparation to analysis to model building with applications in Dask and take a deep dive into fundamentals of distributed computing.

While this book still has something to offer if you've worked with other distributed computing frameworks such as Spark, and you've already mastered the NumPy/SciPy/Pandas stack, you may find that this book is not at the appropriate altitude for you. Dask was designed to make scaling out NumPy and Pandas as simple and painless as possible, so you may be better served by other resources such as the API documentation.

While the majority of this book is centered around hands-on examples of typical tasks that you as a data scientist or data engineer will encounter on most projects, this chapter will cover some fundamental knowledge essential for understanding how Dask works "under the hood." First, we'll examine why a tool like Dask is even necessary to have in your data science toolkit and what makes it unique; then, we'll cover directed acyclic graphs, a concept that Dask uses extensively to control parallel execution of code. With that knowledge, you should have a better understanding of how Dask works when you ask it to crunch through a big dataset; this knowledge will serve you well as you continue through your Dask journey, and we will come back to this knowledge in later chapters when we walk through how to build out your own cluster in the cloud. With that in mind, we'll turn our focus to what makes Dask unique, and why it's a valuable tool for data science.

1.1 Why Dask?

For many modern organizations, the promise of data science's transformative powers is universally alluring—and for good reason. In the right hands, effective data science teams can transform mere ones and zeros into real competitive advantages. Making better decisions, optimizing business processes, and detecting strategic blind spots are all touted as benefits of investing in data science capabilities. However, what we call "data science" today isn't really a new idea. For the past several decades, organizations all over the world have been trying to find better ways to make strategic and tactical decisions. Using names like *decision support, business intelligence, analytics,* or just plain old *operations research,* the goals of each have been the same: keep tabs on what's happening and make better-informed decisions. What has changed in recent years, however, is that the barriers to learning and applying data science have been significantly lowered. Data science is no longer relegated to operations research journals or academic-like research and development arms of large consulting groups. A key enabler of bringing data science to the masses has been the rising popularity of the Python programming language and its powerful collection of libraries called the Python Open Data Science Stack. These libraries, which include NumPy, SciPy, Pandas, and scikit-learn, have become industry-standard tools that boast a large community of developers and plentiful learning materials. Other languages that have been historically favored for this kind of work, such as FORTRAN, MATLAB, and Octave, are more difficult to learn and don't have nearly the same amount of community support. For these reasons, Python and its Open Data Science Stack has become one of the most popular platforms both for learning data science and for everyday practitioners.

Alongside these developments in data science accessibility, computers have continued to become ever more powerful. This makes it easy to produce, collect, store, and process far more data than before, all at a price that continues to march downward. But this deluge of data now has many organizations questioning the value of collecting and storing all that data—and rightfully so! Raw data has no intrinsic value; it must be cleaned, scrutinized, and interpreted to extract actionable information out of it. Obviously, this is where you—the data scientist—come into play. Working with the Python Open Data Science Stack, data scientists often turn to tools like Pandas for data cleaning and exploratory data analysis, SciPy and NumPy to run statistical tests on the data, and scikit-learn to build predictive models. This all works well for relatively small-sized datasets that can comfortably fit into RAM. But because of the shrinking expense of data collection and storage, data scientists are more frequently working on problems that involve analyzing enormous datasets. These tools have upper limits to their feasibility when working with datasets beyond a certain size. Once the threshold is crossed, the problems described in the beginning of the chapter start to appear. But where is that threshold? To avoid the ill-defined and oft-overused term *big data*, we'll use a three-tiered definition throughout the book to describe different-sized datasets and the challenges that come with each. Table 1.1 describes the different criteria we'll use to define the terms *small dataset, medium dataset,* and *large dataset* throughout the book.

Table 1.1   A tiered definition of data sizes

Dataset type	Size range	Fits in RAM?	Fits on local disk?
Small dataset	Less than 2–4 GB	Yes	Yes
Medium dataset	Less than 2 TB	No	Yes
Large dataset	Greater than 2 TB	No	No

Small datasets are datasets that fit comfortably in RAM, leaving memory to spare for manipulation and transformations. They are usually no more than 2–4 GB in size, and complex operations like sorting and aggregating can be done without paging. Paging, or spilling to disk, uses a computer's persistent storage (such as a hard disk or solid-state drive) as an extra place to store intermediate results while processing. It can greatly slow down processing because persistent storage is less efficient than RAM at fast data access. These datasets are frequently encountered when learning data science, and tools like Pandas, NumPy, and scikit-learn are the best tools for the job. In fact, throwing more sophisticated tools at these problems is not only overkill, but can be counterproductive by adding unnecessary layers of complexity and management overhead that can reduce performance.

Medium datasets are datasets that cannot be held entirely in RAM but can fit comfortably in a single computer's persistent storage. These datasets typically range in size from 10 GB to 2 TB. While it's possible to use the same toolset to analyze both small datasets and medium datasets, a significant performance penalty is imposed because these tools must use paging in order to avoid out-of-memory errors. These datasets are also large enough that it can make sense to introduce parallelism to cut down processing time. Rather than limiting execution to a single CPU core, dividing the work across all available CPU cores can speed up computations substantially. However, Python was not designed to make sharing work between processes on multicore systems particularly easy. As a result, it can be difficult to take advantage of parallelism within Pandas.

Large datasets are datasets that can neither fit in RAM nor fit in a single computer's persistent storage. These datasets are typically above 2 TB in size, and depending on the problem, can reach into petabytes and beyond. Pandas, NumPy, and scikit-learn are not suitable at all for datasets of this size, because they were not inherently built to operate on distributed datasets.

Naturally, the boundaries between these thresholds are a bit fuzzy and depend on how powerful your computer is. The significance lies more in the different orders of magnitude rather than hard size limits. For example, on a very powerful computer, small data might be on the order of 10s of gigabytes, but not on the order of terabytes. Medium data might be on the order of 10s of terabytes, but not on the order of petabytes. Regardless, the most important takeaway is that there are advantages (and often necessities) of looking for alternative analysis tools when your dataset is pushing the limits of our definition of small data. However, choosing the right tool for the job can be equally challenging. Oftentimes, this can lead data scientists to get stuck with evaluating unfamiliar technologies, rewriting code in different languages, and generally slowing down the projects they are working on.

Dask was launched in late 2014 by Matthew Rocklin with aims to bring native scalability to the Python Open Data Science Stack and overcome its single-machine restrictions. Over time, the project has grown into arguably one of the best scalable computing frameworks available for Python developers. Dask consists of several different components and APIs, which can be categorized into three layers: the scheduler, low-level APIs, and high-level APIs. An overview of these components can be seen in figure 1.1.

What makes Dask so powerful is how these components and layers are built on top of one another. At the core is the task scheduler, which coordinates and monitors execution of computations across CPU cores and machines. These computations are represented in code as either Dask Delayed objects or Dask Futures objects (the key difference is the former are evaluated *lazily*—meaning they are evaluated just in time when the values are needed, while the latter are evaluated *eagerly*—meaning they are evaluated in real time regardless if the value is needed immediately or not). Dask's high-level APIs offer a layer of abstraction over Delayed and Futures objects. Operations on these high-level objects result in many parallel low-level operations managed by the task schedulers, which provides a seamless experience for the user. Because of this design, Dask brings four key advantages to the table:

- Dask is fully implemented in Python and natively scales NumPy, Pandas, and scikit-learn.
- Dask can be used effectively to work with both medium datasets on a single machine and large datasets on a cluster.
- Dask can be used as a general framework for parallelizing most Python objects.
- Dask has a very low configuration and maintenance overhead.

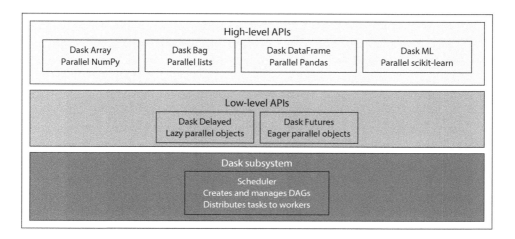

Figure 1.1 The components and layers than make up Dask

The first thing that sets Dask apart from the competition is that it is written and implemented entirely in Python, and its collection APIs natively scale NumPy, Pandas, and scikit-learn. This doesn't mean that Dask merely mirrors common operations and patterns that NumPy and Pandas users will find familiar; it means that the underlying objects used by Dask *are* corresponding objects from each respective library. A Dask DataFrame is made up of many smaller Pandas DataFrames, a Dask Array is made up of many smaller NumPy Arrays, and so forth. Each of the smaller underlying objects, called *chunks* or *partitions*, can be shipped from machine to machine within a cluster, or queued up and worked on one piece at a time locally. We will cover this process much more in depth later, but the approach of breaking up medium and large datasets into smaller pieces and managing the parallel execution of functions over those pieces is fundamentally how Dask is able to gracefully handle datasets that would be too large to work with otherwise. The practical result of using these objects to underpin Dask's distributed collections is that many of the functions, attributes, and methods that Pandas and NumPy users will already be familiar with are syntactically equivalent in Dask. This design choice makes transitioning from working with small datasets to medium and large datasets very easy for experienced Pandas, NumPy, and scikit-learn users. Rather than learning new syntax, transitioning data scientists can focus on the most important aspect of learning about scalable computing: writing code that's robust, performant, and optimized for parallelism. Fortunately, Dask does a lot of the heavy lifting for common use cases, but throughout the book we'll examine some best practices and pitfalls that will enable you to use Dask to its fullest extent.

Next, Dask is just as useful for working with medium datasets on a single machine as it is for working with large datasets on a cluster. Scaling Dask up or down is not at all complicated. This makes it easy for users to prototype tasks on their local machines and seamlessly submit those tasks to a cluster when needed. This can all be done without having to refactor existing code or write additional code to handle cluster-specific issues like resource management, recovery, and data movement. It also gives users a lot of flexibility to choose the best way to deploy and run their code. Oftentimes, using a cluster to work with medium datasets is entirely unnecessary, and can occasionally be slower due to the overhead involved with coordinating many machines to work together. Dask is optimized to minimize its memory footprint, so it can gracefully handle medium datasets even on relatively low-powered machines. This transparent scalability is thanks to Dask's well-designed built-in task schedulers. The local task scheduler can be used when Dask is running on a single machine, and the distributed task scheduler can be used for both local execution and execution across a cluster. Dask also supports interfacing with popular cluster resource managers such as YARN, Mesos, and Kubernetes, allowing you to use an existing cluster with the distributed task scheduler. Configuring the task scheduler and using resource managers to deploy Dask across any number of systems takes a minimal amount of effort. Throughout the book, we'll look at running Dask in different configurations: locally with the local task scheduler, and clustered in the cloud using the distributed task scheduler with Docker and Amazon Elastic Container Service.

One of the most unusual aspects of Dask is its inherent ability to scale most Python objects. Dask's low-level APIs, Dask Delayed and Dask Futures, are the common basis for scaling NumPy arrays used in Dask Array, Pandas DataFrames used in Dask DataFrame, and Python lists used in Dask Bag. Rather than building distributed applications from scratch, Dask's low-level APIs can be used directly to apply all of Dask's scalability, fault tolerance, and remote execution capabilities to any problem.

Finally, Dask is very lightweight and is easy to set up, tear down, and maintain. All its dependencies can be installed using the `pip` or `conda` package manager. It's very easy to build and deploy cluster worker images using Docker, which we will do later in the book, and Dask requires very little configuration out of the box. Because of this, Dask not only does well for handling recurring jobs, but is also a great tool for building proofs of concept and performing ad hoc data analysis.

A common question in the minds of data scientists discovering Dask for the first time is how it compares to other superficially similar technologies like Apache Spark. Spark has certainly become a very popular framework for analyzing large datasets and does quite well in this area. However, although Spark supports several different languages including Python, its legacy as a Java library can pose a few challenges to users who lack Java expertise. Spark was launched in 2010 as an in-memory alternative to the MapReduce processing engine for Apache Hadoop and is heavily reliant on the Java Virtual Machine (JVM) for its core functionality. Support for Python came along a few release cycles later, with an API called PySpark, but this API simply enables you to interact with a Spark cluster using Python. Any Python code that gets submitted to Spark must pass through the JVM using the Py4J library. This can make it quite difficult to fine-tune and debug PySpark code because some execution occurs outside of the Python context.

PySpark users may eventually determine that they need to migrate their codebase to Scala or Java anyway to get the most out of Spark. New features and enhancements to Spark are added to the Java and Scala APIs first, and it typically takes a few release cycles for that functionality to be exposed to PySpark. Furthermore, PySpark's learning curve isn't trivial. Its DataFrame API, while conceptually similar to Pandas, has substantial differences in syntax and structure. This means that new PySpark users must relearn how to do things "the Spark way" rather than draw from existing experience and knowledge of working with Pandas and scikit-learn. Spark is highly optimized to apply computations over collection objects, such as adding a constant to each item in an array or calculating the sum of an array. But this optimization comes at the price of flexibility. Spark is not equipped to handle code that can't be expressed as a map or reduce type operation over a collection. Therefore, you can't use Spark to scale out custom algorithms with the same elegance that you can with Dask. Spark is also notorious for its difficulty to set up and configure, requiring many dependencies such as Apache ZooKeeper and Apache Ambari, which can also be difficult to install and configure in their own right. It's not unusual for organizations that use Spark and Hadoop to have dedicated IT resources whose sole responsibility is to configure, monitor, and maintain the cluster.

This comparison is not intended to be unfair to Spark. Spark is very good at what it does and is certainly a viable solution for analyzing and processing large datasets. However, Dask's short learning curve, flexibility, and familiar APIs make Dask a more attractive solution for data scientists with a background in the Python Open Data Science Stack.

I hope that by now you're starting to see why Dask is such a powerful and versatile toolset. And, if my earlier suspicions were correct—that you decided to pick up this book because you're currently struggling with a large dataset—I hope you feel both encouraged to give Dask a try and excited to learn more about using Dask to analyze a real-world dataset. Before we look at some Dask code, however, it'll be good to review a few core concepts that will help you understand how Dask's task schedulers "divide and conquer" computations. This will be especially helpful if you're new to the idea of distributed computing because understanding the mechanics of task scheduling will give you a good idea of what happens when a computation is executed and where potential bottlenecks may lie.

1.2   *Cooking with DAGs*

Dask's task schedulers use the concept of directed acyclic graphs (or DAGs for short) to compose, control, and express computations. DAGs come from a larger body of mathematics known as *graph theory*. Unlike what you may expect from the name, graph theory doesn't have anything to do with pie charts or bar graphs. Instead, graph theory describes a graph as a representation of a set of objects that have a relationship with one another. While this definition is quite vague and abstract, it means graphs are useful for representing a very wide variety of information. Directed acyclic graphs have some special properties that give them a slightly narrower definition. But rather than continuing to talk about graphs in the abstract, let's have a look at an example of using a DAG to model a real process.

When I'm not busy writing, teaching, or analyzing data, I love cooking. To me, few things in this world can compare to a piping hot plate of pasta. And right up at the top of my all-time-favorite pasta dishes is bucatini all'Amatriciana. If you enjoy Italian cuisine, you'll love the bite of thick bucatini noodles, the sharp saltiness of Pecorino Romano cheese, and the peppery richness of the tomato sauce cooked with guanciale and onion. But I digress! My intent here is not for you to drop the book and run to your kitchen. Rather, I want to explain how making a delicious plate of bucatini all'Amatriciana can be modeled using a directed acyclic graph. First, let's take a quick overview of the recipe, which can be seen in figure 1.2.

Cooking a recipe consists of following a series of sequential steps where raw ingredients are transformed into intermediate states until all the ingredients are ultimately combined into a single complete dish. For example, when you dice an onion, you start

---

BUCATINI ALL'AMATRICIANA

Ingredients
(Serves 4)

2 Tbsp. olive oil
3/4 cup diced onion
2 cloves garlic, minced
4 oz. guanciale, sliced into small pieces
1 28-oz. can San Marzano tomatoes, crushed
Kosher salt
1/2 tsp. red chili flakes
1/2 tsp. freshly ground black pepper
1 lb dried bucatini
1 oz pecorino romano, grated

Instructions

1. Heat oil in a large heavy skillet over medium heat. Add guanciale and fry until crispy (approximately 4 minutes). Add chili flakes, pepper, onion, and garlic. Cook until the onions have softened (approximately 8 minutes). Stir often to avoid burning. Add tomatoes and simmer on low heat until sauce thickens (approximately 15–20 minutes).

2. While the sauce is simmering, bring a large pot of salted water to the boil. Add the pasta and cook for 1–2 minutes less than the cooking time listed on the package. When finished, retain some pasta water (about 1 cup) and drain the pasta into a colander.

3. When the sauce has thickened, add the cooked pasta to the skillet and toss to combine the sauce and noodles. Add half of the retained pasta water and cook until the pasta is al dente (approximately 2 minutes). Stir in grated cheese and serve. Buon appetito!

Figure 1.2   My favorite recipe for bucatini all'Amatriciana

with a whole onion and cut it into pieces, and then you're left with some amount of diced onion. In software engineering parlance, we would describe the process of dicing onions as a *function*.

Dicing onions, while important, is only a very small part of the whole recipe. To complete the entire recipe, we must define many more steps (or functions). Each of these functions is called a *node* in a graph. Since most steps in a recipe follow a logical order (for example, you wouldn't plate the noodles before cooking them), each node can take on dependencies, which means that a prior step (or steps) must be complete before starting the next node's operation. Another step of the recipe is to sauté the diced onions in olive oil, which is represented by another node. Of course, it's not possible to sauté diced onions if you haven't diced any onions yet! Because sautéing the diced onion is directly dependent on and related to dicing the onion, these two nodes are connected by a *line*.

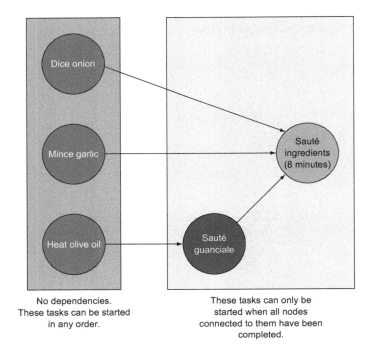

No dependencies.
These tasks can be started
in any order.

These tasks can only be
started when all nodes
connected to them have been
completed.

Figure 1.3   A graph displaying nodes with dependencies

Figure 1.3 represents a graph of the process described so far. Notice that the Sauté Ingredients node has three direct dependencies: the onion and garlic must be diced and the guanciale must be sautéed before the three ingredients can be sautéed together. Conversely, the Dice Onion, Mince Garlic, and Heat Olive Oil nodes do not have any dependencies. The order in which you complete those steps does not matter, but you must complete all of them before proceeding to the final sauté step. Also notice that the lines connecting the nodes have arrows as endpoints. This implies that there is only one possible way to traverse the graph. It makes sense neither to sauté the onion before it's diced, nor to attempt to sauté the onion without a hot, oiled pan ready. This is what's meant by a *directed* acyclic graph: there's a logical, one-way traversal through the graph from nodes with no dependencies to a single terminal node.

Another thing you may notice about the graph in figure 1.3 is that no lines connect later nodes back to earlier nodes. Once a node is complete, it is never repeated or revisited. This is what makes the graph an *acyclic* graph. If the graph contained a feedback loop or some kind of continuous process, it would instead be a *cyclic* graph. This, of course, would not be an appropriate representation of cooking, since recipes have a finite number of steps, have a finite state (finished or unfinished), and deterministically resolve to a completed state, barring any kitchen catastrophes. Figure 1.4 demonstrates what a cyclic graph might look like.

From a programming perspective, this might sound like directed acyclic graphs would not allow looping operations. But this is not necessarily the case: a directed acyclic graph can be constructed from deterministic loops (such as for loops) by copying the nodes to be repeated and connecting them sequentially. In figure 1.3, the guanciale was sautéed in two different steps—first alone, then together with the onions. If the ingredients needed to be sautéed a non-deterministic number of times, the process could not be expressed as an acyclic graph.

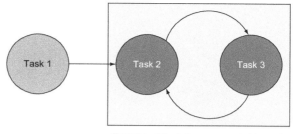

Task 2 and Task 3 are connected to each other in an infinite feedback loop. There is no logical termination point in this graph.

Figure 1.4   An example of a cyclic graph demonstrating an infinite feedback loop

The final thing to note about the graph in figure 1.3 is that it's in a special form known as a *transitive reduction*. This means that any lines that express *transitive dependencies* are eliminated. A transitive dependency simply means a dependency that is met indirectly through completion of another node. Figure 1.5 shows figure 1.3 redrawn without transitive reduction.

Notice that a line is drawn between the nodes containing the operation Heat Olive Oil and Sauté Ingredients (8 minutes). Heating the olive oil is a transitive dependency of sautéing the onion, garlic, and guanciale because the guanciale must be sautéed alone before adding the onion and garlic. In order to sauté the guanciale, you must heat up a pan with olive oil first, so by the time you're ready to sauté all three ingredients together, you already have a hot pan with oil—the dependency is already met!

Figure 1.6 represents the full directed acyclic graph for the complete recipe. As you can see, the graph fully represents the process from start to finish. You can start at any of the red nodes (medium gray in the print version of this book) since they do not have dependencies, and you will eventually reach the terminal node labeled "Buon appetito!" While looking at this graph, it might be easy to spot some bottlenecks, and potentially reorder some nodes to produce a more optimal or

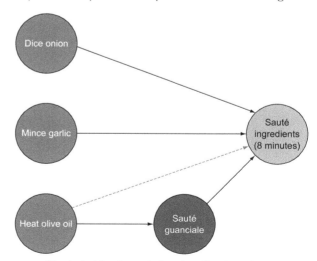

The dashed line demonstrates a transitive dependency. The Sauté Ingredients node is indirectly dependent on the Heat Olive Oil node because it is directly dependent on the Sauté Guanciale node, which is directly dependent on the Heat Olive Oil node.

Figure 1.5   The graph represented in figure 1.3 redrawn without transitive reduction

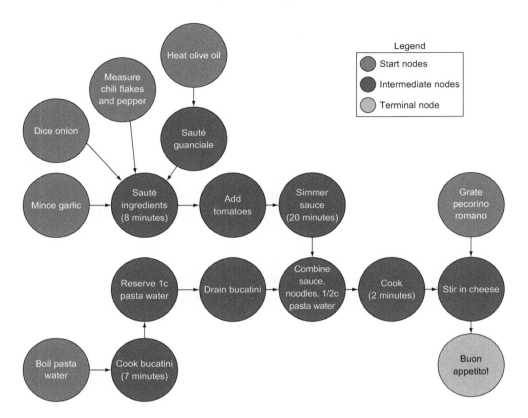

Figure 1.6   The full directed acyclic graph representation of the bucatini all'Amatriciana recipe

time-efficient way of preparing the dish. For instance, if the pasta water takes 20 minutes to come to a rolling boil, perhaps you could draw a graph with a single starting node of putting the water on to boil. Then you wouldn't have to wait for the water to heat up after already preparing the rest of the dish. These are great examples of optimizations that either an intelligent task scheduler or you, the designer of the workload, may come up with. And now that you have the foundational understanding of how directed acyclic graphs work, you should be able to read and understand any arbitrary graph—from cooking pasta to calculating descriptive statistics on a big data set. Next, we'll look at why DAGs are so useful for scalable computing.

1.3   *Scaling out, concurrency, and recovery*

Up to this point, our example of cooking bucatini all'Amatriciana assumed that you were the sole cook in the kitchen. This might be fine if you're only cooking dinner for your family or a small get-together with friends, but if you needed to cook hundreds of servings for a busy dinner service in midtown Manhattan, you would likely reach the limits of your abilities very quickly. It's now time to search for some help!

First, you must decide how you will handle the resource problem: should you upgrade your equipment to help you be more efficient in the kitchen, or should you hire more cooks to help share the workload? In computing, these two approaches are called *scaling up* and *scaling out*, respectively. Just like in our hypothetical kitchen, neither approach is as simple as it may sound. In section 1.3.1, I'll discuss the limitations of scale-up solutions and how scale-out solutions overcome those limitations. Since a key use case of Dask is scaling out complex problems, we'll assume that the best course of action for our hypothetical kitchen is to hire more workers and scale out. Given that assumption, it'll be important to understand some of the challenges that come with orchestrating complex tasks across many different workers. I'll discuss how workers share resources in section 1.3.2, and how worker failures are handled in section 1.3.3.

1.3.1 Scaling up vs. scaling out

Back in our hypothetical kitchen, you're faced with the question of what to do now that you're expected to feed a horde of hungry customers at dinner rush. The first thing you might notice is that as the volume of pasta you need to make increases, the amount of time that each step takes also increases. For example, the original recipe makes four servings and calls for ¾ cup of diced onions. This amount roughly equates to a single medium-sized yellow onion. If you were to make 400 servings of the dish, you would need to dice 100 onions. Assuming you can dice an onion in around two minutes, and it takes you 30 seconds to clear the cutting board and grab another onion, you would be chopping onions for roughly five hours! Forget the time it would take to prepare the rest of the recipe. By the time you merely finish dicing the onions, your angry customers would already have taken their business elsewhere. And to add insult to injury, you'd have cried your eyes dry from spending the last five hours cutting onions! The two potential solutions to this problem are to replace your existing kitchen equipment with faster, more efficient equipment (scale up) or to hire more workers to work in parallel (scale out). Figure 1.7 shows what these two methods would look like.

The decision to scale up or scale out isn't an easy one because there are advantages and trade-offs to both. You might want to consider scaling up, because you would still ultimately oversee the whole process from start to finish. You wouldn't have to deal with others' potential unreliability or variation in skills, and you wouldn't have to worry about bumping into other people in the kitchen. Perhaps you can trade in your trusty knife and cutting board for a food processor that can chop onions in one-tenth the time that it takes you to do it manually. This will suit your needs until you start scaling again. As your business expands and you start serving 800, 1,600, and 3,200 plates of pasta per day, you will start running into the same capacity

Scale up

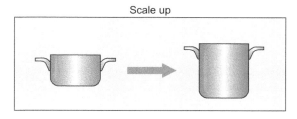

Scale out

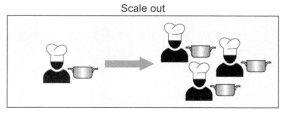

Figure 1.7 Scaling up replaces existing equipment with larger/faster/more efficient equipment, while scaling out divides the work between many workers in parallel.

problems you had before, and you'll eventually outgrow your food processor. There will come a time you will need to buy a new, faster machine. Taking this example to an extreme, you'll eventually hit the limit of current kitchen technology and have to go to great lengths and expense to develop and build better and better food processors. Eventually, your simple food processor will become highly specialized for chopping an extraordinarily large amount of onions and require incredible feats of engineering to build and maintain. Even then, you will reach a point when further innovation is simply not tenable (at some point, the blades will have to rotate so quickly that the onion will just turn to mush!). But hold on a second, let's not get carried away. For most chefs, opening a small checkered-tablecloth joint in the city doesn't entail formulating a plan to become a worldwide pasta magnate and a food processor R&D powerhouse—meaning simply choosing to get the food processor (scaling up) is likely the best option. Likewise, most of the time, upgrading a cheap, low-end workstation to a high-end server will be easier and cheaper than buying a bunch of hardware and setting up a cluster. This is especially true if the size of the problem you're facing sits at the high end of medium datasets or the low end of large datasets. This also becomes an easier choice to make if you're working in the cloud, because it's much easier to scale up a process from one instance type to another instead of paying to acquire hardware that might not end up meeting your needs. That said, scaling out can be the better option if you can take advantage of a lot of parallelism or if you're working with large datasets. Let's look at what scaling out will yield in the kitchen.

Rather than attempt to improve on your own skills and abilities, you hire nine additional cooks to help share the workload. If all 10 of you focused 100% of your time and attention to the process of chopping onions, that five hours of work now comes down to a mere 30 minutes, assuming you have equal skill levels. Of course, you would need to buy additional knives, cutting boards, and other tools, and you would need to provide adequate facilities and pay for your additional cooks, but in the long run this will be a more cost-effective solution if your other alternative is pouring money into development of specialized equipment. Not only can the additional cooks help you with reducing the time it takes to prepare the onions, but because they are non-specialized workers, they can also be trained to do all the other necessary tasks. A food processor, on the other hand, cannot be trained to boil pasta no matter how hard you may try! The trade-offs are that your other cooks can get sick, might need to miss work, or otherwise do things that are unexpected and hinder the process. Getting your team of cooks to work together toward a single goal does not come for free. At first you might be able to supervise if only three or four other cooks are in the kitchen, but eventually you might need to hire a sous chef as the kitchen grows out. Likewise, real costs are associated with maintaining a cluster, and these should be honestly evaluated when considering whether to scale up or scale out.

Pressing on with your new team of cooks, you now must figure out how to relay instructions to each cook and make sure the recipe comes out as intended. Directed acyclic graphs are a great tool for planning and orchestrating complex tasks across a pool of workers. Most importantly, dependencies between nodes help ensure that the work will follow a certain order (remember that a node cannot begin work until all its dependencies have completed), but there are no restrictions on how individual nodes are completed—whether by a single entity or many entities working in parallel. A node is a standalone unit of work, so it's possible to subdivide the work and share it among many workers. This means that you could assign four cooks to chop the onions, while four other cooks sauté the guanciale, and the remaining two cooks mince the garlic. Dividing and supervising the work in the kitchen is the job of the sous chef, which represents Dask's task scheduler. As each cook completes their task, the sous chef can assign them the next available task. To keep food moving through the kitchen in an efficient manner, the sous chef should constantly evaluate what work needs to be done and aim to start tasks closest to the terminal node as soon as possible. For example, rather than waiting for all 100 onions to be chopped, if enough onions, garlic, and guanciale have been prepared to begin making a complete batch of sauce, the sous chef should tell the next available cook to begin preparing a batch of sauce. This strategy allows some customers to be served sooner, rather than keeping all customers waiting until everyone can be served at the same time. It's also more efficient to avoid having all the onions in a chopped state at once, because it can take up a large amount of cutting board space. Likewise, Dask's task scheduler aims to cycle workers between many tasks in order to reduce memory load and emit finished results quickly. It distributes units of work to machines in an efficient manner and aims to minimize the worker pool's idle time. Organizing execution of the graph between workers and assigning an appropriate number of workers to each task is crucial for minimizing the time it takes to complete the graph. Figure 1.8 depicts a possible way the original graph can be distributed to multiple workers.

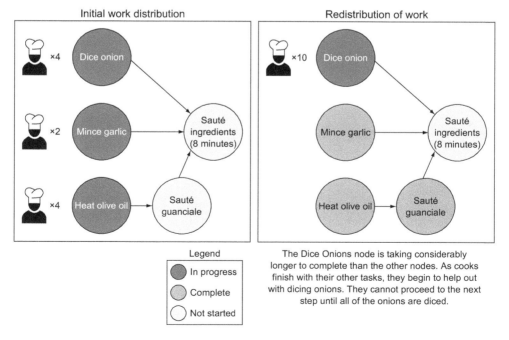

Figure 1.8   A graph with nodes distributed to many workers depicting dynamic redistribution of work as tasks complete at different times

1.3.2   *Concurrency and resource management*

More often than not, you have to consider more constraints than just the number of available workers. In scalable computing, these are called issues of *concurrency*. For example, if you hire more cooks to dice onions, but you only have five knives in the kitchen, only five operations that require a knife can be carried out simultaneously. Some other tasks may require sharing resources, such as the step that calls for minced garlic. Therefore, if all five knives are in use by cooks dicing onions, the garlic can't be minced until at least one knife becomes available. Even if the remaining five cooks have completed all other possible nodes, the garlic-mincing step becomes delayed due to *resource starvation*. Figure 1.9 demonstrates an example of resource starvation in our hypothetical kitchen.

The other cooks are forced to remain idle until the onion-dicing step is complete. When a shared resource is in use, a *resource lock* is placed on it, meaning other workers can't "steal" the resource until the worker who locked the resource is finished using it. It would be quite rude (and dangerous) for one of your cooks to wrestle the knife out of the hands of another cook. If your cooks are constantly fighting over who gets to use the knife next, those disagreements consume time that could be spent working on completing the recipe. The sous chef is responsible for defusing these confrontations by laying the ground rules about who can use certain resources and what happens when a resource becomes available. Similarly, the task scheduler in a scalable computing framework must decide how to deal with resource contention and locking. If not handled properly, resource contention can be very detrimental to performance. But fortunately, most frameworks (including Dask) are pretty good at efficient task scheduling and don't normally need to be hand-tuned.

1.3.3   *Recovering from failures*

Finally, no discussion of scalable computing would be complete without mentioning recovery strategies. Just like it's difficult for a sous chef to closely supervise all her cooks at once, it gets increasingly difficult to orchestrate distribution of processing tasks as the number of machines in a cluster increases. Since the final result consists of the aggregate of all the individual operations, it's important to ensure that all the pieces find their way to where they need to go. But machines, like people, are imperfect and fail at times. Two types of failures must be accounted for: worker failure and data loss. For example, if you've

This cook must wait and remain idle until either a knife becomes available or a new task that doesn't require a knife is available. This is an example of a resource-starved worker.

Figure 1.9   An example of resource starvation

assigned one of your cooks to dice the onions and going into the third hour straight of chopping he decided he can't take the monotony anymore, he might put down his knife, take off his coat, and walk out the door. You're now down a worker! One of your other cooks will need to take up his place in order to finish dicing the onions, but thankfully you can still use the onions that the previous cook diced before he left. This is worker failure without data loss. The work that the failed worker completed does not need to be reproduced, so the impact to performance is not as severe.

When data loss occurs, a significant impact to performance is much more likely. For example, your kitchen staff has completed all the initial prep steps and the sauce is simmering away on the stove. Unfortunately, the pot is accidentally knocked over and spills all over the floor. Knowing that scraping the sauce off the floor and attempting to recover would violate all the health codes in the book, you're forced to remake the sauce. This means going back to dicing more onions, sautéing more guanciale, and so on. The dependencies for the Simmer Sauce node are no longer met, meaning you have to step all the way back to the first dependency-free node and work your way back from there. Although this is a fairly catastrophic example, the important thing to remember is that at any point in the graph, the complete lineage of operations up to a given node can be "replayed" in the event of a failure. The task scheduler is ultimately responsible for stopping work and redistributing the work to be replayed. And because the task scheduler can dynamically redistribute tasks away from failed workers, the specific workers that completed the tasks before don't need to be present to redo the tasks. For example, if the cook who decided to quit earlier had taken some diced onions with him, you would not need to stop the whole kitchen and redo everything from the beginning. You would just need to determine how many additional onions need to be diced and assign a new cook to do that work.

In rare circumstances, the task scheduler might run into problems and fail. This is akin to your sous chef deciding to hang up her hat and walk out the door. This kind of failure can be recovered from, but since only the task scheduler knows the complete DAG and how much was finished, the only option is to start over at step 1 with a brand-new task graph. Admittedly, the kitchen analogy falls apart a bit here. In reality, your cooks would know the recipe well enough to finish service without micromanagement of the sous, but this isn't the case with Dask. The workers simply do what they're told, and if there's no task scheduler around to tell them what to do, they can't make decisions on their own.

Hopefully you now have a good understanding of the power of DAGs and how they relate to scalable computing frameworks. These concepts will certainly come up again through this book since all of Dask's task scheduling is based on the DAG concepts presented here. Before we close out the chapter, we'll take a brief look at the dataset that we'll use throughout the book to learn about Dask's operations and capabilities.

1.4 Introducing a companion dataset

Since the intent of this book is to give you hands-on experience using Dask for data science, it's only natural to have a dataset you can work with alongside the examples in the forthcoming chapters. Rather than proceed through the book working on a number of purpose-built "toy" examples, it will be a lot more valuable to apply your newfound skills to a real, messy dataset. It's also important for you to gain experience using an appropriately large dataset, because you will be better equipped to apply your knowledge to medium and large datasets in the wild. So, over the next several chapters, we'll use a great public domain dataset provided by NYC OpenData (https://opendata.cityofnewyork.us) as a backdrop for learning how to use Dask.

Every third week of the month, the New York City Department of Finance records and publishes a data set of all parking citations issued throughout the fiscal year so far. The data collected by the city is quite rich, even including some interesting geographic features. To make the data more accessible, an archive containing four years of data from NYC OpenData has been collected and published on the popular machine learning website, Kaggle, by Aleksey Bilogur and Jacob Boysen under the City of New York account. The dataset spans from 2013 through June 2017 and is over 8 GB uncompressed. While this dataset may meet the definition of small data if you have a very powerful computer, for most readers it should be a well-sized medium dataset. Although larger datasets are certainly out there, I hope you appreciate not needing to download 2 TB of data before proceeding to the next chapter. You can get the data for yourself at www.kaggle.com/new-york-city/nyc-parking-tickets. After you've downloaded the data, roll up your sleeves and get ready to have a first look at Dask in the next chapter!

Summary

- Dask can be used to scale popular data analysis libraries such as Pandas and NumPy, allowing you to analyze medium and large datasets with ease.
- Dask uses directed acyclic graphs (DAGs) to coordinate execution of parallelized code across CPU cores and machines.
- Directed acyclic graphs are made up of nodes and have a clearly defined start and end, a single traversal path, and no looping.
- Upstream nodes must be completed before work can begin on any dependent downstream nodes.
- Scaling out can generally improve performance of complex workloads, but it creates additional overhead that might substantially reduce those performance gains.
- In the event of a failure, the steps to reach a node can be repeated from the beginning without disturbing the rest of the process.

Introducing Dask

This chapter covers

- Warming up with a short example of data cleaning using Dask DataFrames

- Visualizing DAGs generated by Dask workloads with graphviz

- Exploring how the Dask task scheduler applies the concept of DAGs to coordinate execution of code

Now that you have a basic understanding of how DAGs work, let's take a look at how Dask uses DAGs to create robust, scalable workloads. To do this, we'll use the NYC Parking Ticket data you downloaded at the end of the previous chapter. This will help us accomplish two things at once: you'll get your first taste of using Dask's Data-Frame API to analyze a structured dataset, and you'll start to get familiar with some of the quirks in the dataset that we'll address throughout the next few chapters. We'll also take a look at a few useful diagnostic tools and use the low-level Delayed API to create a simple custom task graph.

Before we dive into the Dask code, if you haven't already done so, check out the appendix for instructions on how to install Dask and all the packages you'll need for the code examples in the remainder of the book. You can also find the complete code notebooks online at www.manning.com/books/data-science-with-python-and-dask and also at http://bit.ly/daskbook. For all the examples throughout the book (unless otherwise noted), I recommend you use a Jupyter Notebook. Jupyter Notebooks will help you keep your code organized and will make it easy to produce visualizations when necessary. The code in the examples has been tested in both Python 2.7 and Python 3.6 environments, so you should be able to use either without issue. Dask is available for both major versions of Python, but I highly recommend that you use Python 3 for any new projects, because the end of support for Python 2 is slated for 2020.

Finally, before we get going, we'll take a moment to set the table for where we'll be headed over the next few chapters. As mentioned before, the objective of this book is to teach you the fundamentals of Dask in a pragmatic way that focuses on how to use it for common data science tasks. Figure 2.1 represents a fairly standard way of approaching data science problems, and we'll use this workflow as a backdrop to demonstrate how to apply Dask to each part of it.

In this chapter, we'll take a look at a few snippets of Dask code that fall into the areas of data gathering, data cleaning, and exploratory analysis. However, chapters 4, 5, and 6 will cover those topics much more in depth. Instead, the focus here is to give you a first glimpse of what Dask syntax looks like. We'll also focus on how the high-level commands we give Dask relate to the DAGs generated by the underlying scheduler. So, let's get going!

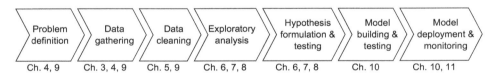

Figure 2.1   Our workflow, at a glance, in *Data Science with Python and Dask*

2.1   *Hello Dask: A first look at the DataFrame API*

An essential step of any data science project is to perform exploratory analysis on the dataset. During exploratory analysis, you'll want to check the data for missing values, outliers, and any other data quality issues. Cleaning the dataset ensures that the analysis you do, and any conclusions you make about the data, are not influenced by erroneous or anomalous data. In our first look at using Dask DataFrames, we'll step through reading in a data file, scanning the data for missing values, and dropping columns that either are missing too much data or won't be useful for analysis.

2.1.1   *Examining the metadata of Dask objects*

For this example, we'll look at just the data collected from 2017. First, you'll need to import the Dask modules and read in your data.

Listing 2.1 Importing relevant libraries and data

```
import dask.dataframe as dd
from dask.diagnostics import ProgressBar
from matplotlib import pyplot as plt
df = dd.read_csv('nyc-parking-tickets/*2017.csv')
df
```

Imports dask as well as matplotlib for generating graphics

Reads the 2017 CSV file into a Dask DataFrame

If you're an experienced Pandas user, listing 2.1 will look very familiar. In fact, it is syntactically equivalent! For simplicity's sake, I've unzipped the data into the same folder as the Python notebook I'm working in. If you put your data elsewhere, you will either need to find the correct path to use or change your working directory to the folder that contains your data using os.chdir. Inspecting the DataFrame we just created yields the output shown in figure 2.2.

The output of listing 2.1 might not be what you expected. While Pandas would display a sample of the data, when inspecting a Dask DataFrame, we are shown the metadata of the DataFrame. The column names are along the top, and underneath is each column's respective datatype. Dask tries very hard to intelligently infer datatypes from the data, just as Pandas does. But its ability to do so accurately is limited by the fact that Dask was built to handle medium and large datasets that can't be loaded into RAM at once. Since Pandas can perform operations entirely in memory, it can quickly and easily scan the entire DataFrame to find the best datatype for each column. Dask, on the other hand, must be able to work just as well with local datasets and large datasets that could be scattered across multiple physical machines in a distributed filesystem. Therefore, Dask DataFrames employ random sampling methods to profile and infer datatypes from a small sample of the data. This works fine if data anomalies, such as letters

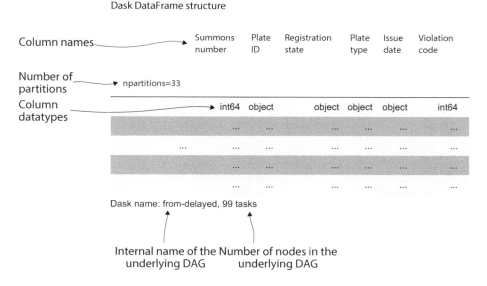

Figure 2.2 Inspecting the Dask DataFrame

appearing in a numeric column, are widespread. However, if there's a single anomalous row among millions or billions of rows, it's very improbable that the anomalous row would be picked in a random sample. This will lead to Dask picking an incompatible datatype, which will cause errors later on when performing computations. Therefore, a best practice to avoid that situation would be to explicitly set datatypes rather than relying on Dask's inference process. Even better, storing data in a binary file format that supports explicit data types, such as Parquet, will avoid the issue altogether and bring some additional performance gains to the table as well. We will return to this issue in a later chapter, but for now we will let Dask infer datatypes.

The other interesting pieces of information about the DataFrame's metadata give us insight into how Dask's scheduler is deciding to break up the work of processing this file. The npartitions value shows how many partitions the DataFrame is split into. Since the 2017 file is slightly over 2 GB in size, at 33 partitions, each partition is roughly 64 MB in size. That means that instead of loading the entire file into RAM all at once, each Dask worker thread will work on processing the file one 64 MB chunk at a time.

Figure 2.3 demonstrates this behavior. Rather than eagerly loading the entire Data-Frame into RAM, Dask breaks the file into smaller chunks that can be worked on independently. These chunks are called *partitions*. In the case of Dask DataFrames, each partition is a relatively small Pandas DataFrame. In the example in figure 2.3, the

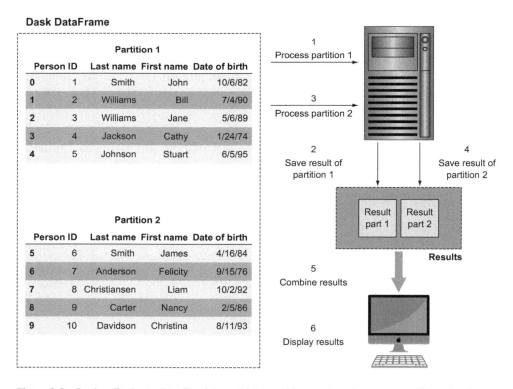

Figure 2.3   Dask splits large data files into multiple partitions and works on one partition at a time.

DataFrame consists of two partitions. Therefore, the single Dask DataFrame is made up of two smaller Pandas DataFrames. Each partition can be loaded into memory and worked on one at a time or in parallel. In this case, the worker node first picks up partition 1 and processes it, and saves the result in a temporary holding space. Next it picks up partition 2 and processes it, saving the result to a temporary holding space. Finally, it combines the results and ships it down to our client, which displays the result. Because the worker node can work on smaller pieces of the data at a time, work can be distributed out to many machines. Or, in the case of a local cluster, work can proceed on very large datasets without resulting in out-of-memory errors.

The last bit of metadata we got from our DataFrame is that it consists of 99 tasks. That's telling us that Dask created a DAG with 99 nodes to process the data. The graph consists of 99 nodes because each partition requires three operations to be created: reading the raw data, splitting the data into the appropriately sized block, and initializing the underlying DataFrame object. In total, 33 partitions with 3 tasks per partition results in 99 tasks. If we had 33 workers in our worker pool, the entire file could be worked on simultaneously. With just one worker, Dask will cycle through each partition one at a time. Now, let's try to count the missing values in each column across the entire file.

Listing 2.2 Counting missing values in the DataFrame

```
missing_values = df.isnull().sum()
missing_values

Dask Series Structure:
npartitions=1
Date First Observed     int64
Violation Time           ...
dtype: int64
Dask Name: DataFrame-sum-agg, 166 tasks
```

The syntax for counting null values again looks a lot like Pandas. But as before, inspecting the resulting Series object doesn't give us the output we might expect. Instead of getting the missing counts, Dask returns some metadata information about the expected result. It looks like `missing_values` is a Series of `int64`s, but where's the actual data? Dask hasn't actually done any processing yet because it uses *lazy computation*. This means that what Dask has actually done under the hood is prepare another DAG, which was then stored in the `missing_values` variable. The data isn't computed until the task graph is explicitly executed. This behavior makes it possible to build up complex task graphs quickly without having to wait for each intermediate step to finish. You might notice that the tasks count has grown to 166 now. That's because Dask has taken the first 99 tasks from the DAG used to read in the data file and create the DataFrame called `df`, added 66 tasks (2 per partition) to check for nulls and sum, and then added a final step to collect all the pieces together into a single Series object and return the answer.

Listing 2.3   Calculating the percent of missing values in the DataFrame

```
missing_count = ((missing_values / df.index.size) * 100)
missing_count

Dask Series Structure:
npartitions=1
Date First Observed     float64
Violation Time              ...
dtype: float64
Dask Name: mul, 235 tasks
```

Before we run the computation, we'll ask Dask to transform these numbers into percentages by dividing the missing value counts (missing_values) by the total number of rows in the DataFrame (df.index.size), then multiplying everything by 100. Notice that the number of tasks has increased again, and the datatype of the resulting Series changed from int64 to float64! This is because the division operation resulted in answers that were not whole (integer) numbers. Therefore, Dask automatically converted the answer to floating-point (decimal) numbers. Just as Dask tries to infer datatypes from files, it will also try to infer how operations will affect the datatype of the output. Since we've added a stage to the DAG that divides two numbers, Dask infers that we'll likely move from integers to floating-point numbers and changes the metadata of the result accordingly.

2.1.2   Running computations with the compute method

Now we're ready to run and produce our output.

Listing 2.4   Computing the DAG

```
with ProgressBar():
    missing_count_pct = missing_count.compute()
missing_count_pct

Summons Number               0.000000
Plate ID                     0.006739
Registration State           0.000000
Plate Type                   0.000000
Issue Date                   0.000000
Violation Code               0.000000
Vehicle Body Type            0.395361
Vehicle Make                 0.676199
Issuing Agency               0.000000
Street Code1                 0.000000
Street Code2                 0.000000
Street Code3                 0.000000
Vehicle Expiration Date      0.000000
Violation Location          19.183510
Violation Precinct           0.000000
```

```
Issuer Precinct                          0.000000
Issuer Code                              0.000000
Issuer Command                          19.093212
Issuer Squad                            19.101506
Violation Time                           0.000583
Time First Observed                     92.217488
Violation County                         0.366073
Violation In Front Of Or Opposite       20.005826
House Number                            21.184968
Street Name                              0.037110
Intersecting Street                     68.827675
Date First Observed                      0.000000
Law Section                              0.000000
Sub Division                             0.007155
Violation Legal Code                    80.906214
Days Parking In Effect                  25.107923
From Hours In Effect                    50.457575
To Hours In Effect                      50.457548
Vehicle Color                            1.410179
Unregistered Vehicle?                   89.562223
Vehicle Year                             0.000000
Meter Number                            83.472476
Feet From Curb                           0.000000
Violation Post Code                     29.530489
Violation Description                   10.436611
No Standing or Stopping Violation      100.000000
Hydrant Violation                      100.000000
Double Parking Violation               100.000000
dtype: float64
```

Whenever you want Dask to compute the result of your work, you need to call the .compute() method of the DataFrame. This tells Dask to go ahead and run the computation and display the results. You may sometimes see this referred to as *materializing* results, because the DAG that Dask creates to run the computation is a logical representation of the results, but the actual results aren't calculated (that is, materialized) until you explicitly compute them. You'll also notice that we wrapped the call to compute within a ProgressBar context. This is one of several diagnostic contexts that Dask provides to help you keep track of running tasks, and especially comes in handy when using the local task scheduler. The ProgressBar context will simply print out a text-based progress bar showing you the estimated percent complete and the elapsed time for the computation.

By the output of our missing-values calculation, it looks like we can immediately throw out a few columns: No Standing or Stopping Violation, Hydrant Violation, and Double Parking Violation are completely empty, so there's no value in keeping them around. We'll drop any column that's missing more than 60% of its values (note: 60% is just an arbitrary value chosen for the sake of example; the threshold you use to throw out columns with missing data depends on the problem you're trying to solve, and usually relies on your best judgement).

Listing 2.5   Filtering sparse columns

```
columns_to_drop = missing_count_pct[missing_count_pct > 60].index
with ProgressBar():
    df_dropped = df.drop(columns_to_drop, axis=1).persist()
```

This is interesting. Since we materialized the data in listing 2.4, `missing_count_pct` is a Pandas Series object, but we can use it with the `drop` method on the Dask DataFrame. We first took the Series we created in listing 2.4 and filtered it to get the columns that have more than 60% missing values. We then got the index of the filtered Series, which is a list of column names. We then used that index to drop columns in the Dask Data-Frame with the same name. You can generally mix Pandas objects and Dask objects because each partition of a Dask DataFrame is a Pandas DataFrame. In this case, the Pandas Series object is made available to all threads, so they can use it in their computation. In the case of running on a cluster, the Pandas Series object will be serialized and broadcasted to all worker nodes.

2.1.3   *Making complex computations more efficient with persist*

Because we've decided that we don't care about the columns we just dropped, it would be inefficient to re-read the columns into memory every time we want to make an additional calculation just to drop them again. We really only care about analyzing the filtered subset of data we just created. Recall that as soon as a node in the active task graph emits results, its intermediate work is discarded in order to minimize memory usage. That means if we want to do something additional with the filtered data (for example, look at the first five rows of the DataFrame), we would have to go to the trouble of re-running the entire chain of transformations again. To avoid repeating the same calculations many times over, Dask allows us to store intermediate results of a computation so they can be reused. Using the `persist()` method of the Dask DataFrame tells Dask to try to keep as much of the intermediate result in memory as possible. In case Dask needs some of the memory being used by the persisted DataFrame, it will select a number of partitions to drop from memory. These dropped partitions will be recalculated on the fly when needed, and although it may take some time to recalculate the missing partitions, it is still likely to be much faster than recomputing the entire DataFrame. Using `persist` appropriately can be very useful for speeding up computations if you have a very large and complex DAG that needs to be reused many times.

   This concludes our first look at Dask DataFrames. You saw how, in only a few lines of code, we were able to read in a dataset and begin preparing it for exploratory analysis. The beauty of this code is that it works the same regardless of whether you're running Dask on one machine or thousands of machines, and regardless of whether you're crunching through a couple gigabytes of data (as we did here) or analyzing petabytes of data. Also, because of the syntactic similarities with Pandas, you can easily transition workloads from Pandas to Dask with a minimum amount of code refactoring (which mostly amounts to adding Dask imports and `compute` calls). We'll go much further into our analysis in the coming chapters, but for now we'll dig a little deeper into how Dask uses DAGs to manage distribution of the tasks that underpin the code we just walked through.

2.2   *Visualizing DAGs*

So far, you've learned how directed acyclic graphs (DAGs) work, and you've learned that Dask uses DAGs to orchestrate distributed computations of DataFrames. However, we haven't yet peeked "under the hood" and seen the actual DAGs that the schedulers create. Dask uses the graphviz library to generate visual representations of the DAGs created by the task scheduler. If you followed the steps in the appendix to install graphviz, you will be able to inspect the DAG backing any Dask Delayed object. You can inspect the DAGs of DataFrames, series, bags, and arrays by calling the `visualize()` method on the object.

2.2.1   *Visualizing a simple DAG using Dask Delayed objects*

For this example, we'll take a step back from the Dask DataFrame objects seen in the previous example to step down a level of abstraction: the Dask Delayed object. The reason we'll move to Delayed objects is because the DAGs that Dask creates for even simple DataFrame operations can grow quite large and be hard to visualize. Therefore, for convenience, we'll use Dask Delayed objects for this example so we have better control over composition of the DAG.

> **Listing 2.6   Creating some simple functions**

```
import dask.delayed as delayed
from dask.diagnostics import ProgressBar

def inc(i):
    return i + 1

def add(x, y):
    return x + y

x = delayed(inc)(1)
y = delayed(inc)(2)
z = delayed(add)(x, y)

z.visualize()
```

Listing 2.6 begins by importing the packages needed for this example: in this case, the `delayed` package and the `ProgressBar` diagnostic we used previously. Next, we define a couple simple Python functions. The first adds one to its given input, and the second adds the two given inputs. The next three lines introduce the `delayed` constructor. By wrapping `delayed` around a function, a Dask Delayed representation of the function is produced. Delayed objects are equivalent to a node in a DAG. The arguments of the original function are passed in a second set of parentheses. For example, the object x represents a Delayed evaluation of the `inc` function, passing in 1 as the value of i. Delayed objects can reference other Delayed objects as well, which can be seen in the definition of the object z. Chaining together these Delayed objects is what ultimately makes up a graph. For the object z to be evaluated, both of the objects x and y must

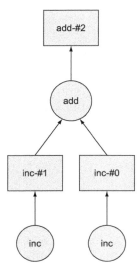

Figure 2.4   A visual representation of the DAG produced in listing 2.6

first be evaluated. If x or y has other Delayed dependencies that must be met as part of their evaluation, those dependencies would need to be evaluated first and so forth. This sounds an awful lot like a DAG: evaluating the object z has a well-known chain of dependencies that must be evaluated in a deterministic order, and there is a well-defined start and end point. Indeed, this is a representation of a very simple DAG in code. We can have a look at what that looks like by using the visualize method.

As you can see in figure 2.4, object z is represented by a DAG. At the bottom of the graph, we can see the two calls to the inc function. That function didn't have any Delayed dependencies of its own, so there are no lines with arrows pointing into the inc nodes. However, the add node has two lines with arrows pointing into it. This represents the dependency on first calculating x and y before being able to sum the two values. Since each inc node is free of dependencies, a unique worker would be able to work on each task independently. Taking advantage of parallelism like this could be very advantageous if the inc function took a long time to evaluate.

2.2.2 *Visualizing more complex DAGs with loops and collections*

Let's look at a slightly more complex example.

Listing 2.7   Performing the add_two operation

```
def add_two(x):
    return x + 2

def sum_two_numbers(x,y):
    return x + y

def multiply_four(x):
    return x * 4
```

```
data = [1, 5, 8, 10]

step1 = [delayed(add_two)(i) for i in data]
total = delayed(sum)(step1)
total.visualize()
```

Now things are getting interesting. Let's unpack what happened here. We started again by defining a few simple functions, and also defined a list of integers to use. This time, though, instead of creating a Delayed object from a single function call, the Delayed constructor is placed inside a list comprehension that iterates over the list of numbers. The result is that `step1` becomes a list of Delayed objects instead of a list of integers.

The next line of code uses the built-in `sum` function to add up all the numbers in the list. The `sum` function normally takes an iterable as an argument, but since it's been wrapped in a Delayed constructor, it can be passed the list of Delayed objects. As before, this code ultimately represents a graph. Let's take a look at what the graph looks like.

Now, the variable total is a Delayed object, which means we can use the `visualize` method on it to draw the DAG that Dask will use if we ask Dask to compute the answer! Figure 2.5 shows the output of the `visualize` method. One thing to notice is that Dask draws DAGs from the bottom up. We started with four numbers in a list called `data`, which corresponds to four nodes at the bottom of the DAG. The circles on the Dask DAGs represent function calls. This makes sense: we had four numbers, and we wanted to apply the `add_two` function to each number so we have to call it four times. Similarly, we call the `sum` function only one time because we're passing in the complete list. The squares on the DAG represent intermediate results. For instance, the result of iterating over the list of numbers and applying the `add_two` function to each of the original numbers is four transformed numbers that had two added to them. Just like with the DataFrame in the previous section, Dask doesn't actually compute the answer until you call the `compute` method on the total object.

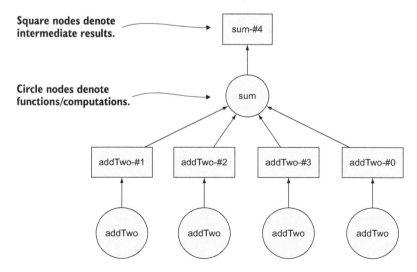

Figure 2.5   The directed acyclic graph representing the computation in listing 2.7

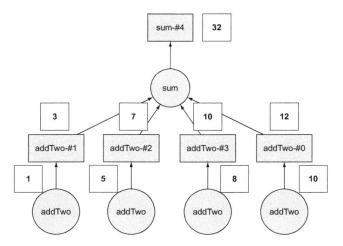

Figure 2.6   The DAG from figure 2.5 with the values superimposed over the computation

In figure 2.6, we've taken the four numbers from the data list and superimposed them over the DAG so you can see the result of each function call. The result, 32, is calculated by taking the original four numbers, applying the addTwo transformation to each, then summing the result.

We'll now add another degree of complexity to the DAG by multiplying every number by four before collecting the result.

Listing 2.8   Multiply each value by four

```
def add_two(x):
    return x + 2

def sum_two_numbers(x,y):
    return x + y

def multiply_four(x):
    return x * 4

data = [1, 5, 8, 10]

step1 = [delayed(add_two)(i) for i in data]
step2 = [delayed(multiply_four)(j) for j in step1]
total = delayed(sum)(step2)
total.visualize()
```

This looks an awful lot like the previous code listing, with one key difference. In the first line of code, we apply the multiply_four function to step1, which was the list of Delayed objects we produced by adding two to the original list of numbers. Just like you saw in the DataFrame example, it's possible to chain together computations without immediately calculating the intermediate results.

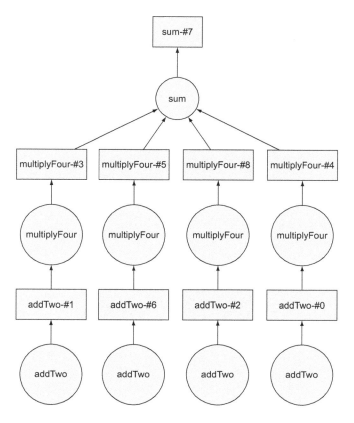

Figure 2.7   The DAG including the multiplyFour step

Figure 2.7 shows the output of the computation in listing 2.8. If you look closely at the DAG, you'll notice another layer has been added between the addTwo nodes and the sum node. This is because we've now instructed Dask to take each number from the list, add two to it, then add four, and *then* sum the results.

2.2.3   Reducing DAG complexity with persist

Let's now take this one step further: say we want to take this sum, add it back to each of our original numbers, then sum all that together.

Listing 2.9   Adding another layer to the DAG

```
data2 = [delayed(sum_two_numbers)(k, total) for k in data]
total2 = delayed(sum)(data2)
total2.visualize()
```

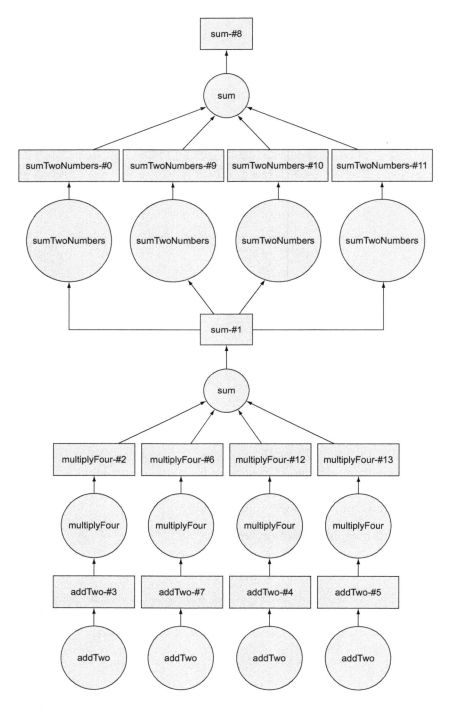

Figure 2.8   The DAG generated by listing 2.9

In this example, we've taken the complete DAG we created in the last example, which is stored in the `total` variable, and used it to create a new list of Delayed objects.

The DAG in figure 2.8 looks like the DAG from listing 2.9 was copied and another DAG was fused on top of it. That's precisely what we want! First, Dask will calculate the sum of the first set of transformations, then add it to each of the original numbers, then finally compute the sum of that intermediate step. As you can imagine, if we repeat this cycle a few more times, the DAG will start to get too large to visualize. Similarly, if we had 100 numbers in the original list instead of 4, the DAG diagram would also be very large (try replacing the data list with a `range[100]` and rerun the code!) But we touched on a more important reason in the last section as to why a large DAG might become unwieldy: persistence.

As mentioned before, every time you call the `compute` method on a Delayed object, Dask will step through the complete DAG to generate the result. This can be okay for simple computations, but if you're working on very large, distributed datasets, it can quickly become inefficient to repeat calculations over and over again. One way around that is to persist intermediate results that you want to reuse. But what does that do to the DAG?

Listing 2.10 Persisting calculations

```
total_persisted = total.persist()
total_persisted.visualize()
```

In this example, we took the DAG we created in listing 2.9 and persisted it. What we get instead of the full DAG is a single result, as seen in figure 2.9 (remember that a rectangle represents a result). This result represents the value that Dask would calculate when the `compute` method is called on the `total` object. But instead of re-computing it every time we need to access its value, Dask will now compute it once and save the result in memory. We can now chain another delayed calculation on top of this persisted result, and we get some interesting results.

Listing 2.11 Chaining a DAG from a persisted DAG

```
data2 = [delayed(sum_two_numbers)(l, total_persisted) for l in data]
total2 = delayed(sum)(data2)
total2.visualize()
```

The resulting DAG in figure 2.10 is much smaller. In fact, it looks like only the top half of the DAG from listing 2.9. That's because the `sum-#1` result is precomputed and persisted. So instead of calculating the whole DAG in listing 2.11, Dask can use the persisted data, thereby reducing the number of calculations needed to produce the result.

Before we move on to the next section, give listing 2.12 a try! Dask can generate very large DAGs. Although the diagram won't fit on this page, it will hopefully give you an appreciation of the complexity that Dask can handle very elegantly.

```
sum-#0
```

Figure 2.9   The DAG generated by listing 2.10

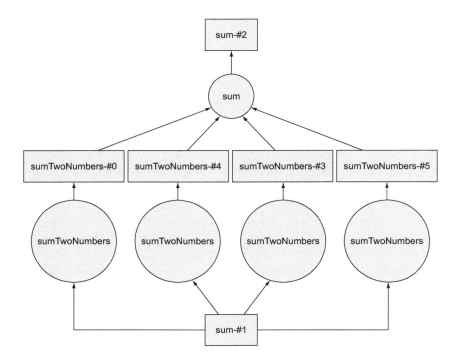

Figure 2.10   The DAG generated by listing 2.11

Listing 2.12   Visualizing the last NYC data DAG

```
missing_count.visualize()
```

2.3   *Task scheduling*

As I've mentioned a few times now, Dask uses the concept of *lazy computations* throughout its API. We've seen the effect of this in action—whenever we perform some kind of action on a Dask Delayed object, we have to call the compute method before anything actually happens. This is quite advantageous when you consider the time it might take to churn through petabytes of data. Since no computation actually happens until you request the result, you can define the complete string of transformations that Dask should perform on the data without having to wait for one computation to finish before defining the next—leaving you to do something else (like dice onions for that pot of bucatini all'Amatriciana I've convinced you to make) while the complete result is computing!

2.3.1   *Lazy computations*

Lazy computations also allow Dask to split work into smaller logical pieces, which helps avoid loading the entire data structure that it's operating on into memory. As you saw with the DataFrame in section 2.1, Dask divided the 2 GB file into 33 64 MB chunks, and operated on 8 chunks at a time. That means the maximum memory consumption for the entire operation didn't exceed 512 MB, yet we were still able to process the entire 2 GB file. This gets even more important as the size of the datasets you work on stretches into the terabyte and petabyte range.

But what actually happens when you request the result from Dask? The computations you defined are represented by a DAG, which is a step-by-step plan for computing the result you want. However, that step-by-step plan doesn't define which physical resources should be used to perform the computations. Two important things still must be considered: where the computations will take place and where the results of each computation should be shipped to if necessary. Unlike relational database systems, Dask does not predetermine the precise runtime location of each task before the work begins. Instead, the task scheduler dynamically assesses what work has been completed, what work is left to do, and what resources are free to accept additional work in real time. This allows Dask to gracefully handle a host of issues that arise in distributed computing, including recovery from worker failure, network unreliability, and workers completing work at different speeds. In addition, the task scheduler can keep track of where intermediate results have been stored, allowing follow-on work to be shipped to the data instead of unnecessarily shipping the data around the network. This results in far greater efficiency when operating Dask on a cluster.

2.3.2 Data locality

Since Dask makes it easy to scale up your code from your laptop to hundreds or thousands of physical servers, the task scheduler must make intelligent decisions about which physical machine(s) will be asked to take place in a specific piece of a computation. Dask uses a centralized task scheduler to orchestrate all this work. To do this, each Dask worker node reports what data it has available and how much load it's experiencing to the task scheduler. The task scheduler constantly evaluates the state of the cluster to come up with fair, efficient execution plans for computations submitted by users. For example, if we split the example from section 2.1 (reading the NYC parking ticket data) between two computers (server A and server B), the task scheduler may state that an operation on partition 26 should be performed by server A, and the same operation should be performed on partition 8 by server B. For the most part, if the task scheduler divides up the work as evenly as possible across machines in the cluster, the computations will complete as quickly and efficiently as possible.

But that rule of thumb does not always hold true in a number of scenarios: one server is under heavier load than the others, has less powerful hardware than the others, or does not have fast access to the data. If any of those conditions is true, the busier/weaker server will lag behind the others, and therefore should be given proportionately fewer tasks to avoid becoming a bottleneck. The dynamic nature of the task scheduler allows it to react to these situations accordingly if they cannot be avoided.

For best performance, a Dask cluster should use a distributed filesystem like S3 or HDFS to back its data storage. To illustrate why this is important, consider the following counterexample, where a file is stored on only one machine. For the sake of our example, the data is stored on server A. When server A is directed to work on partition 26, it can read the partition directly off its hard disk. However, this poses a problem for server B. Before server B can work on partition 8, server A will need to send partition 8 to server B. Any additional partitions that server B is to work on will also need to be sent over to server B before the work can begin. This will cause a considerable slowdown in the computations because operations involving networking (even 10 Gb fiber) are slower than direct reads off of locally attached disks.

Figure 2.11 demonstrates this issue. If Node 1 wants to work on Partition 1, it would be able to do so much more quickly if it had Partition 1 available on local disk. If this wasn't an option, it could read the data over the network from Node 2, but that would be much slower.

The remedy to this problem would be to split the file up ahead of time, store some partitions on server A, and store some partitions on server B. This is precisely what a distributed file system does. Logical files are split up between physical machines. Aside from other obvious benefits, like redundancy in the event one of the servers' hard disks fails, distributing the data across many physical machines allows the workload to be spread out more evenly. It's far faster to bring the computations to the data than to bring the data to the computations!

Dask's task scheduler takes *data locality*, or the physical location of data, into account when considering where a computation should take place. Although it's sometimes not

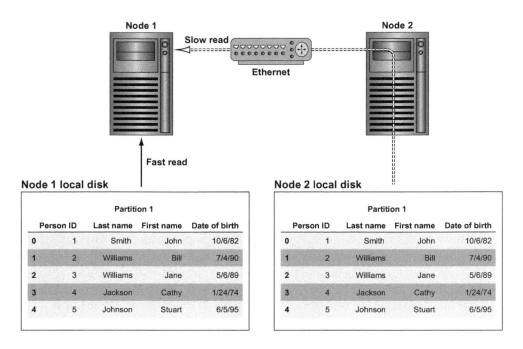

Figure 2.11   Reading data from local disk is much faster than reading data stored remotely.

possible for Dask to completely avoid moving data from one worker to another, such as instances where some data must be broadcast to all machines in the cluster, the task scheduler tries its hardest to minimize the amount of data that moves between physical servers. When datasets are smaller, it might not make much difference, but when datasets are very large, the effects of moving data around the network are much more evident. Therefore, minimizing data movement generally leads to more performant computations.

Hopefully you now have a better understanding of the important role that DAGs play in enabling Dask to break up huge amounts of work into more manageable pieces. We'll come back to the Delayed API in later chapters, but keep in mind that every piece of Dask we touch in this book is backed by Delayed objects, and you can visualize the backing DAG at any time. In practice, you likely won't need to troubleshoot computations in such explicit detail very often, but understanding the underlying mechanics of Dask will help you better identify potential issues and bottlenecks in your workloads. In the next chapter, we'll begin our deep dive into the DataFrame API in earnest.

Summary

- Computations on Dask DataFrames are structured by the task scheduler using DAGs.
- Computations are constructed lazily, and the `compute` method is called to execute the computation and retrieve the results.
- You can call the `visualize` method on any Dask object to see a visual representation of the underlying DAG.
- Computations can be streamlined by using the `persist` method to store and reuse intermediate results of complex computations.
- Data locality brings the computation to the data in order to minimize network and IO latency.

Part 2

Working with structured data using Dask DataFrames

Now that you have a basic understanding of how Dask makes it possible to both work with large datasets and take advantage of parallelism, you're ready to get some hands-on experience working with a real dataset to learn how to solve common data science challenges with Dask. Part 2 focuses on Dask Data-Frames—a parallelized implementation of the ever-popular Pandas DataFrame—and how to use them to clean, analyze, and visualize large structured datasets.

Chapter 3 opens the part by explaining how Dask parallelizes Pandas Data-Frames and describing why some parts of the Dask DataFrame API are different from its Pandas counterpart.

Chapter 4 jumps into the first part of the data science workflow by addressing how to read data into DataFrames from various data sources.

Chapter 5 continues the workflow by diving into common data manipulation and cleaning tasks, such as sorting, filtering, recoding, and filling in missing data.

Chapter 6 demonstrates how to generate descriptive statistics using some built-in functions, as well as how to build your own custom aggregate and window functions.

Chapters 7 and 8 close out part 2 by taking you from basic visualizations through advanced, interactive visualizations, even plotting location-based data on a map.

After completing part 2, you'll be well-versed in how to handle many data prep and analysis tasks common to data science projects, and you'll be in a good position to move into more advanced topics to come!

Introducing
Dask DataFrames

This chapter covers

- Defining structured data and determining when to use Dask DataFrames

- Exploring how Dask DataFrames are organized

- Inspecting DataFrames to see how they are partitioned

- Dealing with some limitations of DataFrames

In the previous chapter, we started exploring how Dask uses DAGs to coordinate and manage complex tasks across many machines. However, we only looked at some simple examples using the Delayed API to help illustrate how Dask code relates to elements of a DAG. In this chapter, we'll begin to take a closer look at the Data-Frame API. We'll also start working through the NYC Parking Ticket data following a fairly typical data science workflow. This workflow and their corresponding chapters can be seen in figure 3.1.

Figure 3.1   The *Data Science with Python and Dask* workflow

Dask DataFrames wrap Delayed objects around Pandas DataFrames to allow you to oper-ate on more sophisticated data structures. Rather than writing your own complex web of functions, the DataFrame API contains a whole host of complex transformation meth-ods such as Cartesian products, joins, grouping operations, and so on, that are useful for common data manipulation tasks. Before we cover those operations in depth, which we will do in chapter 5, we'll start our exploration of Dask by addressing some necessary background knowledge for data gathering. More specifically, we'll look at how Dask DataFrames are well suited to manipulate *structured data*, which is data that consists of rows and columns. We'll also look at how Dask can support parallel processing and han-dle large datasets by chunking data into smaller pieces called *partitions*. Plus, we'll look at some performance-maximizing best practices throughout the chapter.

3.1   *Why use DataFrames?*

The shape of data found "in the wild" is usually described one of two ways: structured or unstructured. Structured data is made up of rows and columns: from the humble spread-sheet to complex relational database systems, structured data is an intuitive way to store information. Figure 3.2 shows an example of a structured dataset with rows and columns.

It's natural to gravitate toward this format when thinking about data because the structure helps keep related bits of information together in the same visual space. A row represents a logical entity: in the spreadsheet, each row represents a person. Rows are made up of one or more columns, which represent things we know about each entity. In the spreadsheet, we've captured each person's last name, first name, date of birth, and a unique identifier. Many kinds of data can be fit into this shape: transactional data from point-of-sale systems, results from a marketing survey, clickstream data, and even image data once it's been specially encoded.

◄──────── **Columns** ────────►

Person ID	Last name	First name	Date of birth
1	Smith	John	10/6/82
2	Williams	Bill	7/4/90
3	Williams	Jane	5/6/89

Rows

Figure 3.2   An example of structured data

Because of the way that structured data is organized and stored, it's easy to think of many different ways to manipulate the data. For example, we could find the earliest date of birth in the dataset, filter people out that don't match a certain pattern, group people together by their last name, or sort people by their first name. Compare that with how the data might look if we stored it in several list objects.

Listing 3.1   A list representation of figure 3.2

```
person_IDs = [1,2,3]
person_last_names = ['Smith', 'Williams', 'Williams']
person_first_names = ['John', 'Bill', 'Jane']
person_DOBs = ['1982-10-06', '1990-07-04', '1989-05-06']
```

In listing 3.1, the columns are stored as separate lists. Although it's still possible to do all the transformations previously suggested, it's not immediately evident that the four lists are related to each other and form a complete dataset. Furthermore, the code required for operations like grouping and sorting on this data would be quite complex and require a substantial understanding of data structures and algorithms to write code that performs efficiently. Python offers many different data structures that we could use to represent this data, but none are as intuitive for storing structured data as the DataFrame.

Like a spreadsheet or a database table, DataFrames are organized into rows and columns. However, we have a few additional terms to be aware of when working with DataFrames: indexes and axes. Figure 3.3 displays the anatomy of a DataFrame.

The example in figure 3.3 shows a DataFrame representation of the structured data from figure 3.2. Notice the additional labels on the diagram: rows are referred to as "axis 0" and columns are referred to as "axis 1." This is important to remember when working with DataFrame operations that reshape the data. DataFrame operations default to working along axis 0, so unless you explicitly specify otherwise, Dask will perform operations row-wise.

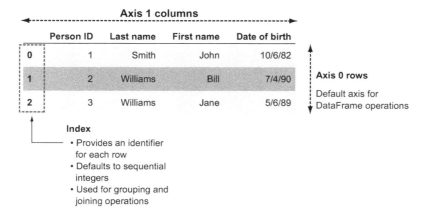

Figure 3.3   A Dask representation of the structured data example from figure 3.2

The other area highlighted in figure 3.3 is the index. The index provides an identifier for each row. Ideally, these identifiers should be unique, especially if you plan to use the index as a key to join with another DataFrame. However, Dask does not enforce uniqueness, so you can have duplicate indices if necessary. By default, DataFrames are created with a sequential integer index like the one seen in figure 3.3. If you want to specify your own index, you can set one of the columns in the DataFrame to be used as an index, or you can derive your own Index object and assign it to be the index of the DataFrame. We cover common indexing functions in-depth in chapter 5, but the importance of indices in Dask cannot be overstated: they hold the key to distributing DataFrame workloads across clusters of machines. With that in mind, we'll now take a look at how indices are used to form partitions.

3.2   *Dask and Pandas*

As mentioned a few times, Pandas is a very popular and powerful framework for analyzing structured data, but its biggest limitation is that it was not designed with scalability in mind. Pandas is exceptionally well suited for handling small structured datasets and is highly optimized to perform fast and efficient operations on data stored in memory. However, as we saw in our hypothetical kitchen scenario in chapter 1, as the volume of work increases substantially it can be a better choice to hire additional help and spread the tasks across many workers. This is where Dask's DataFrame API comes in: by providing a wrapper around Pandas that intelligently splits huge data frames into smaller pieces and spreads them across a cluster of workers, operations on huge datasets can be completed much more quickly and robustly.

The different pieces of the DataFrame that Dask oversees are called *partitions*. Each partition is a relatively small DataFrame that can be dispatched to any worker and maintains its full lineage in case it must be reproduced. Figure 3.4 demonstrates how Dask uses partitioning for parallel processing.

In figure 3.4, you can see the difference between how Pandas would handle the dataset and how Dask would handle the dataset. Using Pandas, the dataset would be loaded into memory and worked on sequentially one row at a time. Dask, on the other hand, can split the data into multiple partitions, allowing the workload to be *parallelized*. This means if we had a long-running function to apply over the DataFrame, Dask could complete the work more efficiently by spreading the work out over multiple machines. However, it should be noted that the DataFrame in figure 3.4 is used only for the sake of example. As mentioned previously, the task scheduler does introduce some overhead into the process, so using Dask to process a DataFrame with only 10 rows would likely not be the fastest solution. Figure 3.5 shows an example of how two hosts might coordinate work on this partitioned dataset in more detail.

As node 1 is driving the computation and telling node 2 what to do, it is currently taking on the role of the task scheduler. Node 1 tells node 2 to work on partition 2 while node 1 works on partition 1. Each node finishes its processing tasks and send its part of the result back to the client. The client then assembles the pieces of the results and displays the output.

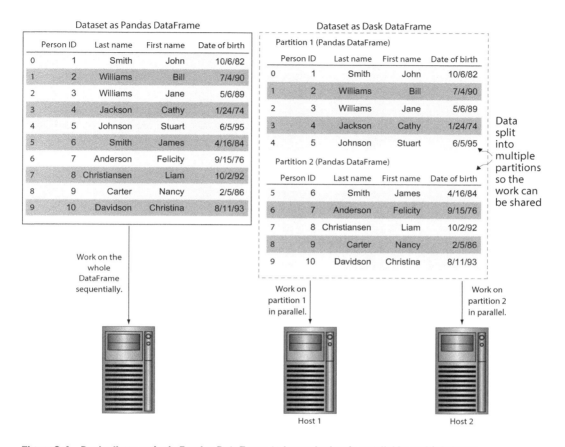

Figure 3.4 Dask allows a single Pandas DataFrame to be worked on in parallel by multiple hosts.

3.2.1 Managing DataFrame partitioning

Since partitioning can have such a significant impact on performance, you might be worried that managing partitioning will be a difficult and tedious part of constructing Dask workloads. However, fear not: Dask tries to help you get as much performance as possible without manual tuning by including some sensible defaults and heuristics for creating and managing partitions. For example, when reading in data using the read_csv method of Dask DataFrames, the default partition size is 64 MB each (this is also known as the default blocksize). While 64 MB might seem quite small given that modern servers tend to have tens of gigabytes of RAM, it is an amount of data that is small enough that it can be quickly transported over the network if necessary, but large enough to minimize the likelihood that a machine will run out of things to do while waiting for the next partition to arrive. Using either the default or a user-specified blocksize, the data will be split into as many partitions as necessary so that each partition is no larger than the blocksize. If you desire to create a DataFrame with a specific number of partitions instead, you can specify that when creating the DataFrame by passing in the npartitions argument.

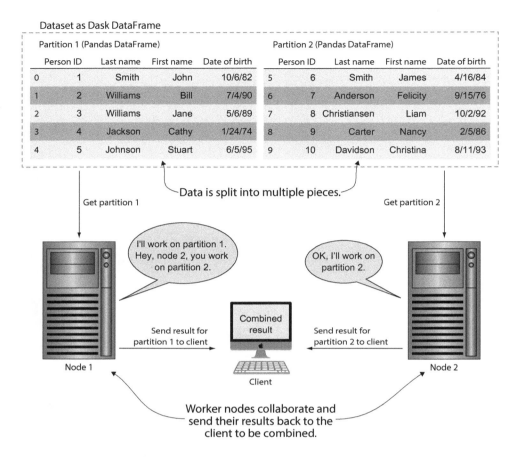

Figure 3.5   Processing data in parallel across several machines

Listing 3.2   Creating a DataFrame with a specific number of partitions

```
import pandas
import dask.dataframe as daskDataFrame

person_IDs = [1,2,3,4,5,6,7,8,9,10]
person_last_names = ['Smith', 'Williams', 'Williams','Jackson','Johnson',
    'Smith','Anderson','Christiansen','Carter','Davidson']
person_first_names = ['John', 'Bill', 'Jane','Cathy','Stuart','James',
    'Felicity','Liam','Nancy','Christina']
person_DOBs = ['1982-10-06', '1990-07-04', '1989-05-06', '1974-01-24',
    '1995-06-05', '1984-04-16', '1976-09-15', '1992-10-02', '1986-02-05',
    '1993-08-11']          Creating all the data as lists

peoplePandasDataFrame = pandas.DataFrame({'Person ID':personIDs,
            'Last Name': personLastNames,
            'First Name': personFirstName,                    Stores the data in a
           'Date of Birth': personDOBs},                      Pandas DataFrame
         columns=['Person ID', 'Last Name', 'First Name', 'Date of Birth'])
```

```
peopleDaskDataFrame = daskDataFrame.from_pandas(peoplePandasDataFrame,
    npartitions=2)
```
Converts the Pandas DataFrame to a Dask DataFrame

In listing 3.2, we created a Dask DataFrame and explicitly split it into two partitions using the npartitions argument. Normally, Dask would have put this dataset into a single partition because it is quite small.

Listing 3.3 Inspecting partitioning of a Dask DataFrame

Shows the boundaries of the partitioning scheme; produces the output: (0, 5, 9)

Shows how many partitions exist in the DataFrame; produces the output: 2; partition 1 holds rows 0 to 4, partition 2 holds rows 5 to 9

```
print(people_dask_df.divisions)
print(people_dask_df.npartitions)
```

Listing 3.3 shows a couple useful attributes of Dask DataFrames that can be used to inspect how a DataFrame is partitioned. The first attribute, divisions, (0, 5, 9), shows the boundaries of the partitioning scheme (remember that partitions are created on the index). This might look strange since there are two partitions but three boundaries. Each partition's boundary consists of pairs of numbers from the list of divisions. The boundary for the first partition is "from 0 up to (but not including) 5," meaning it will contain rows 0, 1, 2, 3, and 4. The boundary for the second partition is "from 5 through (and including) 9," meaning it will contain rows 5, 6, 7, 8, and 9. The last partition always includes the upper boundary, whereas the other partitions go up to but don't include their upper boundary.

The second attribute, npartitions, simply returns the number of partitions that exist in the DataFrame.

Listing 3.4 Inspecting the rows in a DataFrame

```
people_dask_df.map_partitions(len).compute()
```
Counts the number of rows in each partition
```
''' Produces the output:
0    5
1    5
dtype: int64 '''
```

Listing 3.4 shows how to use the map_partitions method to count the number of rows in each partition. map_partitions generally applies a given function to each partition. This means that the result of the map_partitions call will return a Series equal in size to the number of partitions the DataFrame currently has. Since we have two partitions in this DataFrame, we get two items back in the result of the call. The output shows that each partition contains five rows, meaning Dask split the DataFrame into two equal pieces.

Sometimes it may be necessary to change the number of partitions in a Dask Data-Frame. Particularly when your computations include a substantial amount of filtering, the size of each partition can become imbalanced, which can have negative performance consequences on subsequent computations. The reason for this is because if one partition suddenly contains a majority of the data, all the advantages of parallelism are effectively lost. Let's look at an example of this. First, we'll derive a new DataFrame by applying a filter to our original DataFrame that removes all people with the last name Williams. We'll then inspect the makeup of the new DataFrame by using the same map_partitions call to count the rows per partition.

> **Listing 3.5   Repartitioning a DataFrame**

Filters out people with a last name of Williams and recount the rows.

Collapses the two partitions into one

```
people_filtered = people_dask_df[people_dask_df['Last Name'] != 'Williams']
print(people_filtered.map_partitions(len).compute())

people_filtered_reduced = people_filtered.repartition(npartitions=1)
print(people_filtered_reduced.map_partitions(len).compute())
```

Notice what happened: the first partition now only contains three rows, and the second partition has the original five. People with the last name of Williams happened to be in the first partition, so our new DataFrame has become rather unbalanced.

The second two lines of code in the listing aim to fix the imbalance by using the repartition method on the filtered DataFrame. The npartitions argument here works the same way as the npartitions argument used earlier when we created the initial DataFrame. Simply specify the number of partitions you want and Dask will figure out what needs to be done to make it so. If you specify a lower number than the current number of partitions, Dask will combine existing partitions by concatenation. If you specify a higher number than the current number of partitions, Dask will split existing partitions into smaller pieces. You can call repartition at any time in your program to initiate this process. However, like all other Dask operations, it's a lazy computation. No data will actually get moved around until you make a call such as compute, head, and so on. Calling the map_partitions function again on the new DataFrame, we can see that the number of partitions has been reduced to one, and it contains all eight of the rows. Note that if you repartition again, this time increasing the number or partitions, the old divisions (0, 5, 9) will be retained. If you want to split the partitions evenly, you will need to manually update the divisions to match your data.

3.2.2   *What is the shuffle?*

Now that we've learned that partitioning is important, explored how Dask handles partitioning, and learned what you can do to influence it, we'll round out this discussion by learning about a frequent challenge that arises in distributed computing: dealing with the *shuffle*. No, I'm not talking about the dance move—frankly, I wouldn't be the best source of dance advice! In distributed computing, the shuffle is the process of broadcasting all partitions to all workers. Shuffling the data is necessary when performing sorting, grouping, and indexing operations, because each row needs to be compared to every other row in the entire DataFrame to determine its correct relative position. This is a time-expensive operation, because it necessitates transferring large amounts of data over the network. Let's see what this might look like.

In figure 3.6, we're seeing what would happen with our DataFrame if we want to group our data by Last Name. For example, we might want to find the eldest person by last name. For the majority of the data, it's no problem. Most of the last names in this dataset are unique. As you can see in the data in figure 3.6, there are only two cases in which we have multiple people with the same last name: Williams and Smith. For the two people named Williams, they are in the same partition, so server 1 has all the information it needs locally to determine that the oldest Williams was born in 1989. However, for the people named Smith, there's one Smith in partition 1 and one Smith in partition 2. Either server 1 will have to send its Smith to server 2 to make the comparison, or server 2 will have to send server 1 its Smith. In both cases, for Dask to be able to compare the birthdates of each Smith, one of them will have to be shipped over the network.

Depending on what needs to be done with the data, completely avoiding shuffle operations might not be feasible. However, you can do a few things to minimize the need for shuffling the data. First, ensuring that the data is stored in a presorted order will eliminate the need to sort the data with Dask. If possible, sorting the data in a source system, such as a relational database, can be faster and more efficient than sorting the data in a distributed system. Second, using a sorted column as the DataFrame's index will enable greater efficiency with joins. When the data is presorted, lookup operations are very fast because the partition where a certain row is kept can be easily determined by using the divisions defined on the DataFrame. Finally, if you must use an operation that triggers a shuffle, persist the result if you have the resources to do so. This will prevent having to repeat shuffling the data again if the DataFrame needs to be recomputed.

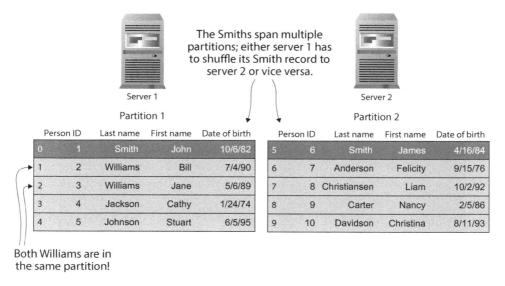

Figure 3.6 A `GroupBy` **operation that requires a shuffle**

3.3   *Limitations of Dask DataFrames*

Now that you have a good idea of what the DataFrame API is useful for, it will be helpful to close the chapter by covering a few limitations that the DataFrame API has.

First and foremost, Dask DataFrames do not expose the entire Pandas API. Even though Dask DataFrames are made up of smaller Pandas DataFrames, some functions that Pandas does well are simply not conducive to a distributed environment. For example, functions that would alter the structure of the DataFrame, such as insert and pop, are not supported because Dask DataFrames are immutable. Some of the more complex window operations are also not supported, such as expanding and EWM methods, as well as complex transposition methods like stack/unstack and melt, because of their tendency to cause a lot of data shuffling. Oftentimes, these expensive operations don't really need to be performed on the full, raw dataset. In those cases, you should use Dask to do all your normal data prep, filtering, and transformation, then dump the final dataset into Pandas. You will then be able to perform the expensive operations on the reduced dataset. Dask's DataFrame API makes it very easy to interoperate with Pandas DataFrames, so this pattern can be very useful when analyzing data using Dask DataFrames.

The second limitation is with relational-type operations, such as `join/merge`, `groupby`, and `rolling`. Although these operations are supported, they are likely to involve a lot of shuffling, making them performance bottlenecks. This can be minimized, again, either by using Dask to prepare a smaller dataset that can be dumped into Pandas, or by limiting these operations to only use the index. For example, if we wanted to join a DataFrame of people to a DataFrame of transactions, that computation would be significantly faster if both datasets were sorted and indexed by the Person ID. This would minimize the likelihood that each person's records are spread out across many partitions, in turn making shuffles more efficient.

Third, indexing has a few challenges due to the distributed nature of Dask. If you wish to use a column in a DataFrame as an index in lieu of the default numeric index, it will need to be sorted. If the data is stored presorted, this becomes no problem at all. If the data is not presorted, it can be very slow to sort the entire DataFrame because it requires a lot of shuffling. Effectively, each partition first needs to be sorted, then needs to be merged and sorted again with every other partition. Sometimes it may be necessary to do this, but if you can proactively store your data presorted for the computations you need, it will save you a lot of time.

The other significant difference you may notice with indexing is how Dask handles the `reset_index` method. Unlike Pandas, where this will recalculate a new sequential index across the entire DataFrame, the method in Dask DataFrames behaves like a `map_partitions` call. This means that each partition will be given its own sequential index that starts at 0, so the whole DataFrame will no longer have a unique sequential index. In figure 3.7, you can see the effect of this.

Each partition contained five rows, so once we called `reset_index`, the index of the first five rows remains the same, but the next five rows, which are contained in the

The Index recycled back to 0 when the partition boundary was reached.

	Person ID	Last name	First name	Date of birth
0	1	Smith	John	10/6/82
1	2	Williams	Bill	7/4/90
2	3	Williams	Jane	5/6/89
3	4	Jackson	Cathy	1/24/74
4	5	Johnson	Stuart	6/5/95
0	6	Smith	James	4/16/84
1	7	Anderson	Felicity	9/15/76
2	8	Christiansen	Liam	10/2/92
3	9	Carter	Nancy	2/5/86
4	10	Davidson	Christina	8/11/93

Figure 3.7   The result of calling `reset_index` on a Dask DataFrame

next partition, start over at 0. Unfortunately, there's no easy way to reset the index in a partition-aware way. Therefore, use the `reset_index` method carefully and only if you don't plan to use the resulting sequential index to join, group, or sort the DataFrame.

Finally, since a Dask DataFrame is made up of many Pandas DataFrames, operations that are inefficient in Pandas will also be inefficient in Dask. For example, iterating over rows by using the `apply` and `iterrows` methods is notoriously inefficient in Pandas. Therefore, following Pandas best practices will give you the best performance possible when using Dask DataFrames. If you're not well on your way to mastering Pandas yet, continuing to sharpen your skills will not only benefit you as you get more familiar with Dask and distributed workloads, but it will help you in general as a data scientist!

Summary

- Dask DataFrames consist of rows (axis 0), columns (axis 1), and an index.
- DataFrame methods tend to operate row-wise by default.
- Inspecting how a DataFrame is partitioned can be done by accessing the `divisions` attribute of a DataFrame.
- Filtering a DataFrame can cause an imbalance in the size of each partition. For best performance, partitions should be roughly equal in size. It's a good practice to repartition a DataFrame using the `repartition` method after filtering a large amount of data.
- For best performance, DataFrames should be indexed by a logical column, partitioned by their index, and the index should be presorted.

Loading data into DataFrames

This chapter covers

- Creating DataFrames from delimited text files and defining data schemas
- Extracting data from a SQL relational database and manipulating it using Dask
- Reading data from distributed filesystems (S3 and HDFS)
- Working with data stored in Parquet format

I've given you a lot of concepts to chew on over the course of the previous three chapters—all of which will serve you well along your journey to becoming a Dask expert. But, we're now ready to roll up our sleeves and get into working with some data. As a reminder, figure 4.1 shows the data science workflow we'll be following as we work through the functionality of Dask.

Figure 4.1 The *Data Science with Python and Dask* workflow

In this chapter, we remain at the very first steps of our workflow: Problem Definition and Data Gathering. Over the next few chapters, we'll be working with the NYC Parking Ticket data to answer the following question:

> *What patterns can we find in the data that are correlated with increases or decreases in the number of parking tickets issued by the New York City parking authority?*

Perhaps we might find that older vehicles are more likely to receive tickets, or perhaps a particular color attracts more attention from the parking authority than other colors. Using this guiding question, we'll gather, clean, and explore the relevant data with Dask DataFrames. With that in mind, we'll begin by learning how to read data into Dask DataFrames.

One of the unique challenges that data scientists face is our tendency to study *data at rest*, or data that wasn't specifically collected for the purpose of predictive modeling and analysis. This is quite different from a traditional academic study in which data is carefully and thoughtfully collected. Consequentially, you're likely to come across a wide variety of storage media and data formats throughout your career. We will cover reading data in some of the most popular formats and storage systems in this chapter, but by no means does this chapter cover the full extent of Dask's abilities. Dask is very flexible in many ways, and the DataFrame API's ability to interface with a very large number of data collection and storage systems is a shining example of that.

As we work through reading data into DataFrames, keep what you learned in previous chapters about Dask's components in mind: the Dask DataFrames we will create are made up of many small Pandas DataFrames that have been logically divided into partitions. All operations performed on the Dask DataFrame result in the generation of a DAG (directed acyclic graph) of Delayed objects which can be distributed to many processes or physical machines. And the task scheduler controls the distribution and execution of the task graph. Now on to the data!

4.1 *Reading data from text files*

We'll start with the simplest and most common format you're likely to come across: delimited text files. Delimited text files come in many flavors, but all share the common concept of using special characters called *delimiters* that are used to divide data up into logical rows and columns.

Every delimited text file format has two types of delimiters: row delimiters and column delimiters. A row delimiter is a special character that indicates that you've reached the end of a row, and any additional data to the right of it should be considered part of the next row. The most common row delimiter is simply a newline character (\n) or a carriage return followed by a newline character (\r\n). Delimiting rows by line is a standard choice because it provides the additional benefit of breaking up the raw data visually and reflects the layout of a spreadsheet.

Likewise, a column delimiter indicates the end of a column, and any data to the right of it should be treated as part of the next column. Of all the popular column delimiters out there, the comma (,) is the most frequently used. In fact, delimited text files that use comma column delimiters have a special file format named for it: *comma-separated values* or CSV for short. Among other common options are pipe (|), tab, space, and semicolon.

In figure 4.2, you can see the general structure of a delimited text file. This one in particular is a CSV file because we're using commas as the column delimiter. Also, since we're using the newline as the row delimiter, you can see that each row is on its own line.

Two additional attributes of a delimited text file that we haven't discussed yet include an optional header row and text qualifiers. A header row is simply the use of the first row to specify names of columns. Here, Person ID, Last Name, and First Name aren't descriptions of a person; they are *metadata* that describe the data structure. While not required, a header row can be helpful for communicating what your data structure is supposed to hold.

Text qualifiers are yet another type of special character used to denote that the contents of the column is a text string. They can be very useful in instances where the actual data is allowed to contain characters that are also being used as row or column delimiters. This is a fairly common issue when working with CSV files that contain text data, because commas normally show up in text. Surrounding these columns with text qualifiers indicates that any instances of the column or row delimiters inside the text qualifiers should be ignored.

Now that you've had a look at the structure of delimited text files, let's have a look at how to apply this knowledge by importing some delimited text files into Dask. The NYC Parking Ticket data we briefly looked at in chapter 2 comes as a set of CSV files, so this will be a perfect dataset to work with for this example. If you haven't downloaded the data already, you can do so by visiting www.kaggle.com/new-york-city/nyc-parking-tickets. As I mentioned before, I've unzipped the data into the same folder as the Jupyter notebook I'm working in for convenience's sake. If you've put your data elsewhere, you'll need to change the file path to match the location where you saved the data.

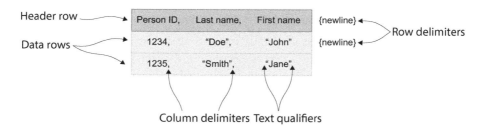

Figure 4.2   The structure of a delimited text file

Dask DataFrame structure:

	Summons number	Plate ID	Registration state	Plate type	Issue date	Violation code	Vehicle body type	Vehicle make	Issuing agency	Street code1	Street code2	Street code3	Vehicle expiration date	Violation location	Violation precinct
npartitions=33															
	int64	object	object	object	object	int64	object	object	object	int64	int64	int64	int64	float64	int64
	...	...	...	...	...	...	...	...	...	...	...	...	...	...	...
...	...	...	...	...	...	...	...	...	...	...	...	...	...	...	...
	...	...	...	...	...	...	...	...	...	...	...	...	...	...	...
	...	...	...	...	...	...	...	...	...	...	...	...	...	...	...

Dask Name: from-delayed, 99 tasks

Figure 4.3 The metadata of the `fy17` DataFrame

Listing 4.1 Importing CSV files using Dask defaults

```
import dask.dataframe as dd
from dask.diagnostics import ProgressBar

fy14 = dd.read_csv('nyc-parking-tickets/Parking_Violations_Issued_-_Fiscal_
    Year_2014__August_2013___June_2014_.csv')
fy15 = dd.read_csv('nyc-parking-tickets/Parking_Violations_Issued_-_Fiscal_
    Year_2015.csv')
fy16 = dd.read_csv('nyc-parking-tickets/Parking_Violations_Issued_-_Fiscal_
    Year_2016.csv')
fy17 = dd.read_csv('nyc-parking-tickets/Parking_Violations_Issued_-_Fiscal_
    Year_2017.csv')

fy17
```

In listing 4.1, the first three lines should look familiar: we're simply importing the DataFrame library and the ProgressBar context. In the next four lines of code, we're reading in the four CSV files that come with the NYC Parking Ticket dataset. For now, we'll read each file into its own separate DataFrame. Let's have a look at what happened by inspecting the fy17 DataFrame.

In figure 4.3, we see the metadata of the fy17 DataFrame. Using the default 64 MB blocksize, the data was split into 33 partitions. You might recall this from chapter 3. You can also see the column names at the top, but where did those come from? By default, Dask assumes that your CSV files will have a header row, and our file indeed has a header row. If you look at the raw CSV file in your favorite text editor, you will see the column names on the first line of the file. If you want to see all the column names, you can inspect the columns attribute of the DataFrame.

Listing 4.2 Inspecting the columns of a DataFrame

```
fy17.columns

'''
Produces the output:
```

```
Index([u'Summons Number', u'Plate ID', u'Registration State', u'Plate Type',
       u'Issue Date', u'Violation Code', u'Vehicle Body Type', u'Vehicle
       Make', u'Issuing Agency', u'Street Code1', u'Street Code2', u'Street
       Code3',u'Vehicle Expiration Date', u'Violation Location',
         u'Violation Precinct', u'Issuer Precinct', u'Issuer Code',
         u'Issuer Command', u'Issuer Squad', u'Violation Time',
         u'Time First Observed', u'Violation County',
         u'Violation In Front Of Or Opposite', u'House Number', u'Street Name',
       u'Intersecting Street', u'Date First Observed', u'Law Section',
         u'Sub Division', u'Violation Legal Code', u'Days Parking In Effect
       ', u'From Hours In Effect', u'To Hours In Effect', u'Vehicle Color',
         u'Unregistered Vehicle?', u'Vehicle Year', u'Meter Number',
         u'Feet From Curb', u'Violation Post Code', u'Violation Description',
         u'No Standing or Stopping Violation', u'Hydrant Violation',
         u'Double Parking Violation'],
       dtype='object')
'''
```

If you happen to take a look at the columns of any other DataFrame, such as fy14 (Parking Tickets for 2014), you'll notice that the columns are different from the fy17 (Parking Tickets for 2017) DataFrame. It looks as though the NYC government changed what data it collects about parking violations in 2017. For example, the latitude and longitude of the violation was not recorded prior to 2017, so these columns won't be useful for analyzing year-over-year trends (such as how parking violation "hotspots" migrate throughout the city). If we simply concatenated the datasets together as is, we would get a resulting DataFrame with an awful lot of missing values. Before we combine the datasets, we should find the columns that all four of the Data-Frames have in common. Then we should be able to simply union the DataFrames together to produce a new DataFrame that contains all four years of data.

We could manually look at each DataFrame's columns and deduce which columns overlap, but that would be terribly inefficient. Instead, we'll automate the process by taking advantage of the DataFrames' columns attribute and Python's set operations. The following listing shows you how to do this.

> **Listing 4.3   Finding the common columns between the four DataFrames**

```
# Import for Python 3.x
from functools import reduce

columns = [set(fy14.columns),
    set(fy15.columns),
    set(fy16.columns),
    set(fy17.columns)]
common_columns = list(reduce(lambda a, i: a.intersection(i), columns))
```

On the first line, we create a list that contains four set objects, respectively representing each DataFrame's columns. On the next line, we take advantage of the intersection method of set objects that returns a set containing the items that exist in both of the sets it's comparing. Wrapping this in a reduce function, we're able to walk through each DataFrame's metadata, pull out the columns that are common to all four DataFrames, and discard any columns that aren't found in all four DataFrames. What we're left with is the following abbreviated list of columns:

```
['House Number',
 'No Standing or Stopping Violation',
 'Sub Division',
 'Violation County',
 'Hydrant Violation',
 'Plate ID',
 'Plate Type',
 'Vehicle Year',
 'Street Name',
 'Vehicle Make',
'Issuing Agency',
...
 'Issue Date']
```

Now that we have a set of common columns shared by all four of the DataFrames, let's take a look at the first couple of rows of the fy17 DataFrame.

Listing 4.4   Looking at the head of the `fy17` DataFrame

```
fy17[common_columns].head()
```

Two important things are happening in listing 4.4: the column filtering operation and the top collecting operation. Specifying one or more columns in square brackets to the right of the DataFrame name is the primary way you can select/filter columns in the Data-Frame. Since common_columns is a list of column names, we can pass that in to the column selector and get a result containing the columns contained in the list. We've also chained a call to the head method, which allows you to view the top *n* rows of a DataFrame. As shown in figure 4.4, by default, it will return the first five rows of the DataFrame, but you

	Feet from curb	No standing or stopping violation	Vehicle color	Meter number	Violation description	Vehicle year	Street code1	Date first observed	To hours in effect	Summons number	...	Street name	Violation legal code	Time first observed	Issuer code	Issuer command	Street code2
0	0	NaN	GY	NaN	FAILURE TO STOP AT RED LIGHT	2001	0	0	NaN	5092469481	...	ALLERTON AVE (W/B) @	T	NaN	0	NaN	0
1	0	NaN	GY	NaN	FAILURE TO STOP AT RED LIGHT	2001	0	0	NaN	5092451658	...	ALLERTON AVE (W/B) @	T	NaN	0	NaN	0
2	0	NaN	BK	NaN	BUS LANE VIOLATION	2004	0	0	NaN	4006265037	...	SB WEBSTER AVE @ E 1	T	NaN	0	NaN	0
3	0	NaN	WH	NaN	47-Double PKG-Midtown	2007	10610	0	0700P	8478629828	...	7th Ave	NaN	NaN	359594	T102	34330
4	0	NaN	WHITE	NaN	69-Failure to Disp Muni Recpt	2007	10510	0	0700P	7868300310	...	6th Ave	NaN	NaN	364832	T102	34310

5 rows x 43 columns

Figure 4.4   The first five rows of the `fy17` DataFrame using the common column set

can specify the number of rows you wish to retrieve as an argument. For example, `fy17`
`.head(10)` will return the first 10 rows of the DataFrame. Keep in mind that when you
get rows back from Dask, they're being loaded into your computer's RAM. So, if you try
to return too many rows of data, you will receive an out-of-memory error. Now let's try
the same call on the `fy14` DataFrame.

Listing 4.5   Looking at the head of the `fy14` DataFrame

```
fy14[common_columns].head()

'''
Produces the following output:

Mismatched dtypes found in `pd.read_csv`/`pd.read_table`.

+-----------------------+---------+----------+
| Column                | Found   | Expected |
+-----------------------+---------+----------+
| Issuer Squad          | object  | int64    |
| Unregistered Vehicle? | float64 | int64    |
| Violation Description | object  | float64  |
| Violation Legal Code  | object  | float64  |
| Violation Post Code   | object  | float64  |
+-----------------------+---------+----------+

The following columns also raised exceptions on conversion:

- Issuer Squad
  ValueError('cannot convert float NaN to integer',)
- Violation Description
  ValueError('invalid literal for float(): 42-Exp. Muni-Mtr (Com. Mtr. Z)',)
- Violation Legal Code
  ValueError('could not convert string to float: T',)
- Violation Post Code
  ValueError('invalid literal for float(): 05 -',)

Usually this is due to dask's dtype inference failing, and
*may* be fixed by specifying dtypes manually
'''
```

Looks like Dask ran into trouble when trying to read the `fy14` data! Thankfully, the
Dask development team has given us some pretty detailed information in this error
message about what happened. Five columns—Issuer Squad, Unregistered Vehicle?,
Violation Description, Violation Legal Code, and Violation Post Code—failed to be
read correctly because their datatypes were not what Dask expected. As we learned in
chapter 2, Dask uses random sampling to infer datatypes to avoid scanning the entire
(potentially massive) DataFrame. Although this usually works well, it can break down
when a large number of values are missing in a column or the vast majority of data can
be classified as one datatype (such as an integer), but a small number of edge cases
break that assumption (such as a random string or two). When that happens, Dask will
throw an exception once it begins to work on a computation. In order to help Dask

read our dataset correctly, we'll need to manually define a schema for our data instead of relying on type inference. Before we get around to doing that, let's review what datatypes are available in Dask so we can create an appropriate schema for our data.

4.1.1 *Using Dask datatypes*

Similar to relational database systems, column datatypes play an important role in Dask DataFrames. They control what kind of operations can be performed on a column, how overloaded operators (+, -, and so on) behave, and how memory is allocated to store and access the column's values. Unlike most collections and objects in Python, Dask DataFrames use explicit typing rather than duck typing. This means that all values contained in a column must conform to the same datatype. As we saw already, Dask will throw errors if values in a column are found that violate the column's datatype.

Since Dask DataFrames consist of partitions made up of Pandas DataFrames, which in turn are complex collections of NumPy arrays, Dask sources its datatypes from NumPy. The NumPy library is a powerful and important mathematics library for Python. It enables users to perform advanced operations from linear algebra, calculus, and trigonometry. This library is important for the needs of data science because it provides the cornerstone mathematics for many statistical analysis methods and machine learning algorithms in Python. Let's take a look at NumPy's datatypes, which can be seen in figure 4.5.

As you can see, many of these reflect the primitive types in Python. The biggest difference is that NumPy datatypes can be explicitly sized with a specified bit-width. For example, the `int32` datatype is a 32-bit integer that allows any integer between –2,147,483,648 and 2,147,483,647. Python, by comparison, always uses the maximum

Basic type	Available NumPy types	Comments
Boolean	`bool`	Elements are 1 byte in size.
Integer	`int8, int16, int32, int64, int128, int`	`int` defaults to the size of `int` in C for the platform.
Unsigned integer	`uint8, uint16, uint32, uint64, uint128, uint`	`uint` defaults to the size of unsigned `int` in C for the platform.
Float	`float32, float64, float, longfloat`	`float` is always a double-precision floating-point value (64 bits). `longfloat` represents large-precision floats. Its size is platform dependent.
Complex	`complex64, complex128, complex`	The real and complex elements of a `complex64` are each represented by a single-precision (32-bit) value for a total size of 64 bits.
Strings	`str, unicode`	Unicode is always UTF32 (UCS4).
Object	`object`	Represents items in arrays as Python objects.
Records	`void`	Used for arbitrary data structures in record arrays.

Figure 4.5   NumPy datatypes used by Dask

bit-width based on your operating system and hardware's support. So, if you're working on a computer with a 64-bit CPU and running a 64-bit OS, Python will always allocate 64 bits of memory to store an integer. The advantage of using smaller datatypes
where appropriate is that you can hold more data in RAM and the CPU's cache at one
time, leading to faster, more efficient computations. This means that when creating a
schema for your data, you should always choose the smallest possible datatype to hold
your data. The risk, however, is that if a value exceeds the maximum size allowed by the
particular datatype, you will experience overflow errors, so you should think carefully
about the range and domain of your data.

For example, consider house prices in the United States: home prices are typically
above $32,767 and are unlikely to exceed $2,147,483,647 for quite some time if histor-
ical inflation rates prevail. Therefore, if you were to store house prices rounded to the
nearest whole dollar, the int32 datatype would be most appropriate. While the int64
and int128 types are wide enough to hold this range of numbers, it would be inefficient
to use more than 32 bits of memory to store each value. Likewise, using int8 or int16
would not be large enough to hold the data, resulting in an overflow error.

If none of the NumPy datatypes are appropriate for the kind of data you have, a column can be stored as an object type, which represents any Python object. This is also
the datatype that Dask will default to when its type inference comes across a column that
has a mix of numbers and strings, or when type inference cannot determine an appropriate datatype to use. However, one common exception to this rule happens when you
have a column with a high percentage of missing data. Take a look at figure 4.6, which
shows part of the output of that last error message again.

Would you really believe that a column called Violation Description should be a
floating-point number? Probably not! Typically, we can expect description columns to
be text, and therefore Dask should use an object datatype. Then why did Dask's type
inference think the column holds 64-bit floating-point numbers? It turns out that a large
majority of records in this DataFrame have missing violation descriptions. In the raw
data, they are simply blank. Dask treats blank records as null values when parsing files,
and by default fills in missing values with NumPy's NaN (not a number) object called
np.nan. If you use Python's built-in type function to inspect the datatype of an object, it

Column	Found	Expected
Issuer squad	object	int64
Unregistered vehicle?	float64	int64
Violation description	object	float64
Violation legal code	object	float64
Violation post code	object	float64

**Dask inferred a text column to
be a floating-point number?
That doesn't look right!**

Figure 4.6   A Dask error showing mismatched datatypes

reports that np.nan is a float type. So, since Dask's type inference randomly selected a bunch of np.nan objects when trying to infer the type of the Violation Description column, it assumed that the column must contain floating-point numbers. Now let's fix the problem so we can read in our DataFrame with the appropriate datatypes.

4.1.2 Creating schemas for Dask DataFrames

Oftentimes when working with a dataset, you'll know each column's datatype, whether it can contain missing values, and its valid range of values ahead of time. This information is collectively known as the data's *schema*. You're especially likely to know the schema for a dataset if it came from a relational database. Each column in a database table must have a well-known datatype. If you have this information ahead of time, using with Dask is as easy as writing up the schema and applying it to the read_csv method. You'll see how to do that at the end of this section. However, sometimes you might not know what the schema is ahead of time, and you'll need to figure it out on your own. Perhaps you're pulling data from a web API which hasn't been properly documented or you're analyzing a data extract and you don't have access to the data source. Neither of these approaches is ideal because they can be tedious and time consuming, but sometimes you may really have no other option. Here are two methods you can try:

- Guess-and-check
- Manually sample the data

The guess-and-check method isn't complicated. If you have well-named columns, such as Product Description, Sales Amount, and so on, you can try to infer what kind of data each column contains using the names. If you run into a datatype error while running a computation like the ones we've seen, simply update the schema and start over again. The advantage of this method is that you can quickly and easily try different schemas, but the downside is that it may become tedious to constantly restart your computations if they continue to fail due to datatype issues.

The manual sampling method aims to be a bit more sophisticated but can take more time up front since it involves scanning through some of the data to profile it. However, if you're planning to analyze the dataset anyways, it's not "wasted" time in the sense that you will be familiarizing yourself with the data while creating the schema. Let's look at how we can do this.

Listing 4.6 Building a generic schema

```
import numpy as np
import pandas as pd

dtype_tuples = [(x, np.str) for x in common_columns]
dtypes = dict(dtype_tuples)
dtypes

'''
```

```
Displays the following output:
{'Date First Observed': str,
 'Days Parking In Effect     ': str,
 'Double Parking Violation': str,
 'Feet From Curb': str,
 'From Hours In Effect': str,
 ...
}
'''
```

First we need to build a dictionary that maps column names to datatypes. This must be done because the `dtype` argument that we'll feed this object into later expects a dictionary type. To do that, in listing 4.6, we first walk through the `common_columns` list that we made earlier to hold all of the column names that can be found in all four Data-Frames. We transform each column name into a tuple containing the column name and the `np.str` datatype, which represents strings. On the second line, we take the list of tuples and convert them into a dict, the partial contents of which are displayed. Now that we've constructed a generic schema, we can apply it to the `read_csv` function to use the schema to load the `fy14` data into a DataFrame.

```
fy14 = dd.read_csv('nyc-parking-tickets/Parking_Violations_Issued_-_Fiscal_
    Year_2014__August_2013___June_2014_.csv', dtype=dtypes)

with ProgressBar():
    display(fy14[common_columns].head())
```

Listing 4.7 looks largely the same as the first time we read in the 2014 data file. However, this time we specified the `dtype` argument and passed in our schema dictionary. What happens under the hood is Dask will disable type inference for the columns that have matching keys in the `dtype` dictionary and use the explicitly specified types instead. While it's perfectly reasonable to include only the columns you want to change, it's best to not rely on Dask's type inference at all whenever possible. Here I've shown you how to create an explicit schema for all columns in a DataFrame, and I encourage you to make this a regular practice when working with big datasets. With this particular schema, we're telling Dask to just assume that all of the columns are strings. Now if we try to view the first five rows of the DataFrame again, using `fy14[common_columns]
.head()`, Dask doesn't throw an error message! But we're not done yet. We now need to have a look at each column and pick a more appropriate datatype (if possible) to maximize efficiency. Let's have a look at the Vehicle Year column.

```
with ProgressBar():
    print(fy14['Vehicle Year'].unique().head(10))

# Produces the following output:
```

```
0      2013
1      2012
2         0
3      2010
4      2011
5      2001
6      2005
7      1998
8      1995
9      2003
Name: Vehicle Year, dtype: object
```

In listing 4.8, we're simply looking at 10 of the unique values contained in the Vehicle Year column. It looks like they are all integers that would fit comfortably in the `uint16` datatype. `uint16` is the most appropriate because years can't be negative values, and these years are too large to be stored in `uint8` (which has a maximum size of 255). If we had seen any letters or special characters, we would not need to proceed any further with analyzing this column. The string datatype we had already selected would be the only datatype suitable for the column.

One thing to be careful about is that a sample of 10 unique values might not be a sufficiently large enough sample size to determine that there aren't any edge cases you need to consider. You could use `.compute()` instead of `.head()` to bring back all the unique values, but this might not be a good idea if the particular column you're looking at has a high degree of uniqueness to it (such as a primary key or a high-dimensional category). The range of 10–50 unique samples has served me well in most cases, but sometimes you will still run into edge cases where you will need to go back and tweak your datatypes.

Since we're thinking an integer datatype might be appropriate for this column, we need to check one more thing: Are there any missing values in this column? As you learned earlier, Dask represents missing values with `np.nan`, which is considered to be a float type object. Unfortunately, `np.nan` cannot be cast or coerced to an integer `uint16` datatype. In the next chapter we will learn how to deal with missing values, but for now if we come across a column with missing values, we will need to ensure that the column will use a datatype that can support the `np.nan` object. This means that if the Vehicle Year column contains any missing values, we'll be required to use a `float32` datatype and not the `uint16` datatype we originally thought appropriate because `uint16` is unable to store `np.nan`.

Listing 4.9 Checking the Vehicle Year column for missing values

```
with ProgressBar():
    print(fy14['Vehicle Year'].isnull().values.any().compute())

# Produces the following output:
True
```

In listing 4.9, we're using the `isnull` method, which checks each value in the specified column for existence of `np.nan`. It returns `True` if `np.nan` is found and `False` if it's not, and then aggregates the checks for all rows into a Boolean Series. Chaining with `.values.any()` reduces the Boolean Series to a single `True` if at least one row is True, and `False` if no rows are True. This means that if the code in listing 4.9 returns `True`, at least one row in the Vehicle Year column is missing. If it returned `False`, it would indicate that no rows in the Vehicle Year column are missing data. Since we have missing values in the Vehicle Year column, we must use the `float32` datatype for the column instead of `uint16`.

Now, we should repeat the process for the remaining 42 columns. For brevity's sake, I've gone ahead and done this for you. In this particular instance, we could also use the data dictionary posted on the Kaggle webpage (at https://www.kaggle.com/new-york-city/nyc-parking-tickets/data) to help speed along this process.

Listing 4.10   The final schema for the NYC Parking Ticket Data

```
dtypes = {
 'Date First Observed': np.str,
 'Days Parking In Effect    ': np.str,
 'Double Parking Violation': np.str,
 'Feet From Curb': np.float32,
 'From Hours In Effect': np.str,
 'House Number': np.str,
 'Hydrant Violation': np.str,
 'Intersecting Street': np.str,
 'Issue Date': np.str,
 'Issuer Code': np.float32,
 'Issuer Command': np.str,
 'Issuer Precinct': np.float32,
 'Issuer Squad': np.str,
 'Issuing Agency': np.str,
 'Law Section': np.float32,
 'Meter Number': np.str,
 'No Standing or Stopping Violation': np.str,
 'Plate ID': np.str,
 'Plate Type': np.str,
 'Registration State': np.str,
 'Street Code1': np.uint32,
 'Street Code2': np.uint32,
 'Street Code3': np.uint32,
 'Street Name': np.str,
 'Sub Division': np.str,
 'Summons Number': np.uint32,
 'Time First Observed': np.str,
 'To Hours In Effect': np.str,
 'Unregistered Vehicle?': np.str,
 'Vehicle Body Type': np.str,
 'Vehicle Color': np.str,
 'Vehicle Expiration Date': np.str,
 'Vehicle Make': np.str,
 'Vehicle Year': np.float32,
 'Violation Code': np.uint16,
 'Violation County': np.str,
 'Violation Description': np.str,
```

```
'Violation In Front Of Or Opposite': np.str,
'Violation Legal Code': np.str,
'Violation Location': np.str,
'Violation Post Code': np.str,
'Violation Precinct': np.float32,
'Violation Time': np.str
}
```

Listing 4.10 contains the final schema for the NYC Parking Ticket data. Let's use it to reload all four of the DataFrames, then union all four years of data together into a final DataFrame.

Listing 4.11 Applying the schema to all four DataFrames

```
data = dd.read_csv('nyc-parking-tickets/*.csv', dtype=dtypes, usecols=common_
    columns)
```

In listing 4.11, we reload the data and apply the schema we created. Notice that instead of loading four separate files into four separate DataFrames, we're now loading all CSV files contained in the nyc-parking-tickets folder into a single DataFrame by using the * wildcard. Dask provides this for convenience since it's common to split large datasets into multiple files, especially on distributed filesystems. As before, we're passing the final schema into the dtype argument, and we're now also passing the list of columns we want to keep into the usecols argument. usecols takes a list of column names and drops any columns from the resulting DataFrame that aren't specified in the list. Since we only care about analyzing the data we have available for all four years, we'll choose to simply ignore the columns that aren't shared across all four years.

usecols is an interesting argument because if you look at the Dask API documentation, it's not listed. It might not be immediately obvious why this is, but it's because the argument comes from Pandas. Since each partition of a Dask DataFrame is a Pandas DataFrame, you can pass along any Pandas arguments through the *args and **kwargs interfaces and they will control the underlying Pandas DataFrames that make up each partition. This interface is also how you can control things like which column delimiter should be used, whether the data has a header or not, and so on. The Pandas API documentation for read_csv and its many arguments can be found at http://pandas.pydata .org/pandas-docs/stable/generated/pandas.read_csv.html.

We've now read in the data and we are ready to clean and analyze this DataFrame. If you count the rows, we have over 42.3 million parking violations to explore! However, before we get into that, we will look at interfacing with a few other storage systems as well as writing data. We'll now look at reading data from relational database systems.

4.2 *Reading data from relational databases*

Reading data from a relational database system (RDBMS) into Dask is fairly easy. In fact, you're likely to find that the most tedious part of interfacing with RDBMSs is setting up and configuring your Dask environment to do so. Because of the wide variety of RDBMSs used in production environments, we can't cover the specifics for each one here. But, a substantial amount of documentation and support is available online for the specific RDBMS you're working with. The most important thing to be aware of is that when using Dask in a multi-node cluster, your client machine is not the only machine that will need access to the database. Each worker node needs to be able to access the database server, so it's important to install the correct software and configure each node in the cluster to be able to do so.

Dask uses the SQL Alchemy library to interface with RDBMSs, and I recommend using the pyodbc library to manage your ODBC drivers. This means you will need to install and configure SQL Alchemy, pyodbc, and the ODBC drivers for your specific RDBMS on each machine in your cluster for Dask to work correctly. To learn more about SQL Alchemy, you can check out www.sqlalchemy.org/library.html. Likewise, you can learn more about pyodbc at https://github.com/mkleehammer/pyodbc/wiki.

Listing 4.12 Reading a SQL table into a Dask DataFrame

```
username = 'jesse'
password = 'DataScienceRulez'
hostname = 'localhost'
database_name = 'DSAS'
odbc_driver = 'ODBC+Driver+13+for+SQL+Server'

connection_string = 'mssql+pyodbc://{0}:{1}@{2}/{3}?driver={4}'.
    format(username, password, hostname, database_name, odbc_driver)

data = dd.read_sql_table('violations', connection_string, index_col='Summons
    Number')
```

In listing 4.12, we first set up a connection to our database server by building a connection string. For this particular example, I'm using SQL Server on Linux from the official SQL Server Docker container on a Mac. Your connection string might look different based on the database server and operating system you're running on. The last line demonstrates how to use the read_sql_table function to connect to the database and create the DataFrame. The first argument is the name of the database table you want to query, the second argument is the connection string, and the third argument is the column to use as the DataFrame's index. These are the three required arguments for this function to work. However, you should be aware of a few important assumptions.

First, concerning datatypes, you might think that Dask gets datatype information directly from the database server since the database has a defined schema already. Instead, Dask samples the data and infers datatypes just like it does when reading a delimited text file. However, Dask sequentially reads the first five rows from the table instead of randomly sampling data across the dataset. Because databases indeed have a well-defined schema, Dask's type inference is much more reliable when reading data from an RDBMS versus a delimited text file. However, it's still not perfect. Because of the way data might be sorted, edge cases can come up that cause Dask to choose incorrect datatypes. For example, a string column might have some rows where the strings contain only numbers ("1456," "2986," and so on.) If the data is sorted in such a way that only these numeric-like strings appear in the sample Dask takes when inferring datatypes, it may incorrectly assume the column should be an integer datatype instead of a string datatype. In these situations, you may still have to do some manual schema tweaking as you learned in the previous section.

The second assumption is how the data should be partitioned. If the `index_col` (currently set to `'Summons Number'`) is a numeric or date/time datatype, Dask will automatically infer boundaries and partition the data based on a 256 MB block size (which is larger than `read_csv`'s 64 MB block size). However, if the `index_col` is not a numeric or date/time datatype, you must either specify the number of partitions or the boundaries to partition the data by.

```
data = dd.read_sql_table('violations', connection_string, index_col='Vehicle
    Color', npartitions=200)
```

In listing 4.13, we chose to index the DataFrame by the Vehicle Color column, which is a string column. Therefore, we have to specify how the DataFrame should be partitioned. Here, using the npartitions argument, we are telling Dask to split the Data-Frame into 200 evenly sized pieces. Alternatively, we can manually specify boundaries for the partitions.

```
partition_boundaries = sorted(['Red', 'Blue', 'White', 'Black', 'Silver',
    'Yellow'])

data = dd.read_sql_table('violations', connection_string, index_col='Vehicle
    Color', divisions=partition_boundaries)
```

Listing 4.14 shows how to manually define partition boundaries. The important thing to note about this is Dask uses these boundaries as an alphabetically sorted half-closed interval. This means that you won't have partitions that *only* contain the color defined by their boundary. For example, because green is alphabetically between blue and red, green cars will fall into the red partition. The "red partition" is actually all colors that are alphabetically greater than blue and alphabetically less than or equal to red. This isn't really intuitive at first and can take some getting used to.

The third assumption that Dask makes when you pass only the minimum required parameters is that you want to select all columns from the table. You can limit the columns you get back using the columns argument, which behaves similarly to the usecols argument in read_csv. While you are allowed to use SQL Alchemy expressions in the argument, I recommend that you avoid offloading any computations to the database server, since you lose the advantages of parallelizing that computation that Dask gives you.

Listing 4.15   Selecting a subset of columns

```
# Equivalent to:
# SELECT [Summons Number], [Plate ID], [Vehicle Color] FROM dbo.violations
column_filter = ['Summons Number', 'Plate ID', 'Vehicle Color']
data = dd.read_sql_table('violations', connection_string, index_col='Summons
    Number', columns=column_filter)
```

Listing 4.15 shows how to add a column filter to the connection query. Here we've created a list of column names that exist in the table; then we pass them to the columns argument. You can use the column filter even if you are querying a view instead of a table.

The fourth and final assumption made by providing the minimum arguments is the schema selection. When I say "schema" here, I'm not referring to the datatypes used by the DataFrame; I'm referring to the database schema object that RDBMSs use to group tables into logical clusters (such as dim/fact in a data warehouse or sales, hr, and so on, in a transactional database). If you don't provide a schema, the database driver will use the default for the platform. For SQL Server, this results in Dask looking for the violations table in the dbo schema. If we had put the table in a different schema, perhaps one called chapterFour, we would receive a "table not found" error.

Listing 4.16   Specifying a database schema

```
# Equivalent to:
# SELECT * FROM chapterFour.violations
data = dd.read_sql_table('violations', connection_string, index_col='Summons
    Number', schema='chapterFour')
```

Listing 4.16 shows you how to select a specific schema from Dask. Passing the schema name into the schema argument will cause Dask to use the provided database schema rather than the default.

Like read_csv, Dask allows you to forward along arguments to the underlying calls to the Pandas read_sql function being used at the partition level to create the Pandas DataFrames. We've covered all the most important functions here, but if you need an extra degree of customization, have a look at the API documentation for the Pandas read_sql function. All its arguments can be manipulated using the *args and **kwargs interfaces provided by Dask DataFrames. Now we'll look at how Dask deals with distributed filesystems.

4.3   *Reading data from HDFS and S3*

While it's very likely that many datasets you'll come across throughout your work will be stored in relational databases, powerful alternatives are rapidly growing in popularity. Most notable are the developments in distributed filesystem technologies from 2006 onward. Powered by technologies like Apache Hadoop and Amazon's Simple Storage System (or S3 for short), distributed filesystems bring the same benefits to file storage that distributed computing brings to data processing: increased throughput, scalability, and robustness. Using a distributed computing framework alongside a distributed filesystem technology is a harmonious combination: in the most advanced distributed filesystems, such as the Hadoop Distributed File System (HDFS), nodes are aware of data locality, allowing computations to be shipped to the data rather than the data shipped to the compute resources. This saves a lot of time and back-and-forth communication over the network. Figure 4.7 demonstrates why keeping data isolated so a single node can have some performance consequences.

A significant bottleneck is caused by the need to chunk up and ship data to the other nodes in the cluster. Under this configuration, when Dask reads in the data, it will partition the DataFrame as usual, but the other worker nodes can't do any work until a partition of data is sent to them. Because it takes some time to transfer these 64 MB chunks over the network, the total computation time will be increased by the time it takes to ship data back and forth between the node that has the data and the other workers. This becomes even more problematic if the size of the cluster grows by any significant amount. If we had several hundred (or more) worker nodes vying for chunks of data all at once, the networking stack on the data node could easily get saturated with requests and slow to a crawl. Both of these problems can be mitigated by using a distributed

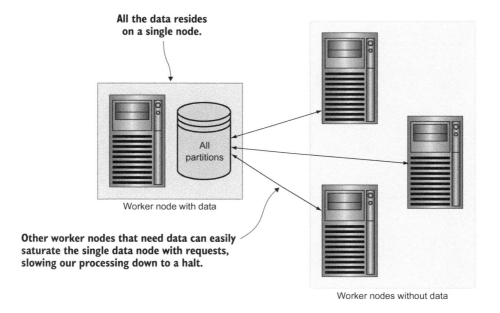

Figure 4.7   Running a distributed computation without a distributed filesystem

filesystem. Figure 4.8 shows how distributing the data across worker nodes makes the process more efficient.

Instead of creating a bottleneck by holding data on only one node, the distributed filesystem chunks up data ahead of time and spreads it across multiple machines. It's standard practice in many distributed filesystems to store redundant copies of chunks/partitions both for reliability and performance. From the perspective of reliability, storing each partition in triplicate (which is a common default configuration) means that two separate machines would have to fail before any data loss occurs. The probability of two machines failing in a short amount of time is much lower than the probability of one machine failing, so it adds an extra layer of safety at a nominal cost of additional storage.

From the performance perspective, spreading the data out across the cluster makes it more likely that a node containing the data will be available to run a computation when requested. Or, in the event that all worker nodes that hold that partition are already busy, one of them can ship the data to another worker node. In this case, spreading out the data avoids any single node getting saturated by requests for data. If one node is busy serving up a bunch of data, it can offload some of those requests to other nodes that hold the requested data. Figure 4.9 demonstrates why data-local distributed filesystems are even more advantageous.

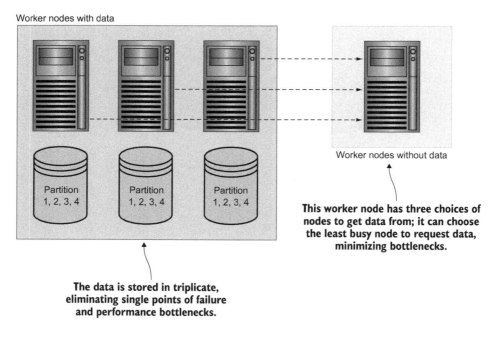

Figure 4.8   Running a distributed computation on a distributed filesystem

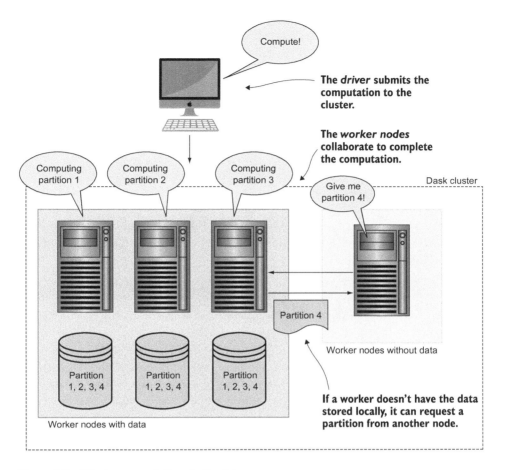

Figure 4.9   Shipping computations to the data

The node controlling the orchestration of the distributed computation (called the *driver*) knows that the data it wants to process is available in a few locations because the distributed filesystem maintains a catalogue of the data held within the system. It will first ask the machines that have the data locally whether they're busy or not. If one of the nodes is not busy, the driver will instruct the worker node to perform the computation. If all the nodes are busy, the driver can either choose to wait until one of the worker nodes is free, or instruct another free worker node to get the data remotely and run the computation. HDFS and S3 are two of the most popular distributed filesystems, but they have one key difference for our purposes: HDFS is designed to allow computations to run on the same nodes that serve up data, and S3 is not. Amazon designed S3 as a web service dedicated solely to file storage and retrieval. There's absolutely no way to execute application code on S3 servers. This means that when you work with data stored in S3, you will always have to transmit partitions from S3 to a Dask worker node in order to process it. Let's now take a look at how we can use Dask to read data from these systems.

```
data = dd.read_csv('hdfs://localhost/nyc-parking-tickets/*.csv',
    dtype=dtypes, usecols=common_columns)
```

In listing 4.17, we have a `read_csv` call that should look very familiar by now. In fact, the only thing that's changed is the file path. Prefixing the file path with `hdfs://` tells Dask to look for the files on an HDFS cluster instead of the local filesystem, and `local-host` indicates that Dask should query the local HDFS NameNode for information on the whereabouts of the file.

All the arguments for `read_csv` that you learned before can still be used here. In this way, Dask makes it extremely easy to work with HDFS. The only additional requirement is that you install the hdfs3 library on each of your Dask workers. This library allows Dask to communicate with HDFS; therefore, this functionality won't work if you haven't installed the package. You can simply install the package with pip or conda (hdfs3 is on the conda-forge channel).

```
data = dd.read_csv('s3://my-bucket/nyc-parking-tickets/*.csv', dtype=dtypes,
    usecols=common_columns)
```

In listing 4.18, our `read_csv` call is (again) almost exactly the same as listing 4.17. This time, however, we've prefixed the file path with `s3://` to tell Dask that the data is located on an S3 filesystem, and `my-bucket` lets Dask know to look for the files in the S3 bucket associated with your AWS account named "my-bucket".

In order to use the S3 functionality, you must have the s3fs library installed on each Dask worker. Like hdfs3, this library can be installed simply through pip or conda (from the conda-forge channel). The final requirement is that each Dask worker is properly configured for authenticating with S3. s3fs uses the boto library to communicate with S3. You can learn more about configuring boto at http://boto.cloudhackers.com/en/latest/getting_started.html. The most common S3 authentication configuration consists of using the AWS Access Key and AWS Secret Access Key. Rather than injecting these keys in your code, it's a better idea to set these values using environment variables or a configuration file. Boto will check both the environment variables and the default configuration paths automatically, so there's no need to pass authentication credentials directly to Dask. Otherwise, as with using HDFS, the call to `read_csv` allows you to do all the same things as if you were operating on a local filesystem. Dask really makes it easy to work with distributed filesystems!

Now that you have some experience working with a few different storage systems, we'll round out the "reading data" part of this chapter by talking about a special file format that is very useful for fast computations.

4.4   *Reading data in Parquet format*

CSV and other delimited text files are great for their simplicity and portability, but they aren't really optimized for the best performance, especially when performing complex data operations such as sorts, merges, and aggregations. While a wide variety of file formats attempt to increase efficiency in many different ways, with mixed results, one of the more recent high-profile file formats is Apache Parquet. Parquet is a high-performance columnar storage format jointly developed by Twitter and Cloudera that was designed with use on distributed filesystems in mind. Its design brings several key advantages to the table over text-based formats: more efficient use of IO, better compression, and strict typing. Figure 4.10 shows the difference in how data is stored in Parquet format versus a row-oriented storage scheme like CSV.

With row-oriented formats, values are stored on disk and in memory sequentially based on the row position of the data. Consider what we'd have to do if we wanted to perform an aggregate function over x, such as finding the mean. To collect all the values of x, we'd have to scan over 10 values in order to get the 4 values we want. This means we spend more time waiting for IO completion just to throw away over half of the values read from disk. Compare that with the columnar format: in that format, we'd simply grab the sequential chunk of x values and have all four values we want. This seeking operation is much faster and more efficient.

Another significant advantage of applying column-oriented chunking of the data is that the data can now be partitioned and distributed by column. This leads to much faster and more efficient shuffle operations, since only the columns that are necessary for an operation can be transmitted over the network instead of entire rows.

Finally, efficient compression is also a major advantage of Parquet. With column-oriented data, it's possible to apply different compression schemes to individual columns so the data becomes compressed in the most efficient way possible. Python's Parquet library supports many of the popular compression algorithms such as gzip, lzo, and snappy.

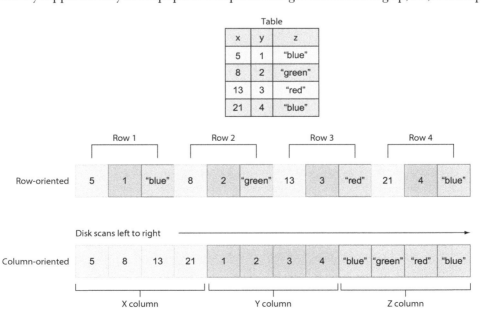

Figure 4.10   The structure of Parquet compared with delimited text files

To use Parquet with Dask, you need to make sure you have the fastparquet or pyarrow library installed, both of which can be installed either via pip or conda (conda-forge). I would generally recommend using pyarrow over fastparquet, because it has better support for serializing complex nested data structures. You can also install the compression libraries you want to use, such as python-snappy or python-lzo, which are also available via pip or conda (conda-forge). Now let's take a look at reading the NYC Parking Ticket dataset one more time in Parquet format. As a side note, we will be using Parquet format extensively through the book, and in the next chapter you will write some of the NYC Parking Ticket dataset to Parquet format. Therefore, you will see the read_parquet method many more times! This discussion is here to simply give you a first look at how to use the method. Now, without further ado, here's how to use the read_parquet method.

Listing 4.19   Reading in Parquet data

```
data = dd.read_parquet('nyc-parking-tickets-prq')
```

Listing 4.19 is about as simple as it gets! The read_parquet method is used to create a Dask DataFrame from one or more Parquet files, and the only required argument is the path. One thing to notice about this call that might look strange: nyc-parking-tickets-prq is a directory, not a file. That's because datasets stored as Parquet are typically written to disk pre-partitioned, resulting in potentially hundreds or thousands of individual files. Dask provides this method for convenience so you don't have to manually create a long list of filenames to pass in. You can specify a single Parquet file in the path if you want to, but it's much more typical to see Parquet datasets referenced as a directory of files rather than individual files.

Listing 4.20   Reading Parquet files from distributed filesystems

```
data = dd.read_parquet('hdfs://localhost/nyc-parking-tickets-prq')

# OR

data = dd.read_parquet('s3://my-bucket/nyc-parking-tickets-prq')
```

Listing 4.20 shows how to read Parquet from distributed filesystems. Just as with delimited text files, the only difference is specifying a distributed filesystem protocol, such as hdfs or s3, and specifying the relevant path to the data.

Parquet is stored with a predefined schema, so there are no options to mess with datatypes. The only real relevant options that Dask gives you to control importing Parquet data are column filters and index selection. These work the same way as with the other file formats. By default, they will be inferred from the schema stored alongside the data, but you can override that selection by manually passing in values to the relevant arguments.

Listing 4.21 Specifying Parquet read options

```
columns = ['Summons Number', 'Plate ID', 'Vehicle Color']

data = dd.read_parquet('nyc-parking-tickets-prq', columns=columns,
    index='Plate ID')
```

In listing 4.21, we pick a few columns that we want to read from the dataset and put them in a list called columns. We then pass in the list to the columns argument, and we specify Plate ID to be used as the index by passing it in to the index argument. The result of this will be a Dask DataFrame containing only the three columns shown here and sorted/indexed by the Plate ID column.

We've now covered a number of ways to get data into Dask from a myriad array of systems and formats. As you can see, the DataFrame API offers a great deal of flexibility to ingest structured data in fairly simple ways. In the next chapter, we'll cover fundamental data transformations and, naturally, writing data back out in a number of different ways.

Summary

- Inspecting the columns of a DataFrame can be done with the columns attribute.
- Dask's datatype inference shouldn't be relied on for large datasets. Instead, you should define your own schemas based on common NumPy datatypes.
- Parquet format offers good performance because it's a column-oriented format and highly compressible. Whenever possible, try to get your dataset in Parquet format.

Cleaning and transforming DataFrames

This chapter covers

- Selecting and filtering data
- Creating and dropping columns
- Finding and fixing columns with missing values
- Indexing and sorting DataFrames
- Combining DataFrames using join and union operations
- Writing DataFrames to delimited text files and Parquet

In the previous chapter, we created a schema for the NYC Parking Ticket dataset and successfully loaded the data into Dask. Now we're ready to get the data cleaned up so we can begin analyzing and visualizing it! As a friendly reminder, figure 5.1 shows what we've done so far and where we're going next within our data science workflow.

Figure 5.1 The *Data Science with Python and Dask* workflow

Data cleaning is an important part of any data science project because anomalies and outliers in the data can negatively influence many statistical analyses. This could lead us to make bad conclusions about the data and build machine learning models that don't stand up over time. Therefore, it's important that we get the data cleaned up as much as possible before moving on to exploratory analysis.

As we work on cleaning and prepping the data for analysis, you'll also learn a lot of methods that Dask gives you to manipulate DataFrames. Given the syntactic similarity of many methods in the Dask DataFrame API, it should become very evident in this chapter that Dask DataFrames are made up of Pandas DataFrames. Some of the operations look exactly the same, but we will also see how some operations differ due to the distributed nature of Dask and how to cope with these differences.

Before we get to work, here's a recap of the code we've run so far to import the data into Dask. You'll want to run this code if you're working along with the chapter.

Listing 5.1 Importing the NYC Parking Ticket data

```
import dask.dataframe as dd
from dask.diagnostics import ProgressBar
import numpy as np

dtypes = {
 'Date First Observed': np.str,
 'Days Parking In Effect    ': np.str,
 'Double Parking Violation': np.str,
 'Feet From Curb': np.float32,
 'From Hours In Effect': np.str,
 'House Number': np.str,
 'Hydrant Violation': np.str,
 'Intersecting Street': np.str,
 'Issue Date': np.str,
 'Issuer Code': np.float32,
 'Issuer Command': np.str,
 'Issuer Precinct': np.float32,
 'Issuer Squad': np.str,
 'Issuing Agency': np.str,
 'Law Section': np.float32,
 'Meter Number': np.str,
 'No Standing or Stopping Violation': np.str,
 'Plate ID': np.str,
 'Plate Type': np.str,
 'Registration State': np.str,
 'Street Code1': np.uint32,
```

```
        'Street Code2': np.uint32,
        'Street Code3': np.uint32,
        'Street Name': np.str,
        'Sub Division': np.str,
        'Summons Number': np.uint32,
        'Time First Observed': np.str,
        'To Hours In Effect': np.str,
        'Unregistered Vehicle?': np.str,
        'Vehicle Body Type': np.str,
        'Vehicle Color': np.str,
        'Vehicle Expiration Date': np.str,
        'Vehicle Make': np.str,
        'Vehicle Year': np.float32,
        'Violation Code': np.uint16,
        'Violation County': np.str,
        'Violation Description': np.str,
        'Violation In Front Of Or Opposite': np.str,
        'Violation Legal Code': np.str,
        'Violation Location': np.str,
        'Violation Post Code': np.str,
        'Violation Precinct': np.float32,
        'Violation Time': np.str
}

nyc_data_raw = dd.read_csv('nyc-parking-tickets/*.csv', dtype=dtypes,
        usecols=dtypes.keys())
```

Listing 5.1 should look very familiar. With the first couple of lines we're importing the modules we'll need for the chapter. Next, we're loading the schema dictionary we created in chapter 4. Finally, we create a DataFrame called `nyc_data_raw` by reading the four CSV files, applying the schema, and selecting the columns that we defined in the schema (`usecols=dtypes.keys()`). Now we're ready to go!

5.1   *Working with indexes and axes*

In chapter 3 you learned that Dask DataFrames have three structural elements: an index and two axes (rows and columns). To refresh your memory, figure 5.2 shows a visual guide to the structure of a DataFrame.

5.1.1   *Selecting columns from a DataFrame*

So far, we haven't done much with the NYC Parking Ticket dataset beyond choosing appropriate datatypes for each column and reading the data into Dask. Now that the data is loaded and ready for us to start exploring, a good place for us to ease into our exploration is by learning how to navigate the DataFrame's index and axes. Let's start with something simple: selecting and filtering columns.

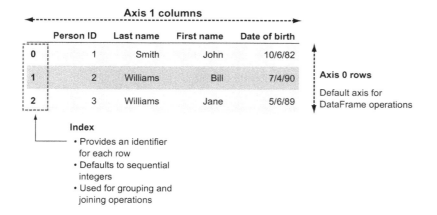

Figure 5.2 The structure of a DataFrame

```
with ProgressBar():
    display(nyc_data_raw['Plate ID'].head())

# Produces the following output:
# 0     GBB9093
# 1     62416MB
# 2     78755JZ
# 3     63009MA
# 4     91648MC
# Name: Plate ID, dtype: object
```

You've already seen a few times that the head method will retrieve the first *n* rows of a DataFrame, but in those examples we've retrieved the entire DataFrame's first *n* rows. In listing 5.2 you can see that we've put a pair of square brackets ([...]) to the right of nyc_data_raw and inside those square brackets we specified the name of one of the DataFrame's columns (Plate ID). The column selector accepts either a string or a list of strings and applies a filter to the DataFrame that returns only the requested columns. In this particular case, since we specified only one column, what we get back is not another DataFrame. Instead, we get back a Series object, which is like a DataFrame that doesn't have a column axis. You can see that, like a DataFrame, a Series object has an index, which is actually copied over from the DataFrame. Oftentimes when selecting columns, however, you'll want to bring back more than one. Listing 5.3 demonstrates how to select more than one column from a DataFrame, and figure 5.3 shows the output of the listing.

Listing 5.3   Selecting multiple columns from a DataFrame using an inline list

```
with ProgressBar():
    print(nyc_data_raw[['Plate ID', 'Registration State']].head())
```

Here we've used the `head` method to ask Dask to bring back the first five rows of the Plate ID column and the Registration State column. The column selector might look a little strange—why did we double up on the square brackets? That's because we're creating an inline list of strings. To get multiple columns back, you need to pass a list of column names (as strings) to the column selector. The outer pair of square brackets denotes that we're using the column selector, and the inner pair of square brackets is the inline constructor for the list of column names. You can also pass a list of column names that's stored as a variable. Listing 5.4 should make the differentiation between the column selector and the list constructor more apparent—and notice that the output shown in figure 5.4 is exactly the same as figure 5.3.

	Plate ID	Registration State
0	GBB9093	NY
1	62416MB	NY
2	78755JZ	NY
3	63009MA	NY
4	91648MC	NY

Figure 5.3   The output of listing 5.3

Listing 5.4   Selecting multiple columns from a DataFrame using a declared list

```
columns_to_select = ['Plate ID', 'Registration State']

with ProgressBar():
    display(nyc_data_raw[columns_to_select].head())
```

Since we first create a list of column names and store it to a variable called `columns_to_select`, we can pass that previously declared list of column names to the column selector. An important thing to note about the column selector: every column name you reference must exist in the DataFrame. This runs counter to the behavior we saw before with the `dtype` and `usecols` arguments of the DataFrame constructor. With those arguments, we can pass a list of column names where some column names don't exist in the data and Dask will simply ignore those columns. On the other hand, if we pass a column name to the column selector that doesn't exist in the DataFrame, Dask will return a Key Error.

	Plate ID	Registration State
0	GBB9093	NY
1	62416MB	NY
2	78755JZ	NY
3	63009MA	NY
4	91648MC	NY

Figure 5.4   The output of listing 5.4

5.1.2 *Dropping columns from a DataFrame*

Quite often, instead of selecting a small subset of columns, you might instead want to keep all but a few columns. You could do this using the column selector method you just learned, but that would be an awful lot of typing, especially if your DataFrame has a lot of columns like this one! Fortunately, Dask gives you a way to selectively drop columns from your DataFrame, keeping all but the columns you specify. Listing 5.5 demonstrates how to use the `drop` method to get rid of the Violation Code column in the DataFrame, and the output of the new DataFrame can be seen in figure 5.5.

Listing 5.5 Dropping a single column from a DataFrame

```
with ProgressBar():
    display(nyc_data_raw.drop('Violation Code', axis=1).head())
```

Similar to the column selector, the `drop` method accepts either a single string or a list of strings representing column names that you wish to drop. Also, notice that we had to specify that the drop operation should be performed on axis 1 (columns) since we want to drop a column from the DataFrame.

Since Dask operations default to axis 0 (rows), the expected behavior of the drop operation, had we not specified `axis=1`, would be to try to locate and drop a row with an index of "Violation Code." This is exactly how Pandas behaves. But, this behavior hasn't been implemented in Dask. Instead, if you forget to specify `axis=1`, you receive an error message that states `NotImplementedError: Drop currently only works for axis=1`.

Similar to specifying multiple columns in the column selector, you can specify multiple columns to drop as well. The effect of this operation on the DataFrame can be seen in figure 5.6.

Listing 5.6 Dropping multiple columns from a DataFrame

```
violationColumnNames = list(filter(lambda columnName: 'Violation' in
    columnName, nyc_data_raw.columns))

with ProgressBar():
    display(nyc_data_raw.drop(violationColumnNames, axis=1).head())
```

	Summons Number	Plate ID	Registration State	Plate Type	Issue Date	Vehicle Body Type	Vehicle Make	Issuing Agency	Street Code1	Street Code2	...	Vehicle Color	Unregistered Vehicle?	Vehicle Year	Meter Number	Feet From Curb	Violation Post Code
0	1283294138	GBB9093	NY	PAS	08/04/2013	SUBN	AUDI	P	37250	13610	...	GY	0	2013.0	-	0.0	NaN
1	1283294151	62416MB	NY	COM	08/04/2013	VAN	FORD	P	37290	40404	...	WH	0	2012.0	-	0.0	NaN
2	1283294163	78755JZ	NY	COM	08/05/2013	P-U	CHEVR	P	37030	31190	...	NaN	0	0.0	-	0.0	NaN
3	1283294175	63009MA	NY	COM	08/05/2013	VAN	FORD	P	37270	11710	...	WH	0	2010.0	-	0.0	NaN
4	1283294187	91648MC	NY	COM	08/08/2013	TRLR	GMC	P	37240	12010	...	BR	0	2012.0	-	0.0	NaN

Figure 5.5 The output of listing 5.5

	Summons Number	Plate ID	Registration State	Plate Type	Issue Date	Vehicle Body Type	Vehicle Make	Issuing Agency	Street Code1	Street Code2	...	Law Section	Sub Division	Days Parking In Effect	From Hours In Effect	To Hours In Effect	Vehicle Color
0	1283294138	GBB9093	NY	PAS	08/04/2013	SUBN	AUDI	P	37250	13610	...	408.0	F1	BBBBBBB	ALL	ALL	GY
1	1283294151	62416MB	NY	COM	08/04/2013	VAN	FORD	P	37290	40404	...	408.0	C	BBBBBBB	ALL	ALL	WH
2	1283294163	78755JZ	NY	COM	08/05/2013	P-U	CHEVR	P	37030	31190	...	408.0	F7	BBBBBBB	ALL	ALL	NaN
3	1283294175	63009MA	NY	COM	08/05/2013	VAN	FORD	P	37270	11710	...	408.0	F1	BBBBBBB	ALL	ALL	WH
4	1283294187	91648MC	NY	COM	08/08/2013	TRLR	GMC	P	37240	12010	...	408.0	E1	BBBBBBB	ALL	ALL	BR

5 rows × 31 columns

Figure 5.6 The output of listing 5.6

In listing 5.6, we're getting a bit fancier with our column list generation. We've decided to drop any columns that contain the word "Violation" in the column name. On the first line, we've defined an anonymous function to check each column name for the presence of "Violation" and applied that to the `nyc_data_raw.columns` list (which contains a list of all of the `nyc_data_raw` DataFrame's column names) using the `filter` function. We then take this list of column names that matched our filter criteria and passed it into the `drop` method of the `nyc_data_raw` DataFrame. All told, that operation will drop 13 columns from the resulting DataFrame.

Now that you've seen two ways to select subsets of columns from Dask DataFrames, you may wonder, when should I use `drop` and when should I use the column selector? They are equivalent from a performance standpoint, so it really comes down to the question of whether you intend to drop more columns than you want to keep or keep more columns than you want to drop. If you intend to drop more columns than you want to keep (for example, you want to keep 2 columns and drop 42 columns), it will be more convenient to use the column selector. Conversely, if you intend to keep more columns than you want to drop (for example, you want to keep 42 columns and drop 2 columns), it will be more convenient to use the `drop` method.

5.1.3 *Renaming columns in a DataFrame*

The last thing to cover on navigating columns, for now, is renaming columns. Sometimes you might be working with data that doesn't have very descriptive/friendly column names in the header and you want to clean them up. While we fortunately do have pretty good column names in the NYC Parking Ticket dataset, we'll look at an example of how to rename columns in the event you need to do so in the future. In the following listing, we use the `rename` method to change the name of the Plate ID column to License Plate, and the result of this can be seen in figure 5.7.

```
Listing 5.7  Renaming a column
```

```
nyc_data_renamed = nyc_data_raw.rename(columns={'Plate ID':'License Plate'})
nyc_data_renamed
```

The `columns` argument simply takes a dictionary where the key is the old column name and the value is the new column name. Dask will make a one-for-one swap, returning a DataFrame with the new column names. Columns that aren't specified in the

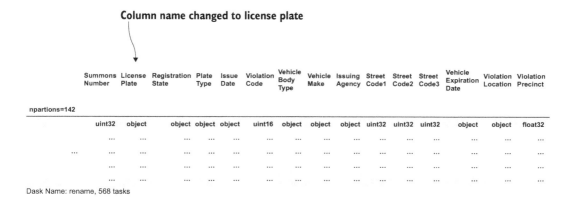

Figure 5.7 The output of listing 5.7

dictionary will not be renamed or dropped. Note that these operations are not altering the source data on disk, only the data that Dask holds in memory. Later in the chapter, we'll cover how to write the modified data back to disk.

5.1.4 Selecting rows from a DataFrame

Next, we'll have a look at how to select data across the rows axis. Later in the chapter we'll talk about searching and filtering rows, which is a more common way to navigate the rows axis. But you are likely to run across situations where you know the range of rows you want to retrieve ahead of time, in which case selecting by index is the appropriate way to get the data. This occurs most frequently when your data is indexed by a date or time. Keep in mind that indexes do not need to be unique, so you can use an index to select a chunk of data. For example, you may want to get all rows that occurred between April 2015 and November 2015. Just like with a clustered index in a relational database, selecting data by index offers a performance boost over search and filter methods. This is largely due to the fact that Dask stores and partitions data sorted in order of the index. Therefore, when seeking specific information, Dask doesn't have to scan through the entire dataset to make sure it brings back all the data you ask for. In the following listing, we use the `loc` method to specify the index of the row we want to retrieve, and the output is displayed in figure 5.8.

Listing 5.8 Getting a single row by index

```
with ProgressBar():
    display(nyc_data_raw.loc[56].head(1))
```

Since the DataFrame hasn't been indexed by a specific column, the index we're selecting is the default sequential numeric index of the DataFrame (which starts at 0). This means we've retrieved the 56th row in the DataFrame if we counted up from the first row. `loc` is syntactically similar to the column selector in that it uses square brackets to accept arguments. Unlike the column selector, however, it will not accept a list of

	Summons Number	Plate ID	Registration State	Plate Type	Issue Date	Violation Code	Vehicle Body Type	Vehicle Make	Issuing Agency	Street Code1	...	Vehicle Color	Unregistered Vehicle?	Vehicle Year	Meter Number	Feet From Curb
56	1293090530	GES3519	NY	PAS	07/07/2013	40	SDN	HONDA	F	70630	...	BLACK	0	1997.0	-	0.0

1 rows × 43 columns

Figure 5.8   The output of listing 5.8

values. You can either pass it a single value or a range of values using Python's standard slice notation.

Listing 5.9   Getting a sequential slice of rows by index

```
with ProgressBar():
    display(nyc_data_raw.loc[100:200].head(100))
```

Listing 5.9 demonstrates using a slice to return rows between 100 and 200. This is the same notation as slicing a list or an array in plain-old Python. One effect of accessing rows using this slicing notation is that the rows that are returned will be sequential. As we've already seen, the drop function does not work across the rows axis, so there's no way to select just rows 1, 3, and 5, for example, without using filtering. You can, however, retrieve the slice you want to reduce further from Dask and use Pandas to do the final filtering.

Listing 5.10   Filtering a slice of rows using Dask and Pandas

```
with ProgressBar():
    some_rows = nyc_data_raw.loc[100:200].head(100)
some_rows.drop(range(100, 200, 2))
```

In listing 5.10, we're taking our Dask DataFrame (nyc_data_raw) and getting a slice of rows between index 100 and 200. Using the head method triggers the computation in Dask and returns the result as a Pandas DataFrame. You could also use the collect method, since you're selecting a small range of data, but using the head method is a good habit to get into in order to avoid accidentally retrieving too much data. We store this result to a variable called some_rows. We're then using the drop method on some_rows (which is a *Pandas* DataFrame) to drop every other row and display the result. The drop method is implemented for the rows axis in Pandas, so if you need to drop rows from a DataFrame, bringing a subset of your Dask data down to Pandas is a good idea. However, be aware that if the slice you're trying to pull down is too big to fit into your computer's memory, the operation will fail with an out-of-memory error. Therefore, this method is only suitable if you're working on a fairly small slice of the Dask DataFrame. Otherwise, you'll need to rely on more advanced filtering methods that we'll cover a bit later in the chapter.

Now that you're getting more comfortable with navigating the data, we'll jump into an important step in the data-cleaning process: finding and fixing missing values in our dataset.

5.2 Dealing with missing values

Oftentimes you'll come across datasets that have missing values due to deficiencies in the data collection process, evolving needs over time, or data processing and storage issues. Whatever the cause, you'll need to decide what to do to eliminate these data-quality issues. When fixing missing values, you have three options to choose from:

- Remove the rows/columns with missing data from your dataset.
- Assign the missing values a default value.
- Impute the missing values.

For example, imagine that you have a dataset containing height measurements of various people, and a few of those height measurements are missing. Depending on the objectives of your analysis, you could decide to either throw out the records with missing height measurements or assume that those people are about average height by finding the arithmetic mean of the measurements you have. Unfortunately, there isn't a "silver bullet" approach to selecting the best method to deal with missing values. It largely depends on the context and domain of the missing data. A good rule of thumb is to work with the stakeholders who will be interpreting and using your analyses to come up with an agreed-upon approach that makes the most sense in the context of the problem you're trying to solve. However, to give you some options, we'll cover how to do all three in this section.

5.2.1 Counting missing values in a DataFrame

We'll start by having a look at what columns in the NYC Parking Ticket data have missing values.

Listing 5.11 Calculating the percentage of missing values by column

```
missing_values = nyc_data_raw.isnull().sum()

with ProgressBar():
    percent_missing = ((missing_values / nyc_data_raw.index.size) * 100).
      compute()
percent_missing


# Produces the following output:

Summons Number                   0.000000
Plate ID                         0.020867
Registration State               0.000000
Plate Type                       0.000000
Issue Date                       0.000000
Violation Code                   0.000000
Vehicle Body Type                0.564922
Vehicle Make                     0.650526
Issuing Agency                   0.000000
Street Code1                     0.000000
Street Code2                     0.000000
Street Code3                     0.000000
Vehicle Expiration Date          0.000002
```

```
Violation Location                          15.142846
Violation Precinct                           0.000002
Issuer Precinct                              0.000002
Issuer Code                                  0.000002
Issuer Command                              15.018851
Issuer Squad                                15.022566
Violation Time                               0.019207
Time First Observed                         90.040886
Violation County                            10.154892
Violation In Front Of Or Opposite           15.953282
House Number                                16.932473
Street Name                                  0.054894
Intersecting Street                         72.571929
Date First Observed                          0.000007
Law Section                                  0.000007
Sub Division                                 0.012412
Violation Legal Code                        84.970398
Days Parking In Effect                      23.225424
From Hours In Effect                        44.821011
To Hours In Effect                          44.821004
Vehicle Color                                1.152299
Unregistered Vehicle?                       88.484122
Vehicle Year                                 0.000012
Meter Number                                81.115883
Feet From Curb                               0.000012
Violation Post Code                         26.532350
Violation Description                       11.523098
No Standing or Stopping Violation           99.999998
Hydrant Violation                           99.999998
Double Parking Violation                    99.999998
dtype: float64
```

Listing 5.11 should look a bit familiar—we did the same thing on just the 2017 data in chapter 2. To recap what's going on here, the first line creates a new Series that contains a count of missing values by column. The `isnull` method scans each row and returns `True` if a missing value is found and `False` if a missing value isn't found. The `sum` method counts up all the `True` values to give us a total count of missing rows per column. We then take that Series of counts and divide it by the number of rows in the DataFrame using `nyc_data_raw.index.size`, and multiply each value by 100. Calling the compute method triggers the calculation and stores the result as a Pandas Series named `percent_missing`.

5.2.2   *Dropping columns with missing values*

Now that we know what we have to work with, we'll start by dropping any columns that have more than 50% of their values missing.

Listing 5.12   Dropping columns that have more than 50% missing values

```
columns_to_drop = list(percent_missing[percent_missing >= 50].index)
nyc_data_clean_stage1 = nyc_data_raw.drop(columns_to_drop, axis=1)
```

In listing 5.12, we start by filtering the `percent_missing` Series to find the names of the columns that have 50% or more missing values. That produces a list that looks like this:

```
['Time First Observed',
 'Intersecting Street',
 'Violation Legal Code',
 'Unregistered Vehicle?',
 'Meter Number',
 'No Standing or Stopping Violation',
 'Hydrant Violation',
 'Double Parking Violation']
```

We then use the `drop` method you learned in the last section to drop the columns from the DataFrame and save the result as the DataFrame called `nyc_data_clean_stage1`. We picked 50% arbitrarily here, but it's quite typical to drop columns with a very high amount of missing data. Take the Double Parking Violation column, for example: it's missing 99.9% of its values. We don't likely stand to gain much information by keeping such a sparse column around, so we'll remove it from our dataset.

5.2.3 Imputing missing values

When you have columns that only have a small amount of missing data, it's more appropriate to discard the rows that have missing data. Before we do that, though, we'll *impute* a value for the Vehicle Color column. *Imputing* means we will use the data that we do have to make a reasonable guess at what the missing data might be. In this instance, we'll find the most frequently occurring color in the dataset. While this assumption might not always hold true, using the most frequently occurring value in a dataset maximizes the probability that you chose correctly.

Listing 5.13 Imputing missing values

```
with ProgressBar():
    count_of_vehicle_colors = nyc_data_clean_stage1['Vehicle Color'].value_
    counts().compute()
most_common_color = count_of_vehicle_colors.sort_values(ascending=False).
    index[0]         ◄────── Finds the most common vehicle color

nyc_data_clean_stage2 = nyc_data_clean_stage1.fillna({'Vehicle Color': most_
    common_color})    ◄──── Fills the missing vehicle color with
                            the most common color
```

Listing 5.13 aims to fill in missing values in the Vehicle Color column by assuming that they were the most common color in the dataset. Filling in missing values by using the most common element of a categorical variable or the arithmetic mean of a continuous variable is a common way to deal with missing values in a way that minimizes the effect on the statistical distribution of the data. On the first line of listing 5.13, we select the Vehicle Color column using the column selector and use the `value_counts` method, which counts the unique occurrences of data. Here's what the contents of count_of_vehicle_colors look like:

```
GY        6280314
WH        6074770
WHITE     5624960
BK        5121030
BLACK     2758479
BL        2193035
GREY      1668739
RD        1383881
SILVE     1253287
...
MATH            1
MARY            1
$RY             1
Name: Vehicle Color, Length: 5744, dtype: int64
```

As you can see, the results of value_counts give us a Series containing each color on the index and how many times the color appeared in the data as values. In the second line of listing 5.13, we sort all the vehicle colors from most occurrences to fewest and grab the name of the most common occurring color. As you can see, GY (gray) is the most commonly occurring color code with over 6.2 million occurrences. On the last line of listing 5.13, we use the fillna method to replace the missing colors with GY. fillna takes a dictionary of key-value pairs where the name of each column you want to fill is used as a key and what you want to fill the occurrences of missing values with is used as a value. Columns that you don't specify in the dictionary will not be modified.

5.2.4   *Dropping rows with missing data*

Now that we've filled in missing values in the Vehicle Color column, we'll take care of the other low missing value columns by dropping the rows that are missing values in those columns.

> **Listing 5.14   Dropping rows with missing data**

```
rows_to_drop = list(percent_missing[(percent_missing > 0) & (percent_missing
    < 5)].index)
nyc_data_clean_stage3 = nyc_data_clean_stage2.dropna(subset=rows_to_drop)
```

Subset argument specifies which columns to check for null values

Listing 5.14 starts by finding all the columns that have missing values but no more than 5% missing values. We put this result in a list called rows_to_drop. The contents of the list look like this:

```
['Plate ID',
 'Vehicle Body Type',
 'Vehicle Make',
 'Vehicle Expiration Date',
 'Violation Precinct',
 'Issuer Precinct',
```

```
'Issuer Code',
'Violation Time',
'Street Name',
'Date First Observed',
'Law Section',
'Sub Division',
'Vehicle Color',
'Vehicle Year',
'Feet From Curb']
```

Note that we're not going to drop these columns! We're just going to drop any rows from our DataFrame that have missing values in these columns. Also notice that Vehicle Color shows up. However, because we're going to apply our dropping function to nyc_data_clean_stage2, no rows will be dropped on account of missing vehicle colors because they've already been filled in. To do the actual dropping, we use the dropna method on the DataFrame. If we don't specify any arguments, dropna will drop all rows with any missing values, so use with caution! The subset argument allows us to specify the columns Dask will check for missing values. If a row has missing values in columns that aren't specified, Dask won't drop them.

5.2.5 *Imputing multiple columns with missing values*

We're almost done now. The last thing we'll do is fill in our remaining columns that have missing data with default values. One thing we'll need to make sure of is that the default value we set for a column is appropriate for that column's datatype. Let's check what columns we have left to clean up and what their datatypes are.

Listing 5.15 Finding the datatypes of the remaining columns

```
remaining_columns_to_clean = list(percent_missing[(percent_missing >= 5) &
    (percent_missing < 50)].index)
nyc_data_raw.dtypes[remaining_columns_to_clean]
```

The first thing we'll do in listing 5.15, like some of the listings before it, is find the columns that we still need to clean up. For any columns that have more than 5% missing values and less than 50% missing values, we'll fill the missing values with a default value. That list of columns is stored in the remaining_columns_to_clean variable, and we use that with the dtypes parameter of the nyc_data_raw DataFrame to find the datatype of each column. Here's what the output looks like:

```
Violation Location                   object
Issuer Command                       object
Issuer Squad                         object
Violation County                     object
Violation In Front Of Or Opposite    object
House Number                         object
Days Parking In Effect               object
From Hours In Effect                 object
To Hours In Effect                   object
Violation Post Code                  object
Violation Description                object
dtype: object
```

As you can see, all the columns we have left to clean up are strings. You may be wondering why they are displayed as `object` instead of `np.str`. This is just cosmetic—Dask only explicitly shows numeric (`int`, `float`, and so on) datatypes. Any non-numeric datatypes will show as `object`. We'll fill in each column with the string "Unknown" to signify that the value was missing. We'll use `fillna` again to fill in the values, so we need to prepare a dictionary with the values for each column.

Listing 5.16   Making a dictionary of values for `fillna`

```
unknown_default_dict = dict(map(lambda columnName: (columnName, 'Unknown'),
    remaining_columns_to_clean))
```

Listing 5.16 show how to build this dictionary. We're simply taking each value in the `remaining_columns_to_clean` list and spitting out a tuple of the column name and the string "Unknown." Finally, we convert the list of tuples to a dictionary, which yields an object that looks like this:

```
{'Days Parking In Effect     ': 'Unknown',
 'From Hours In Effect': 'Unknown',
 'House Number': 'Unknown',
 'Issuer Command': 'Unknown',
 'Issuer Squad': 'Unknown',
 'To Hours In Effect': 'Unknown',
 'Violation County': 'Unknown',
 'Violation Description': 'Unknown',
 'Violation In Front Of Or Opposite': 'Unknown',
 'Violation Location': 'Unknown',
 'Violation Post Code': 'Unknown'}
```

Now that we have a dictionary representing each column we want to fill in and the value to fill with, we can pass it to `fillna`.

Listing 5.17   Filling the DataFrame with default values

```
nyc_data_clean_stage4 = nyc_data_clean_stage3.fillna(unknown_default_dict)
```

Nice and simple. We've now built up our final DataFrame, `nyc_data_clean_stage4`, which has been sequentially built up by starting from `nyc_data_raw` and lazily applying each of the four missing value techniques on various columns. Now it's time to check our work.

Listing 5.18   Checking the success of the filling/dropping operations

```
with ProgressBar():
    print(nyc_data_clean_stage4.isnull().sum().compute())
nyc_data_clean_stage4.persist()

# Produces the following output:

Summons Number              0
Plate ID                    0
Registration State          0
```

```
Plate Type                             0
Issue Date                             0
Violation Code                         0
Vehicle Body Type                      0
Vehicle Make                           0
Issuing Agency                         0
Street Code1                           0
Street Code2                           0
Street Code3                           0
Vehicle Expiration Date                0
Violation Location                     0
Violation Precinct                     0
Issuer Precinct                        0
Issuer Code                            0
Issuer Command                         0
Issuer Squad                           0
Violation Time                         0
Violation County                       0
Violation In Front Of Or Opposite      0
House Number                           0
Street Name                            0
Date First Observed                    0
Law Section                            0
Sub Division                           0
Days Parking In Effect                 0
From Hours In Effect                   0
To Hours In Effect                     0
Vehicle Color                          0
Vehicle Year                           0
Feet From Curb                         0
Violation Post Code                    0
Violation Description                  0
dtype: int64
```

In listing 5.18, we kick off the computation and get back a count of how many missing values remain after applying all our transformations. Looks like we got everything! If you're running the code as you're reading, you might have noticed that the computation took some time to complete. Now would be an opportune time to persist the Data-Frame. Remember that persisting the DataFrame will precompute the work you've done up to this point and store it in a processed state in memory. This will make sure that we don't have to recompute all those transformations as we continue our analysis. The last line of listing 5.18 reviews how to do that. Now that we've taken care of all the missing values, we'll look at a few methods for cleaning up erroneous-looking values.

5.3 Recoding data

Like missing values, it's not unusual to also have some instances in your dataset where the data is not missing but its validity is suspect. For instance, if we came across a vehicle in the NYC Parking Ticket dataset whose color was purportedly Rocky Road, that might raise a few eyebrows. It's more likely that the parking enforcement officer had the local scoop shop's flavor of the day in mind when writing the ticket rather than the job at hand! We need to have a way to clean up those kinds of data anomalies, and one way to do that is by either recoding those values to a more likely choice (such as the most frequent value or arithmetic mean) or placing the anomalous data in an Other category. Just like methods for filling missing data, it's worth it to discuss this with the consumers of your analyses and agree upon a plan for identifying and dealing with anomalous data.

Dask gives you two methods to recode values.

Listing 5.19   Getting value counts of the Plate Type column

```
with ProgressBar():
    license_plate_types = nyc_data_clean_stage4['Plate Type'].value_counts().
    compute()
license_plate_types
```

Listing 5.19 uses the `value_counts` method again that you learned about in the last section. Here we're using it to take a distinct count of all the license plate types that have been recorded over the past four years. The Plate Type column records whether the vehicle in question was a passenger vehicle, commercial vehicle, and so forth. Here's an abbreviated output of the computation:

```
PAS     30452502
COM      7966914
OMT      1389341
SRF       394656
OMS       368952
        . . .
SNO            2
Name: Plate Type, Length: 90, dtype: int64
```

As you can see, the vast majority of license plate types are PAS (passenger vehicles). Combined with COM (commercial vehicles), these two plate types make up over 92% of the entire DataFrame (~38M out of ~41M rows). However, we can also see that there are 90 distinct license plate types (Length: 90)! Let's collapse the Plate Type column so we only have three types: PAS, COM, and Other.

Listing 5.20   Recoding the Plate Type column

```
condition = nyc_data_clean_stage4['Plate Type'].isin(['PAS', 'COM'])
plate_type_masked = nyc_data_clean_stage4['Plate Type'].where(condition,
    'Other')
nyc_data_recode_stage1 = nyc_data_clean_stage4.drop('Plate Type', axis=1)
nyc_data_recode_stage2 = nyc_data_recode_stage1.assign(PlateType=plate_type_
    masked)
nyc_data_recode_stage3 = nyc_data_recode_stage2.
    rename(columns={'PlateType':'Plate Type'})
```

We have a lot of things going on in listing 5.20. First, we need to build a Boolean condition that we'll use to compare with each row. To build the condition, we use the `isin` method. This method will return `True` if the value it's checking is contained in the list of objects passed in as the argument. Otherwise, it will return `False`. When applied over the whole Plate Type column, it will return a Series of `True` and `False` values. In the next line, we pass the Series of `True`/`False` values to the `where` method and apply it to the Plate Type column. The where method keeps the existing value for all rows that are True and replaces any rows that are False with the value passed in the second argument. This means that any row that doesn't have a Plate Type of PAS or COM will have its Plate Type replaced with Other. This results in a new Series that we store in the plate_type_masked variable.

Now that we have the new Series, we need to put it back in the DataFrame. To do that, we'll first drop the old Plate Type column using the drop method that you've seen a few times now. Then we use the assign method to add the Series to the DataFrame as a new column. Because the assign method uses **kwargs for passing column names instead of a dictionary, like many of the other column-based methods do, we can't add a column that has spaces in the column name. Therefore, we create the column as "Plate-Type" and use the rename method you learned earlier in the chapter to give the column the name we want.

If we take a look at the value counts now, you can see we successfully collapsed the column.

Listing 5.21 Looking at value counts after recoding

```
with ProgressBar():
    display(nyc_data_recode_stage3['Plate Type'].value_counts().compute())
```

Here's what the output looks like:

```
PAS      30452502
COM       7966914
Other     3418586
Name: Plate Type, dtype: int64
```

This looks much better now! We've successfully reduced the number of distinct license plate classes to three.

The other method for recoding that we have at our disposal is the mask method. It works largely the same as the where method, but with one key difference: the where method replaces values when the condition passed to it evaluates False, and the mask method replaces values when the condition passed to it evaluates True. To give an example of how this is used, let's now look at the Vehicle Color column again, starting with examining the value counts of the column:

```
GY       6280314
WH       6074770
WHITE    5624960
BK       5121030
           . . .
MARUE          1
MARUI          1
MBWC           1
METBL          1
METBK          1
MET/O          1
MERWH          1
MERON          1
```

```
MERL         1
MERG         1
MEDS         1
MDE          1
MD-BL        1
MCNY         1
MCCT         1
MBROW        1
MARVN        1
MBR          1
MAZOO        1
MAZON        1
MAXOO        1
MAX          1
MAWE         1
MAVEN        1
MAUL         1
MAU          1
MATOO        1
MATH         1
MARY         1
$RY          1
Name: Vehicle Color, Length: 5744, dtype: int64
```

This dataset contains more than 5,744 unique colors, but it looks like some colors are quite strange. Just over 50% of the colors in this dataset have only a single entry like the many you see here. Let's reduce the number of unique colors by putting all the single-color entries in a category called Other.

Listing 5.22   Using `mask` to put unique colors in an "Other" category

```
single_color = list(count_of_vehicle_colors[count_of_vehicle_colors ==
    1].index)
condition = nyc_data_clean_stage4['Vehicle Color'].isin(single_color)
vehicle_color_masked = nyc_data_clean_stage4['Vehicle Color'].mask(condition,
    'Other')
nyc_data_recode_stage4 = nyc_data_recode_stage3.drop('Vehicle Color', axis=1)
nyc_data_recode_stage5 = nyc_data_recode_stage4.assign(VehicleColor=vehicle_
    color_masked)
nyc_data_recode_stage6 = nyc_data_recode_stage5.
    rename(columns={'VehicleColor':'Vehicle Color'})
```

In listing 5.22, we first get a list of all of the colors that appear only once in our dataset by filtering down the value counts of Vehicle Colors. Then, as before, we use the `isin` method to build a Series of `True`/`False` values. This will result in `True` for any rows that have one of the unique colors and `False` for rows that don't. We pass this condition into the `mask` method along with the alternative value of `Other`. This will return a Series where all rows that have one of the unique colors will be replaced with `Other`, and the rows that don't will retain their original value. We then simply follow the same process we did before to put the new column back in the DataFrame: drop the old column, add the new column, and rename it to what we want.

You're probably wondering when you should use one method over the other. They both fundamentally do the same thing and share the same performance characteristics, but sometimes it's more convenient to use one over the other. If you have many unique values, but you want to keep only a few around, using the where method is more convenient. Conversely, if you have many unique values but you want to get rid of only a few of them, using the mask method is more convenient.

Now that you've learned some methods for replacing one value with another static value, we'll look at some more sophisticated methods to create derived columns using functions.

5.4   *Elementwise operations*

While the methods for recoding values that you learned in the previous section are very useful, and you're likely to use them often, it's also good to know how to create new columns that are derived from other existing columns in the DataFrame. One scenario that comes up often with structured data, like our NYC Parking Ticket dataset, is the need to parse and work with date/time dimensions. Back in chapter 4, when we constructed our schema for the dataset, we opted to import the date columns as strings. However, to properly use dates for our analyses, we need to change those strings to datetime objects. Dask gives you the ability to automatically parse dates when reading data, but it can be finicky with formatting. An alternative approach that gives you more control over how the dates are parsed is to import the date columns as strings and manually parse them as part of your data prep workflow. In this section, we'll learn how to use the apply method on DataFrames to apply generic functions to our data and create derived columns. More specifically, we'll parse the Issue Date column, which represents the date that the parking citation was issued and converts that column to a datetime datatype. We'll then create a new column containing the month and year that the citation was issued, which we'll use again later in the chapter. With that in mind, let's get to it!

Listing 5.23   Parsing the Issue Date column

```
from datetime import datetime
issue_date_parsed = nyc_data_recode_stage6['Issue Date'].apply(lambda x:
    datetime.strptime(x, "%m/%d/%Y"), meta=datetime)
nyc_data_derived_stage1 = nyc_data_recode_stage6.drop('Issue Date', axis=1)
nyc_data_derived_stage2 = nyc_data_derived_stage1.assign(IssueDate=issue_
    date_parsed)
nyc_data_derived_stage3 = nyc_data_derived_stage2.
    rename(columns={'IssueDate':'Issue Date'})
```

In listing 5.23, we first need to import the datetime object from Python's standard library. Then, as you've seen in a few previous examples, we create a new Series object by selecting the Issue Date series from our DataFrame (nyc_data_recode_stage6) and use the apply method to perform the transformation. In this particular call to apply, we create an anonymous (lambda) function that takes a value from the input

Series, runs it through the `datetime.strptime` function, and returns a parsed date-time object. The `datetime.strptime` function simply takes a string as input and parses it into a datetime object using the specified format. The format we specified was `"%m/%d/%Y"`, which is equivalent to an mm/dd/yyyy date. The last thing to note about the `apply` method is the `meta` argument we had to specify. Dask tries to infer the output type of the function passed into it, but it's better to explicitly specify what the datatype is. In this case, datatype inference will fail so we're required to pass an explicit datetime datatype. The next three lines of code should be very familiar by now: drop, assign, rename—the pattern we learned before to add a column to our DataFrame. Let's take a look at what happened.

Listing 5.24   Inspecting the result of date parsing

```
with ProgressBar():
    display(nyc_data_derived_stage3['Issue Date'].head())
```

Looking at the column, we get the following output:

```
0    2013-08-04
1    2013-08-04
2    2013-08-05
3    2013-08-05
4    2013-08-08
Name: Issue Date, dtype: datetime64[ns]
```

The column is no longer a string type—just what we wanted! Now let's use our new datetime column to extract just the month and year.

Listing 5.25   Extracting the month and year

```
issue_date_month_year = nyc_data_derived_stage3['Issue Date'].apply(lambda
    dt: dt.strftime("%Y%m"), meta=int)
nyc_data_derived_stage4 = nyc_data_derived_stage3.
    assign(IssueMonthYear=issue_date_month_year)
nyc_data_derived_stage5 = nyc_data_derived_stage4.
    rename(columns={'IssueMonthYear':'Citation Issued Month Year'})
```

This time, in listing 5.25, we again create a new Series based on the Issue Date column in the DataFrame. However, the function we pass through apply now uses the `strftime` method of Python's datetime objects to extract the month and year from the date-time and return a formatted string. We've opted to format our month/year strings as "yyyyMM," as specified in the `strftime` argument. We also specify that the output type of this function is an integer, as denoted by the `meta=int` argument. Finally, we follow the familiar assign-rename pattern as usual to add the column to the DataFrame. However, we didn't need to drop any columns because we don't want to replace an existing column with this new column. We'll simply add it alongside our other columns in the DataFrame. Let's take a look at the contents of this new column now.

Listing 5.26 Inspecting the new derived column

```
with ProgressBar():
    display(nyc_data_derived_stage5['Citation Issued Month Year'].head())
```

Looking at the column, we get the following output:

```
0    201308
1    201308
2    201308
3    201308
4    201308
Name: Citation Issued Month Year, dtype: object
```

Perfect! Just what we wanted: a nice string representation of the month/year that the citation was issued. Now that we've created this column, we're going to finally replace our sequential numeric index with the month/year of the citation! That will allow us to easily look up citations by month/year and do other neat things in coming chapters like look at the ebb and flow of ticket citations month-over-month.

5.5 *Filtering and reindexing DataFrames*

Earlier in the chapter, you learned how to look up values by index slicing using the `loc` method. However, we have a few more-sophisticated ways to search and filter data using Boolean expressions. Let's have a look at finding all citations for the month of October.

Listing 5.27 Finding all citations that occurred in October

```
months = ['201310','201410','201510','201610','201710']
condition = nyc_data_derived_stage5['Citation Issued Month Year'].
    isin(months)
october_citations = nyc_data_derived_stage5[condition]

with ProgressBar():
    display(october_citations.head())
```

In listing 5.27, we first create a list of month-year combinations we want to search for (October for years 2013–2017). We then use the familiar `isin` method to create a Boolean series that returns `True` for each row that matches one of the month-year combinations in the `months` list, and `False` for each row that doesn't match. This Boolean series is then passed into the selector. When the result is computed, you'll get a DataFrame back with only the citations that happened in October.

Any kind of Boolean expression that creates a Boolean series can be used this way. For example, instead of picking certain months, perhaps we want to find all citations that happened after a given date. We can use Python's built-in inequality operators to do this.

Listing 5.28   Finding all citations after 4/25/2016

```
bound_date = '2016-4-25'
condition = nyc_data_derived_stage5['Issue Date'] > bound_date
citations_after_bound = nyc_data_derived_stage5[condition]

with ProgressBar():
    display(citations_after_bound.head())
```

In listing 5.28, we use the greater-than operator to find all records with an Issue Date greater than 4-25-2016. These Boolean filter expressions can also be chained together using the AND (&) and OR (|) operators to create quite complex filters! We'll take a look at how to do that in the next code listing, in which we'll also create a custom index for our DataFrame.

Up to this point, we've relied solely on Dask's default numeric index for our dataset. This has served us fine so far, but we've reached a point where ignoring the benefits of using a more suitable index could cause some serious performance issues. This becomes especially important when we want to combine multiple DataFrames, which is precisely what we'll talk about in the next section of the chapter. While it's possible to combine DataFrames that aren't index aligned, Dask must scan both DataFrames for every possible unique combination of keys used to join the two DataFrames together, making it quite a slow process. When joining two DataFrames that have the same index, and are both sorted and partitioned in index order, the join operation is much faster. Therefore, to prepare our data for joining to another dataset, we'll adjust the index and partitions to align with the other dataset.

Setting an index on a DataFrame will sort the entire dataset by the specified column. While the sorting process can be quite slow, you can persist the result of the sorted DataFrame and even write your data back to disk in a sorted Parquet file so you only have to sort the data once. To set an index on a DataFrame, we use the set_index method.

Listing 5.29   Setting an index on a DataFrame

```
with ProgressBar():
    condition = (nyc_data_derived_stage5['Issue Date'] > '2014-01-01') &
    (nyc_data_derived_stage5['Issue Date'] <= '2017-12-31')
    nyc_data_filtered = nyc_data_derived_stage5[condition]
    nyc_data_new_index = nyc_data_filtered.set_index('Citation Issued Month
    Year')
```

Set the DataFrame index to the Month/Year column.

Filter the data to retain only tickets that were issued between 2014-01-01 and 2017-12-31.

In listing 5.29, we're taking the month-year column we created in the previous section of the chapter and sorting the DataFrame on that value. This will return a new DataFrame that's sorted by that column, enabling us to use it for searching, filtering, and joining much more quickly. If you're working with a dataset that was sorted before it was stored, you can pass the optional argument, sorted=True, to tell Dask that the data is already sorted. Also, you have an opportunity to adjust the partitioning similar to the repartition options you learned previously. You can specify a number of partitions to evenly split the data into using the `npartitions` argument, or you can manually specify the partition boundaries using the `divisions` argument. Since we've sorted the data by month/year, let's repartition the data so each partition contains one month of data. The following listing demonstrates how to do this.

Listing 5.30   Repartitioning the data by month/year

> **Create a list of all month/year combinations to use as keys.**

```
years = ['2014', '2015', '2016', '2017']
months = ['01','02','03','04','05','06','07','08','09','10','11','12']
divisions = [year + month for year in years for month in months]

with ProgressBar():
    nyc_data_new_index.repartition(divisions=divisions) \
        .to_parquet('nyc_data_date_index', compression='snappy')

nyc_data_new_index = dd.read_parquet('nyc_data_date_index')
```

Apply the partitioning scheme to the DataFrame and write the results to a file.   **Read the sorted data back into a DataFrame.**

In listing 5.30, we first produce a list of month/year keys, which is used to define our partition scheme (201401, 201402, 201403, and so forth). Next, we pass the list of partitions into the `repartition` method to apply it to our newly reindexed DataFrame. Finally, we write the results out to a Parquet file to avoid needing to repeatedly sort the data every time subsequent computations are needed and read the sorted data into a new DataFrame called `nyc_data_new_index`. Now that we've set an index on our DataFrame, let's round out the chapter by talking about using the index to combine DataFrames.

5.6   Joining and concatenating DataFrames

If you've worked with a relational database management system (RDBMS) before, such as SQL Server, you likely already have an appreciation for the power of join and union operations. Regardless of whether you're an expert DBA or just getting your first taste of data engineering, it's important to cover these operations in depth because they offer a whole different host of potential performance pitfalls in a distributed environment. First, let's briefly review how join operations work. Figure 5.9 displays the visual result of a join operation.

In a join operation, two data objects (such as tables and DataFrames) are combined into a single object by adding the columns from the left object to the columns of the right object. When we joined the Person table with the Pet table, the resulting object added the columns from the Pet table to the right of the columns from the Person table. Using the combined table, we can determine relationships between the objects, such as Jack is my family's ever-hungry brown tiger tabby. These two objects are logically connected by keys, or a column in one table that's used to look up values in another table.

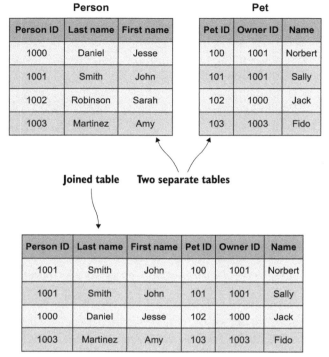

Person

Person ID	Last name	First name
1000	Daniel	Jesse
1001	Smith	John
1002	Robinson	Sarah
1003	Martinez	Amy

Pet

Pet ID	Owner ID	Name
100	1001	Norbert
101	1001	Sally
102	1000	Jack
103	1003	Fido

Joined table   Two separate tables

Person ID	Last name	First name	Pet ID	Owner ID	Name
1001	Smith	John	100	1001	Norbert
1001	Smith	John	101	1001	Sally
1000	Daniel	Jesse	102	1000	Jack
1003	Martinez	Amy	103	1003	Fido

Figure 5.9   A join operation combines two datasets by adding the columns of the right table to the columns of the left table.

In figure 5.10, you can see the key relationship between these two tables. Jack has an Owner ID of 1000, which corresponds to my Person ID of 1000. Therefore, if you wanted additional information about Jack, like who his owner is, you could use this relationship to look up my information. This kind of relational model is the primary way complex structured datasets are stored in the real world. Since people, places, things, and events typically have some degree of relationship to one another, this relational model is an intuitive way to structure and organize interrelated datasets. Let's take a closer look at that combined table again.

Notice in figure 5.11 that Sarah Robinson doesn't appear in the joined table. It also happens that she doesn't have a pet. What we're seeing here is called an *inner join.* This means that only records between the two objects that have relationships with one another are put in the combined table. Records that have no relationships are

Person

Person ID	Last name	First name
1000	Daniel	Jesse
1001	Smith	John
1002	Robinson	Sarah
1003	Martinez	Amy

Pet

Pet ID	Owner ID	Name
100	1001	Norbert
101	1001	Sally
102	1000	Jack
103	1003	Fido

Figure 5.10   We can tell that Jack is my cat because his Owner ID is a key that points to my Person ID.

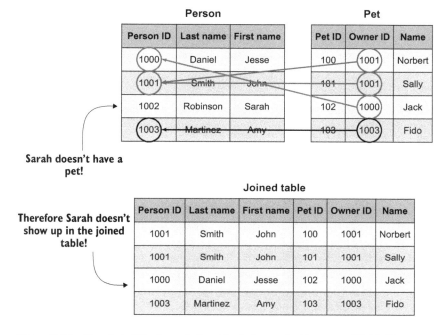

Person

Pet

Person ID	Last name	First name
1000	Daniel	Jesse
1001	Smith	John
1002	Robinson	Sarah
1003	Martinez	Amy

Pet ID	Owner ID	Name
100	1001	Norbert
101	1001	Sally
102	1000	Jack
103	1003	Fido

Sarah doesn't have a pet!

Therefore Sarah doesn't show up in the joined table!

Joined table

Person ID	Last name	First name	Pet ID	Owner ID	Name
1001	Smith	John	100	1001	Norbert
1001	Smith	John	101	1001	Sally
1000	Daniel	Jesse	102	1000	Jack
1003	Martinez	Amy	103	1003	Fido

Figure 5.11 Showing all the key relationships between the Person and Pet tables

discarded. If the purpose of combining these two tables is to learn more about each pet's owner, it wouldn't make sense to include people that don't have any pets. To perform an inner join, you must specify how=inner as an argument of the join method. Let's see an example of this in action.

5.6.1 Joining two DataFrames

Returning to our NYC Parking Ticket Data example, I collected some average monthly temperature data for New York City from the National Oceanic and Atmospheric Administration (NOAA), and have included this data along with the code notebooks. Since we've indexed our parking citation data by month/year, let's add on the average monthly temperature for the month in which the citation was given. Perhaps we'll see a trend that parking citations happen more in warm weather months when parking enforcement can hit the streets. Figure 5.12 displays a sample of the temperature data.

Since the average temperature data and the parking citation data are indexed by the same value (a string representation of month/year), the two datasets are index aligned and joining them will be a rather quick operation! The next listing shows what that looks like.

monthYear	Temp
01-2000	31.3
01-2001	33.6
01-2002	39.9
01-2003	27.5
01-2004	24.7
01-2005	31.3
01-2006	40.9
01-2007	37.5
01-2008	36.5
01-2009	27.9

Figure 5.12 New York City average monthly temperature

```
import pandas as pd
nyc_temps = pd.read_csv('nyc-temp-data.csv')
nyc_temps_indexed = nyc_temps.set_index(nyc_temps.monthYear.astype(str))

nyc_data_with_temps = nyc_data_new_index.join(nyc_temps_indexed, how='inner')

with ProgressBar():
    display(nyc_data_with_temps.head(15))
```

We use how = 'inner' to tell Dask to use an inner join.

In listing 5.31, we first read in the other dataset using Pandas. I've opted to read this file with Pandas because it's very small (only a few KBs). It's also worth demonstrating that Pandas DataFrames can be joined to Dask DataFrames. Of course, Dask DataFrames can be joined to other Dask DataFrames the exact same way, so you have a degree of flexibility here. I've next set the index on the nyc_temps DataFrame to make it index aligned with the Dask DataFrame. Finally, we call the join method on the nyc_data_new_index DataFrame and pass in the temperature DataFrame as the first argument. We also specify how=inner to denote that this is an inner join. Figure 5.13 displays the output of listing 5.31.

As you can see, the Temp column was added to the right of the original DataFrame. We'll keep our eye on that one as we move into the next chapter. Because the weather data overlaps the entire timeframe of the parking citation data, we didn't lose any rows in the join process. And, because the DataFrames were index aligned, it was a very fast

Out[57]:

Registration State	Violation Code	Vehicle Body Type	Vehicle Make	Issuing Agency	Street Code1	Street Code2	Street Code3	...	Vehicle Year	Feet From Curb	Violation Post Code	Violation Description	Plate Type	Vehicle Color	Issue Date	Citation Issued Month Year	Temp	monthYear
NY	46	SUBN	AUDI	P	37250	13610	21190	...	2013.0	0.0	Unknown	Unknown	PAS	GY	2013-08-04	08-2013	74.6	08-2013
NY	46	VAN	FORD	P	37290	40404	40404	...	2012.0	0.0	Unknown	Unknown	COM	WH	2013-08-04	08-2013	74.6	08-2013
NY	46	P-U	CHEVR	P	37030	31190	13610	...	0.0	0.0	Unknown	Unknown	COM	GY	2013-08-05	08-2013	74.6	08-2013
NY	46	VAN	FORD	P	37270	11710	12010	...	2010.0	0.0	Unknown	Unknown	COM	WH	2013-08-05	08-2013	74.6	08-2013
NY	41	TRLR	GMC	P	37240	12010	31190	...	2012.0	0.0	Unknown	Unknown	COM	BR	2013-08-08	08-2013	74.6	08-2013
NJ	14	P-U	DODGE	P	37250	10495	12010	...	0.0	0.0	Unknown	Unknown	PAS	RD	2013-08-11	08-2013	74.6	08-2013
NJ	24	DELV	FORD	X	63430	0	0	...	0.0	0.0	Unknown	Unknown	PAS	WHITE	2013-08-07	08-2013	74.6	08-2013
NY	24	SDN	TOYOT	X	63430	0	0	...	2001.0	0.0	Unknown	Unknown	PAS	WHITE	2013-08-07	08-2013	74.6	08-2013
NY	24	SDN	NISSA	X	23230	41330	83330	...	2012.0	0.0	Unknown	Unknown	PAS	WHITE	2013-08-12	08-2013	74.6	08-2013
NY	20	SDN	VOLKS	T	28930	27530	29830	...	2012.0	0.0	Unknown	Unknown	PAS	WHITE	2013-06-12	08-2013	74.6	08-2013
LA	17	SUBN	HONDA	T	0	0	0	...	0.0	0.0	Unknown	Unknown	PAS	TAN	2013-08-07	08-2013	74.6	08-2013
IL	40	SDN	SCIO	T	26630	40930	18630	...	0.0	6.0	Unknown	Unknown	PAS	BK	2013-08-10	08-2013	74.6	08-2013
PA	20	SDN	TOYOT	T	21130	71330	89930	...	0.0	0.0	Unknown	Unknown	PAS	GR	2013-08-06	08-2013	74.6	08-2013
NY	40	VAN	MERCU	T	23190	27290	20340	...	2003.0	0.0	Unknown	Unknown	COM	RD	2013-08-07	08-2013	74.6	08-2013
NY	51	VAN	TOYOT	X	93230	74830	67030	...	2013.0	0.0	Unknown	Unknown	PAS	GY	2013-08-06	08-2013	74.6	08-2013

Figure 5.13   The output of listing 5.31

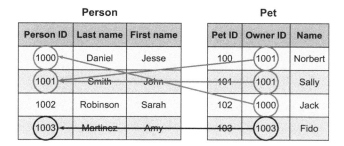

Joined table

Person ID	Last name	First name	Pet ID	Owner ID	Name
1001	Smith	John	100	1001	Norbert
1001	Smith	John	101	1001	Sally
1000	Daniel	Jesse	102	1000	Jack
1003	Martinez	Amy	103	1003	Fido
1002	Robinson	Sarah	*NULL*	*NULL*	*NULL*

With an outer join, unrelated records are kept.

But since Sarah doesn't have any pets, her pet columns are NULL.

Figure 5.14　The result of an outer join preserves records that don't have any relationships.

operation. It's possible to join DataFrames that aren't index aligned, but it can be so detrimental to performance that it's not really worth covering in this book. I'd strongly recommend against it.

If you don't want to discard records that are unrelated, then you will want to perform an *outer join*.

In figure 5.14, you can see that as a result of the outer join, the pets that have owners are connected as before, but now Sarah shows up in our joined table. That's because an outer join does not discard unrelated records. What happens instead is columns that come from the unrelated table will contain missing values. You can see in figure 5.14 that, since Sarah doesn't have any pets, information about her pets is NULL, which represents missing/unknown data. Dask's default behavior is to perform an outer join, so unless you specify otherwise, joining two tables will yield a result like this.

5.6.2　Unioning two DataFrames

The other way to combine datasets is along the row axis. In RDBMSs, this is called a union operation, but in Dask it's called *concatenating* DataFrames.

Figure 5.15 shows the result of concatenating the Person and More People tables. Whereas joins add more data by increasing the number of columns, you can see that concatenation adds more data by increasing the number of rows. Columns that share the same column name across both tables are aligned to each other and the rows are

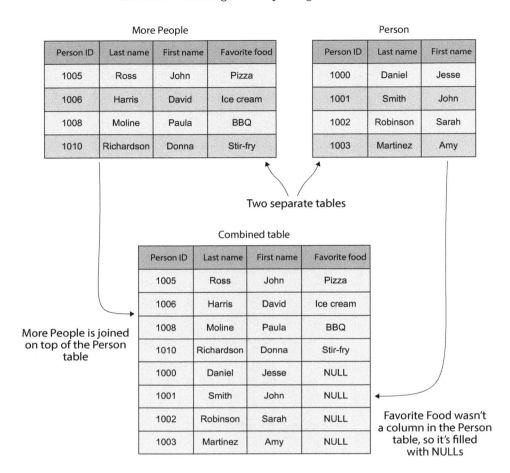

Figure 5.15   The result of concatenating the Person and More People tables

merged. You can also see the result of what happens when the two tables don't have the exact same columns. In this case, the Favorite Food column didn't overlap between both tables, so the values for the people originating from the Person table are assigned a missing value for Favorite Food. Let's see at what this looks like in Dask.

Listing 5.32   Concatenating two DataFrames

```
fy16 = dd.read_csv('nyc-parking-tickets/Parking_Violations_Issued_-_Fiscal_
    Year_2016.csv', dtype=dtypes, usecols=dtypes.keys())
fy17 = dd.read_csv('nyc-parking-tickets/Parking_Violations_Issued_-_Fiscal_
    Year_2017.csv', dtype=dtypes, usecols=dtypes.keys())

fy1617 = fy16.append(fy17)

with ProgressBar():
    print(fy16['Summons Number'].count().compute())
```

```
with ProgressBar():
    print(fy17['Summons Number'].count().compute())

with ProgressBar():
    print(fy1617['Summons Number'].count().compute())
```

In listing 5.32, we're momentarily going all the way back to our raw data. Because we don't need to have a common index we will concatenate the raw data from the two sources. An alternative to the schema building and combined loading (using *.csv in the file path) we did in chapter 4 would be to load each of the files individually and concatenate them with the append method. Syntactically, this is very simple, and no additional arguments exist for the append method. You can see that `fy16` contains 10,626,899 rows, `fy17` contains 10,803,028 rows, and together `fy1617` contains 21,429,927 rows.

5.7 *Writing data to text files and Parquet files*

Now that we've put in a considerable amount of work to clean the dataset, it would be an opportune time to save your progress. While using the `persist` method on your DataFrames from time to time is a good idea to maximize performance, its persistence is only temporary. If you shut down your notebook server and end your Python session, the persisted DataFrames will be cleared from memory, meaning that you'll have to re-run all the computations when you're ready to resume working with the data.

Writing data out of Dask is pretty simple but has one caveat: since Dask divides data into partitions when working on computations, its default behavior is to write one file per partition. This isn't really an issue if you're writing to a distributed filesystem or you're going to consume the data with another distributed system such as Spark or Hive, but if you want to save a single file that you can import into another data analysis tool like Tableau or Excel, you'll have to fold all the data into a single partition using the `repartition` method before saving it.

In this section we'll look at writing data in both of the formats you learned to read in the previous chapter: delimited text files and Parquet.

5.7.1 *Writing to delimited text files*

First, we'll look at how to write data back to delimited text files.

Listing 5.33   Writing a CSV file

```
with ProgressBar():
    if not os.path.exists('nyc-final-csv'):        ◄——  Check if the nyc-final-csv folder
        os.makedirs('nyc-final-csv')                     exists; create it if it doesn't.
    nyc_data_with_temps.repartition(npartitions=1).to_csv('nyc-final-csv/
      part*.csv')     ◄——  Collapse the data down to a single
                            partition (file) and save it in CSV format.
```

Listing 5.33 shows how to save the combined dataset we created in the previous sections of the chapter to a single CSV file. One thing to notice is the filename we've given the data: part*.csv. The * wildcard will be filled in automatically by Dask, indicating the partition number that corresponds to that file. Since we've collapsed all the data together into a single partition, only one CSV file will be written, and it will be called part0.csv. Producing a single CSV file may be useful for exporting data to be used in other applications, but Dask is a distributed library. It makes much more sense from a performance standpoint to keep the data broken into multiple files, which can be read in parallel. In fact, Dask's default behavior is to save each partition to a separate file. Next, we'll look at a few other important options that can be set in the to_csv method, and we'll write out the data into multiple CSV files.

Using the default settings in both the methods makes a few assumptions about the shape of the output file. Namely, by default, the to_csv method will create files that

- Use a comma (,) as a column delimiter
- Save missing (np.nan) values as an empty string ("")
- Include a header row
- Include the index as a column
- Do not use compression

Listing 5.34   Writing a delimited text file with custom options

```
with ProgressBar():
    if not os.path.exists('nyc-final-csv-compressed'):
        os.makedirs('nyc-final-csv-compressed')
    nyc_data_with_temps.to_csv(
        filename='nyc-final-csv-compressed/*',
        compression='gzip',
        sep='|',
        na_rep='NULL',
        header=False,
        index=False)
```

Listing 5.34 demonstrates how to change and customize these assumptions. This particular line of code will write the data DataFrame to 48 files, which will be compressed using gzip, will use the pipe (|) as a column delimiter instead of the comma, will write any missing values as NULL, and will not write a header row or an index column. You can adjust any of these options to suit your needs.

5.7.2   *Writing to Parquet files*

Writing to Parquet is very similar to writing to delimited text files. The key difference is that instead of specifying a scheme for individual filenames, Parquet is simply saved to a directory. Since Parquet is best used by distributed systems, it's not really worth it to adjust partitioning like we did when saving delimited text files. Parquet's option set is very simple.

Listing 5.35 Writing a DataFrame to Parquet

```
with ProgressBar():
    nyc_data_with_temps.to_parquet('nyc_final', compression='snappy')
```

Listing 5.35 demonstrates writing data to Parquet on a local filesystem using the snappy compression codec. It's also possible to save to HDFS or S3 simply by following the path mechanics you've already learned in the previous chapter. As with non-repartitioned text files, Dask will write one Parquet file per partition.

There you have it. In this chapter we've covered many techniques for manipulating data, as well as a very large part of the Dask DataFrame API. I hope you feel much more confident in your ability to manipulate DataFrames now. We have our data cleaned up and are ready to begin analyzing it. Since you've saved your DataFrame, feel free to take a break, grab a coffee, and get ready for the fun part: data analysis!

Summary

- Selecting columns from a DataFrame uses square bracket ([...]) notation. You can select more than one column by passing a list of column names into the column selector brackets.
- The head method shows the first 10 rows of a DataFrame by default. You can also specify a number of rows you want to view.
- Columns can be dropped from a DataFrame by using the drop method. However, since DataFrames are immutable, the column is not dropped from the original DataFrame.
- Null values can be removed from DataFrames using the dropna method.
- Use the drop-assign-rename pattern to replace columns in a DataFrame, such as when parsing or recoding values in a column.
- Transformation functions can be performed elementwise over a DataFrame using the apply method.
- Boolean operators (such as >, <, =) are supported for filtering DataFrames. If your filter condition requires more than one input value, you can use NumPy-style Boolean functions such as isin.
- Two DataFrames can be relationally joined using the merge method. You can even merge a Pandas DataFrame to a Dask DataFrame!
- DataFrames can be concatenated (unioned) using the append method.

Summarizing and
analyzing DataFrames

This chapter covers

- Producing descriptive statistics for a Dask Series

- Aggregating/grouping data using Dask's built-in aggregate functions

- Creating your own custom aggregation functions

- Analyzing time series data with rolling window functions

At the end of the previous chapter we arrived at a dataset ready for us to start digging in and analyzing. However, we didn't perform an exhaustive search for every possible issue with the data. In reality, the data cleaning and preparation process can take a far longer time to complete. It's a common adage among data scientists that data cleaning can take 80% or more of the total time spent on a project. With the skills you learned in the previous chapter, you have a good foundation to address all the most common data-quality issues you'll come across in the wild. As a friendly reminder, figure 6.1 shows how we're progressing through our workflow—we're almost at the halfway point!

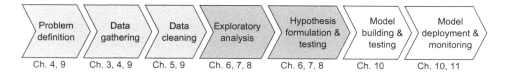

Figure 6.1 The *Data Science with Python and Dask* workflow

We'll now turn our attention to my favorite part of any data science project—exploratory data analysis. The goals of exploratory data analysis are to understand the "shape" of your data, find interesting patterns and correlations in your dataset, and identify significant relationships in your dataset that could be useful for predicting your target variable. As with the previous chapter, we'll highlight the differences and special considerations necessary to perform data analysis in the distributed paradigm of Dask.

6.1 Descriptive statistics

In the final dataset we created at the end of chapter 5, we have somewhere in the neighborhood of 41 million parking citations—that's a lot of observations! One thing that might be interesting to know is the average age of cars parked (illegally) on New York City streets. Are there more newer cars than older cars? How old was the oldest illegally parked car—are we talking Model T or Thunderbird? Using descriptive statistics, we'll answer the following questions:

> *Using the NYC Parking Ticket data, what is the average age of vehicles parked illegally on the streets of New York City? What can we infer about the age of the vehicles?*

6.1.1 What are descriptive statistics?

Before jumping into the code, we'll start with a brief overview of how to understand the shape of our data. This is typically defined by seven mathematical properties used to describe it:

- The smallest value (also called the *minimum*)
- The largest value (also called the *maximum*)
- The average of all data points (also called the *mean*)
- The middle point between the minimum and maximum value (also called the *median*)
- How spread out the data is from the mean (also called the *standard deviation*)
- The most commonly occurring observation (also called the *mode*)
- How balanced the number of data points to the left and right of the central point is (also called the *skewness*)

You've undoubtedly heard some of these terms before, because these concepts are typically taught as the foundation of any basic statistics course. These *descriptive statistics*, while simple, are very powerful ways to describe all kinds of data and tell us important things about our data. As a refresher, here's a visual guide to descriptive statistics.

Figure 6.2 shows a histogram of a hypothetical variable in which 100,000 observations were made. The values that were observed are along the X axis, and the relative *frequency* (how often each value was observed as a percent of all observations) is plotted along the Y axis. What you can take away from this is that we observed a range of values. Sometimes we observed a value of 0, sometimes 5.2, sometimes –3.48, and many more in between. Since we know that the observed value of this hypothetical variable doesn't always stay the same, we call this a *randomly distributed variable.* In order to cope with this variable's randomness, it would be useful to set some expectations about the range of possibilities that we could observe and the value that we'll most likely observe. This is precisely what descriptive statistics aim to achieve!

Back to figure 6.2, take a look at the minimum and maximum. As they are intuitively named, they serve as boundary points for the range of observations that were made. There were no observations made that fell below the minimum (of –10), and likewise, there were no observations that fell above the maximum (of 10). This tells us that it would be very unlikely to see any future observations outside this range. Next, have a look at the mean. This is the "center of mass" of the distribution, meaning if we make a random observation, the value is most likely to be near this point. You can see that the probability is 0.16, meaning that roughly 16% of the time we can expect to observe a value of 0. But what's likely to occur the other 80% of the time? This is where the standard deviation comes into play. The higher the standard deviation, the greater the likelihood that we'll observe values that are far away from the mean.

You can see this behavior in figure 6.3. With a small standard deviation, the probability drops off sharply as you move away from the mean, meaning values far away

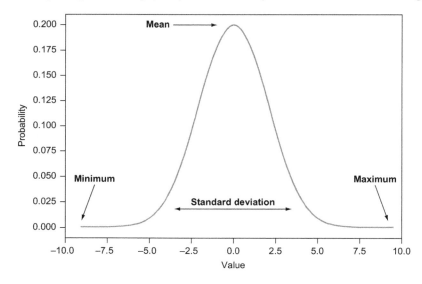

Figure 6.2 A visual guide to descriptive statistics

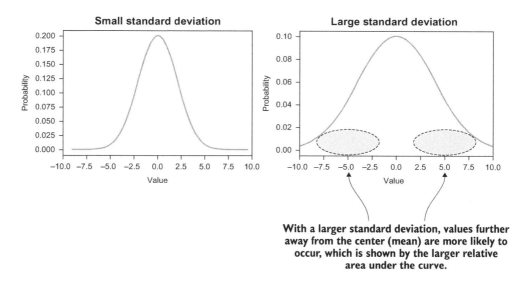

With a larger standard deviation, values further
away from the center (mean) are more likely to
occur, which is shown by the larger relative
area under the curve.

Figure 6.3   A comparison of standard deviation

from the mean are very unlikely to be observed. Conversely, with a large standard deviation, the drop off is much smoother, indicating that values far away from the mean are more likely to be observed. In the extreme case, a standard deviation of 0 would indicate that the value is constant and is not a randomly distributed variable. If we observed a small standard deviation of vehicle ages, we could conclude that many vehicles parked illegally in New York are roughly the same age—or, put another way, little variation exists in the observed age of the vehicles. If we observed a high standard deviation, it would mean that a highly diverse mix of new and old vehicles exists. In figure 6.3, notice that both the distributions are symmetrical. This means that the probability of observing a value of 1 is equal to observing a value of –1 and so on. The rate of drop-off in probability does not differ based on the direction we move away from the highest point on the curve (which represents the most commonly observed value, or the *mode*). This symmetry (or potential asymmetry) is what skewness describes.

In figure 6.4, you can see what the difference in skewness does to the shape of the distribution. With a skewness of 0, as shown in the upper center of figure 6.4, the distribution is symmetrical. Movement away from the mode in either direction causes the same drop-off in probability. This also makes the mean and mode of this distribution equal. Conversely, when skewness is negative, as seen in the lower left of figure 6.4, the drop-off in probability is extremely steep for values greater than the mode and more gradual for values less than the mode. This means that values less than the mode are more likely to be observed than values above the mode (but the mode is still the most likely value to be observed). Also, notice that with this skewness, the mean sits to the left of its original value. Instead of a mean of 0, as before, it's now somewhere around –2.5. Positive skewness, as seen in the lower right of figure 6.4, is the mirror opposite of negative skewness.

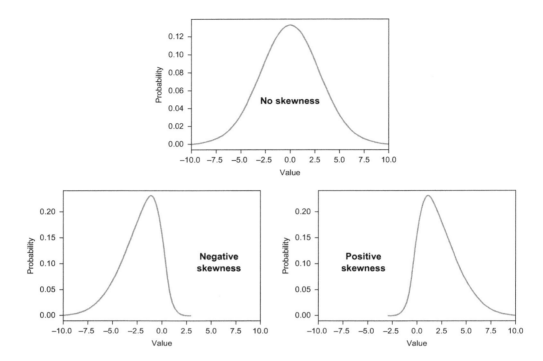

Figure 6.4   A visual comparison of skewness

Values greater than the mode are more likely to be observed than values less than the mode. The mean also sits to the right of 0. Put in terms of analyzing vehicle ages, if we observed a negative skewness, it would indicate that more vehicles are newer than the average age. Conversely, a positive skewness would indicate that more vehicles are older than the average age. Typically, when skewness is greater than 1 or less than −1, we would determine that the distribution is substantially skewed and far from symmetrical.

6.1.2   Calculating descriptive statistics with Dask

Now that you have a good idea of how to understand and interpret these descriptive statistics, let's have a look at how to calculate these values using Dask. To do this, we will first need to calculate the age of each vehicle when it was issued a citation. We have the citation date and the car's model year in the data, so we will use that to create a derived column. As always, we'll start with loading the data we produced in the previous chapter.

Listing 6.1   Loading the data for analysis

```
import dask.dataframe as dd
import pyarrow
from dask.diagnostics import ProgressBar

nyc_data = dd.read_parquet('nyc_final', engine='pyarrow')
```

Everything in listing 6.1 should look familiar; we're simply importing the libraries we need and then reading the Parquet file we generated at the end of chapter 5. Since we didn't previously look at the Vehicle Year column to make sure there aren't any weird values, let's do that first.

Listing 6.2   Checking the Vehicle Year column for anomalies

```
with ProgressBar():
    vehicle_age_by_year = nyc_data['Vehicle Year'].value_counts().compute()
vehicle_age_by_year

# Produces the following (abbreviated) output
0.0         8597125
2013.0      2847241
2014.0      2733114
2015.0      2423991
             ...
2054.0           61
2058.0           58
2041.0           56
2059.0           55
```

As you can see in listing 6.2, our value counts shows some vehicles that were allegedly made in year 0 as well as long into the future. Barring any likelihood of time travel or other aberrations in the space-time continuum, these are likely bad data. We'll filter them out to avoid introducing bad data into our statistical analysis.

Listing 6.3   Filtering out the bad data

Create a filter expression that will remove rows where the vehicle year is less than 0 or greater than 2018.

Apply the filter expression to the data, and count the number of vehicles by vehicle year.

```
with ProgressBar():
    condition = (nyc_data['Vehicle Year'] > 0) & (nyc_data['Vehicle Year'] <=
      2018)
    vehicle_age_by_year = nyc_data[condition]['Vehicle Year'].value_counts().
      compute().sort_index()
vehicle_age_by_year

# Produces the following abbreviated output
1970.0          775
1971.0          981
1972.0          971
...
2014.0      2733114
2015.0      2423991
2016.0      1280707
2017.0       297496
2018.0         2491
Name: Vehicle Year, dtype: int64
```

Display the output.

In listing 6.3, we use the same Boolean filtering you learned how to use in chapter 5 to filter out any vehicles made in the year 0 or beyond 2018. I've selected 2018 as my

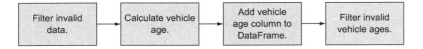

Figure 6.5 Calculating the age of each vehicle at the time a citation was issued

upper bound rather than 2017, because it's common practice for auto manufacturers to be ahead one model year. Since this dataset spans 2017, it's likely that most (if not all) of the observations for 2018 model year vehicles are legitimate. The output now looks much better!

Now let's create the derived column in the filtered data. To do that, we'll apply a custom function that subtracts the Vehicle Year column from the date column to the filtered data, and then add the result to the DataFrame. We'll perform that in the four steps listed in figure 6.5.

Now we'll implement those four steps in code.

Listing 6.4 Calculating the vehicle age at the date of citation

Apply the calculation to each row, creating a derived column.

Apply the filter condition to the data.

Define a function that will subtract the Vehicle Year column from the date column.

```
nyc_data_filtered = nyc_data[condition]

def age_calculation(row):
    return int(row['Issue Date'].year - row['Vehicle Year'])

vehicle_age = nyc_data_filtered.apply(age_calculation, axis=1, meta=('Vehicle
    Age', 'int'))

nyc_data_vehicle_age_stg1 = nyc_data_filtered.assign(VehicleAge=vehicle_age)
nyc_data_vehicle_age_stg2 = nyc_data_vehicle_age_stg1.
    rename(columns={'VehicleAge':'Vehicle Age'})

nyc_data_with_vehicle_age = nyc_data_vehicle_age_stg2[nyc_data_vehicle_age_
    stg2['Vehicle Age'] >= 0]
```

Use the assign-rename pattern to add the new column to the original DataFrame.

Filter out any rows where the vehicle age is negative.

Listing 6.4 should look very familiar as well. On the first line, we apply the filter condition to our data, thereby getting rid of observations with an invalid Vehicle Year. Next, we create our age calculation function. This function takes each DataFrame row as input, gets the year from the Issue Date column, and finds the difference between the year the ticket was issued and the year the car was built. Because `row['Issue Date']` represents a datetime object, we can access just its year value using its `year` attribute. The function is applied to each row of the DataFrame in the third line, which returns a Series containing the age of each vehicle. As a reminder, the `meta` parameter in the `apply` method takes a tuple with a name for the new Series as the first element and the datatype as the second element. The next two lines use the assign-rename pattern you learned in chapter 5 to add a column to a DataFrame and rename it to a friendly name. On the last line, we apply one more filter to get rid of any rows that result in an invalid age calculation. For example, if the citation was written in 2014 and the vehicle year was recorded as 2018, that would result in an invalid vehicle age of –4.

We're now ready to calculate the descriptive statistics! However, we should address one thing before we run the calculations. Each of these calculations (such as mean and standard deviation) requires fully scanning over the entire dataset, so they can take a long time to complete. For example, the mean requires summing all values in the DataFrame, then dividing the sum by the number of rows in the DataFrame. The calculation to produce the vehicle's age is also reasonably complex because of the object manipulation we need to do with the datetime column (datetime operations are typically slow). This would be a good opportunity to use the `persist` method to hold the results of this expensive computation in memory. However, we will instead save the intermediate result as a Parquet file, because we will use this data again in a later chapter. By saving the data to disk, you can come back to the data later without needing to recalculate it, and you won't need to keep your Jupyter notebook server up indefinitely until you need the data again. As a brief reminder, the two parameters we need to pass to the `to_parquet` method are the filename and the Parquet library we want to use to write the data. As with other examples, we'll stick to using PyArrow.

Listing 6.5 Saving the intermediate results to Parquet

```
with ProgressBar():
    files = nyc_data_with_vehicle_age.to_parquet('nyc_data_vehicleAge',
        engine='pyarrow')

nyc_data_with_vehicle_age = dd.read_parquet('nyc_data_vehicleAge',
        engine='pyarrow')
```

Once these two lines finish executing (which took about 45 minutes on my system), we'll be in good shape to calculate the descriptive statistics more quickly and efficiently. For convenience, Dask provides built-in descriptive statistics functions so you don't have to write your own algorithms. We'll take a look at the five descriptive statistics we covered earlier in the section: mean, standard deviation, minimum, maximum, and skewness.

Listing 6.6 Calculating descriptive statistics

```
from dask.array import stats as dask_stats
with ProgressBar():
    mean = nyc_data_with_vehicle_age['Vehicle Age'].mean().compute()
    stdev = nyc_data_with_vehicle_age['Vehicle Age'].std().compute()
    minimum = nyc_data_with_vehicle_age['Vehicle Age'].min().compute()
    maximum = nyc_data_with_vehicle_age['Vehicle Age'].max().compute()
    skewness = float(dask_stats.skew(nyc_data_with_vehicle_age['Vehicle
      Age'].values).compute())
```

Compute the skewness by feeding the Vehicle Age column into the dask_stats.skew function, and cast the result to a float.

As you can see in listing 6.6, for the mean, standard deviation, minimum, and maximum, you can simply call them as built-in methods of the Vehicle Age series. The exception to the set is calculating the skewness. There is no `skew` method as you might expect. However, Dask contains a myriad of statistical tests in the `dask.array` package, which we haven't yet explored (chapter 9 is a deep dive into Dask Array functions). To calculate the skewness for this example, we must convert Vehicle Age from a Dask Series object to a Dask Array object, since the skew function from `dask.array` requires a Dask Array as input. To do this, we can simply use the `values` attribute of the Vehicle Age series. We can then feed that into the `skew` function to calculate the skewness. Inspecting the results of our calculations, we find the values listed in table 6.1.

Table 6.1 **Descriptive statistics of the Vehicle Age column**

Statistic	Vehicle age
Mean	6.74
Standard deviation	5.66
Minimum	0
Maximum	47
Skewness	1.01

How interesting! Ticketed vehicles, on average, are about seven years old. There are some brand-new vehicles (denoted by a minimum age of 0 years), and the oldest vehicle was 47 years old. The standard deviation of 5.66 indicates that, on average, vehicles in this dataset tend to be +/– 5.66 years from the average age of 6.74 years. Finally, the data has a positive skew, meaning vehicles that were newer that 6.74 years were more common than vehicles that were older than 6.74 years.

Given some basic intuition about cars, all these numbers should make sense. When you consider that many vehicles older than 12 years are starting to face the end of their reliable lifespan, it's expected that there would be a significant drop-off in the number of vehicles on the road that are older than this as they become more likely to break down and get junked. Given that new vehicles are expensive and depreciate rapidly for the first several years of their lifespan, it's more economical to purchase lightly used vehicles that are three to five years old. This helps explain the average vehicle age of 6.74 years, as buyers would face the least-severe depreciation by purchasing vehicles of this age, but still have a reliable vehicle for the next five or more years. Likewise, although some vehicles were observed that are extremely old, we can see that the maximum age is many times the standard deviation away from the mean, indicating that seeing a 47-year-old vehicle on the streets of New York City is exceedingly rare.

6.1.3   Using the describe method for descriptive statistics

Dask also gives you another shortcut for calculating descriptive statistics if you don't want to write out the code for each statistic.

> **Listing 6.7   Calculating a bunch of descriptive statistics**

```
with ProgressBar():
    descriptive_stats = nyc_data_with_vehicle_age['Vehicle Age'].describe().
      compute()                         ◄──── Compute descriptive statistics
descriptive_stats.round(2)    ◄────            using the describe method.

# Produces the following output            Round the descriptive stats
count    28777416.00                       to two decimal places.
mean            6.74
std             5.66
min             0.00
25%             4.00
50%             8.00
75%            13.00
max            47.00
dtype: float64
```

In listing 6.7, you can see that the `describe` method produces the following Series containing a variety of common descriptive statistics. You get the count of non-null values, as well as the mean, standard deviation, minimum, and maximum. You also get the 25th percentile, 75th percentile, and median, which are also useful for understanding the spread of the data. One advantage of using the `describe` method is that it's actually more efficient than making four separate `compute` calls to get the mean, standard deviation, and so on. This is because Dask can apply a limited amount of code optimization when you request multiple aggregate functions all in one go.

Now that you've learned how to produce descriptive statistics, you can use these methods for understanding numeric variables in any dataset. Being able to quantify and describe the random behavior of variables is a good start, but another important angle of exploratory data analysis is understanding if any of that perceived randomness can actually be explained. To do this, we'll need to look at the relationships between variables in our dataset. This is our second goal of exploratory data analysis: finding interesting patterns and correlations. We'll head there next.

6.2   Built-In aggregate functions

You may recall from the chapter 5 that we joined some temperature data to the NYC Parking Violation dataset, and to do that, we created a column that holds the month and year in which each citation was issued. Let's use that data to answer the following questions:

> *Using the NYC Parking Ticket data, how many parking citations were issued each month?*
> *Does the average temperature correlate with the number of citations issued?*

6.2.1   *What is correlation?*

When we talk about patterns and relationships in data, we're usually talking more specifically about the *correlation* of two variables. Correlation quantifies how variables move with respect to one another. It can help us answer questions like, "Are the number of issued citations higher when the weather is warmer and lower when it's colder outside?" That might be interesting to know: perhaps the NYC Parking Authority doesn't put as many officers out on the beat in inclement weather. Correlation will tell us about both the strength and direction of the relationship between temperature and number of tickets issued.

Figure 6.6 shows what we mean by strength and direction of the relationship. Scatterplot A demonstrates positive correlation: as the variable on the X axis increases (moves to the right), the variable on the Y axis also tends to increase (moves up). This is a positive correlation—as one variable increases, the other variable also increases. This is also a *strong* correlation because the points are all relatively close to the red line. A very definitive pattern is easy to spot. Scatterplot B shows uncorrelated variables. As the X variable increases, the value of Y sometimes increases, sometimes decreases, and sometimes stays the same. We find no discernable pattern here, so this data is uncorrelated. Finally, scatterplot C shows a strong negative correlation. As the X variable increases, the Y variable decreases. Put in terms of the correlation between citations and temperature that we want to investigate, if the two are positively correlated, that would mean we would typically observe more citations issued in warmer months and fewer citations issued in colder months. If the two were negatively correlated, we would observe the opposite: more citations in colder months and fewer citations in warmer months. And if the two were uncorrelated, then we wouldn't see any discernable pattern. We would sometimes see a large number of citations in warm months and other times see very few citations issued when it's hot outside. We would also sometimes see a large number of citations issued in cold months and other times see very few citations issued in cold months.

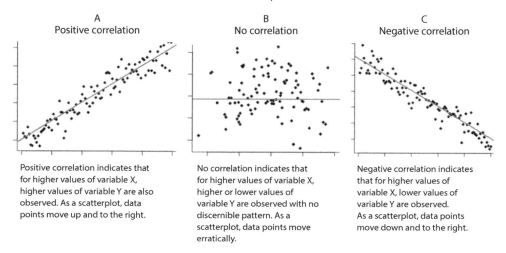

Figure 6.6   **A visual guide to correlation**

A note about correlation and causation

To avoid the ire of any statisticians who may be reading this book, it would be prudent of me to regurgitate an old adage that you may have heard before: "correlation does not imply causation." What does this mean? Simply put, you should *never* assume one variable causes a change in the other just because they're correlated. For example, think about the possibly silly conclusions we could come to if we misinterpreted a positive correlation between number of citations per month and average monthly temperature. This tells us that when we observe a higher number of citations issued in any month, we also tend to observe a higher average temperature. But it would be absurd to think that the NYC Parking Authority is single-handedly causing global climate change by writing parking tickets! It would be far more likely that warmer temperatures make it more pleasant for parking enforcement officers to be outside, leading to more productive shifts (read: more citations issued). However, correlation does not help you define causality in any way, so you should be careful when interpreting and explaining correlations in your data. While this example is obvious enough to understand that our conclusion would be silly, it's not unusual to run across situations where it's much harder to come up with a reasonable explanation for why two variables are correlated. This is one of many cases where having domain-specific knowledge about your data is invaluable to making good decisions in modeling and coming to reasonable conclusions about your data.

6.2.2 Calculating correlations with Dask DataFrames

Now let's have a look at how to perform these calculations in Dask. As mentioned earlier, we'll first need to calculate how many citations were issued per month. Before we do that, we'll create a custom sorting function to help display the results in chronological order. Because the month-year column we created in chapter 5 are strings, simply sorting by that column won't return the results in chronological order. To fix that issue, our custom sort function will map a sequential integer to each month in the correct order and sort the data by the numeric column before dropping it.

Listing 6.8   Custom sorting for the month-year column

Map the month/year strings to sequential integers, which will be used to sort.

Create a list containing all combinations (Cartesian product) of months/years.

Create lists of all months and the years we want to investigate.

```
import pandas as pd

years = ['2014', '2015', '2016', '2017']
months = ['01','02','03','04','05','06','07','08','09','10','11','12']
years_months = [year + month for year in years for month in months]

sort_order = pd.Series(range(len(years_months)), index=years_months,
    name='custom_sort')

def sort_by_months(dataframe, order):
    return dataframe.join(order).sort_values('custom_sort').drop('custom_
    sort', axis=1)
```

Create a function that takes a DataFrame as input, and returns a sorted DataFrame as output.

Listing 6.8 has quite a bit going on in it. Let's unpack it line by line. First, we're going to build a list of month-year values for all months in 2014 through 2017. To do this, we've constructed two lists, one containing the months and one containing the years. In line 5, we use a list comprehension to calculate the Cartesian product of the `months` list and the `years` list. This will create every possible combination of months and years. Because of the way we set up the list comprehension, the list of month-year values will be in the correct chronological order. Next, we turn the list into a Pandas Series. We use the month-year values as the index so we can join it to other DataFrames that have the same index and create a sequential integer value using the `range` function so we can sort the joined data correctly. Finally, we define a quick function called `sortBy-Months`, which will take any index-aligned DataFrame as input, join our sorting map to it, sort chronologically using the integer value we've mapped to each month-year, and drop the numeric column. This will result in a DataFrame sorted chronologically by month-year.

USING AGGREGATE FUNCTIONS IN DASK

Now that we have our sorting logic fleshed out, let's look at how to count the number of citations by month and year. To do this, we'll use an *aggregate function*. Aggregate functions, as you may expect given the name, combine (or aggregate) raw data into some kind of grouping and apply a function over that group. You may already be familiar with aggregate functions if you've worked with GROUP BY statements in SQL. Many of the same functions are available in Dask: counting, summing, finding the minimum/maximum, and so on, by group. In fact, the operations we used in the previous section for descriptive statistics (`min`, `max`, `mean`, and so on) are technically aggregate functions! The only difference is that we applied those functions over the entire, ungrouped dataset. For example, we looked at the average vehicle age overall— but we could have looked at the average vehicle age *by vehicle type* or *by license plate state*. Similarly, we can use the `count` function to count all the citations issued in the whole dataset, or we could count by some sort of grouping like month-year. Unsurprisingly, the function to define the groupings for aggregate functions is `groupby`. From a code perspective, it's quite simple and concise to use, but it's important to understand what goes on behind the scenes. What happens when you call an aggregate function with a defined grouping is an algorithm known as split-apply-combine. Let's take a look at how this works.

For the sake of a simple example, we have four rows of data in the table at the top of figure 6.7 showing a list of pets and their owners' IDs. If we wanted to count the number of pets owned by each owner, we would group by the Owner ID and apply the `count` function to each group. What happens in the background is the original table is *split* into partitions, where each partition contains only pets owned by a single owner. The original table is split into three partitions. Next, we *apply* the aggregate function to each partition. Count will simply find how many rows are in each partition. We're left with a

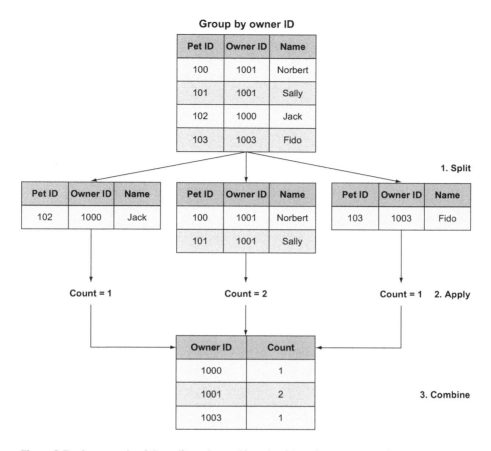

Figure 6.7 An example of the split-apply-combine algorithm of an aggregate function

count of 1 for the left partition, a count of 2 for the center partition, and a count of 1 for the right partition. To reassemble the result, we'll need to *combine* the results from each partition. Here, the result from each partition is simply concatenated to produce the final output.

Based on what you've learned so far about shuffle performance and partitioning, you might be wondering how efficient these split-apply-combine operations can be. Since we have to split the data into unique partitions over the grouping column, you'd be correct to be concerned that this operation will cause a lot of shuffling if you don't choose a group by column that's also used as a partitioning column. These operations can be slightly more efficient if you're working on data stored in compressed Parquet format, but ultimately, it's best practice to only group by the column used to partition your data. Fortunately, we've saved our prepared NYC Parking Ticket data partitioned by month-year, so using that column to group on should be quite fast!

Listing 6.9   Counting citations by month-year

Count the number of citations in each group.

Group by the monthYear column.

Apply the custom sorting function to the result.

```
with ProgressBar():
    nyc_data_by_month = nyc_data.groupby('monthYear')
    citations_per_month = nyc_data_by_month['Summons Number'].count().
     compute()
sort_by_months(citations_per_month.to_frame(), sort_order)
```

In listing 6.9, we use the groupby method to define the column we want to group the data on. Next, we choose one column to apply our count function to and compute it. With the count function, it typically doesn't matter which column you specify. Just be aware that the Dask count function will count only non-null values, so if you apply count to a column that has null values, you will not get a true row count. If you don't specify a column, you'll get a DataFrame that has a count for each column, which is not really what we want here. Finally, we'll take the citationsPerMonth result, which is a Pandas Series, convert it to a DataFrame using the to_frame method, and apply our custom sort function to it. An abbreviated output can be seen in figure 6.8.

If you run the code and look at the full output, you'll notice that the count of citations past June 2017 is far lower than previous months. At the time of writing, this dataset wasn't complete for 2017. In the following code we will filter it out from our correlation calculation; otherwise, it might negatively influence our results. We'll also need to get the average monthly temperature back in our resulting DataFrame, since we want to compare the count of citations to the average temperature.

Listing 6.10   Calculating the correlation between citations and temperature

Create a filter expression that only keeps data not (~) in the last months of 2017.

Group by the Citation Issued Month Year column, count the number of citations in each group, and calculate the average temperature for each group.

```
with ProgressBar():
    condition = ~nyc_data['monthYear'].
     isin(['201707','201708','201709','201710','201711','201712'])
    nyc_data_filtered = nyc_data[condition]
    citations_and_temps = nyc_data_filtered.groupby('monthYear').
     agg({'Summons Number': 'count', 'Temp': 'mean'})
    correlation_matrix = citations_and_temps.corr().compute()
correlation_matrix
```

Show the output.

Apply the filter expression.

Calculate the correlation matrix for the two variables.

Listing 6.10 shows how to calculate the correlation between the temperature and count of citations. First, we build the filter condition to get rid of the months with missing data. To do that, we pass a list of the months we don't want to the isin method. This Boolean expression would normally filter the data so we *only* get the rows back that are contained in the isin list. However, since we prefaced the expression with the negation operator (~), this filter will return all months that are not contained in the isin

Summons Number

Citation Issued Month Year	
01-2014	708136
02-2014	641438
03-2014	899639
04-2014	879840
05-2014	941133
06-2014	940743
07-2014	961567
08-2014	901624

Figure 6.8   An abbreviated count of citations by month-year

list. After building the expression, we apply it to the data in the same way you've seen many times now.

On line 3, we group up the data by monthYear as before, but this time we'll use the agg method on the grouped data. The agg method allows you to apply more than one aggregate operation at once to the same data grouping. To use it, you simply pass in a dictionary containing keys that equate to column names and values that equate to the name of an aggregate function. Here, we're applying the count function to the Summons Number column and the mean function to the Temp column.

You may be wondering why we apply the mean function to the Temp column when the Temp column already contains the average temperature for the month. This is because we stamped the temperature on each raw record, but in our result we want only one temperature value per month. Since the mean of a series of constant numbers is just the constant number, we use mean simply to pass through the average temperature for the month to the result.

Finally, we use the corr method to calculate the correlation between the variables. The output of the correlation matrix can be seen in figure 6.9. It shows us that the correlation between Count of Summons and Temp is 0.14051. This indicates a positive correlation because the correlation coefficient is positive, and it is a *weak* correlation because the correlation coefficient is less than 0.5. We can interpret this to mean that in months where the temperature is warmer on average, more citations are typically issued than in months where the temperature is colder on average. However, a weak correlation indicates that a large amount of variation still isn't neatly explained by these two variables. Put another way, if we observed two different months that had the exact same average temperature, they would likely still have very different counts of citations issued. This means that there could be other variables in the dataset that we can use to help further explain some of this variation.

	Summons Number	Temp
Summons Number	1.00000	0.14051
Temp	0.14051	1.00000

Figure 6.9   The correlation matrix for Count of Summons and Temp

6.3   *Custom aggregate functions*

While correlation is useful for understanding the relationship between two continuous numeric variables, you're likely to also encounter categorical variables that you want to analyze. For example, in section 1, we looked at the average age of the vehicle when a citation was issued and found that the average vehicle was 6.74 years old. But are all kinds of vehicles the same? Let's add another dimension to this analysis by answering the following question:

> Given the NYC Parking Ticket data, is the average age of privately owned vehicles the same as it is for commercially owned vehicles?

6.3.1   *Testing categorical variables with the t-test*

To answer this question, we'll be looking at two different variables in the dataset: average vehicle age and vehicle type. Even though we're interested in how the average age moves as we change our focus from one type of vehicle to another, correlation is not appropriate here. Correlation can only be used to describe how two continuous variables "move" with respect to one another. Vehicle type is not a continuous variable—it's either PAS for a privately owned passenger vehicle or COM for a commercially owned vehicle. It would be strange to say that the average age increases or decreases as the vehicle type increases or decreases. We might simply answer this question by grouping the data by vehicle type and calculating the means, but that poses its own issue: If the means are different, how can you be sure that the difference isn't simply due to random chance? We can turn to a different statistical test, known as the two-sample t-test, to help answer this question.

STATISTICAL HYPOTHESIS TESTING 101

The two-sample t-test is in a family of statistical tests known as *statistical hypothesis tests*. Statistical hypothesis tests help answer predefined hypotheses about certain aspects of data. In every statistical hypothesis test, we start by making a declaration about the data. That declaration, known as the *null hypothesis*, is accepted to be a true statement by default. The test attempts to provide sufficient evidence to the contrary. If the evidence is convincing enough, you may reject the null hypothesis as a true statement. This is measured by a probability that the significance of the evidence is due to random chance. If this probability, called the *p-value*, is sufficiently low enough, the evidence against the null hypothesis is strong enough that it can be rejected. Figure 6.10 shows a flowchart representing the decision processes around hypothesis testing.

The null hypothesis of the two-sample t-test is that "no difference in means exists between the two categories." The test determines if convincing-enough evidence exists to reject that statement. If we find convincing-enough evidence to reject the null hypothesis, we can confidently say that it's likely that there is a difference in the average vehicle age based on its type. Otherwise, we can say that the two types of vehicles do not truly have a different average age.

ASSUMPTIONS OF STATISTICAL HYPOTHESIS TESTS

As with many statistical hypothesis tests, two-sample t-tests typically make a few assumptions about the underlying data we will be testing. These assumptions depend on which two-sample t-test we will use. The two most common kinds of two-sample t-tests are Student's T-Test and Welch's T-Test, named respectively for the statisticians who developed each method (although "Student" was actually a pseudonym adopted by statistician and Guinness Brewery employee William Sealy Gosset).

An important assumption of Student's T-Test is that the variance of each group being tested is equal. Variance, like standard deviation, has to do with how spread-out observations are from the mean. Higher variance means the typical observation tends to lie far away from the mean, and a small variance means the typical observations tends to lie close to the mean. This also means that a distribution with a larger variance has a higher probability of containing observa-

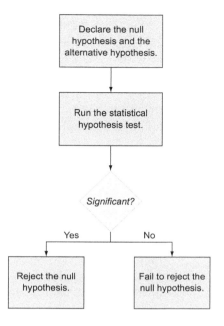

Figure 6.10   The process of statistical hypothesis tests

tions close to the minimum/maximum points of the distribution. Think about what this means in the context of vehicle ages: if we take our two groups, private and commercial vehicles, and they both have the same mean vehicle age, but commercial vehicles have a much higher variance, that would mean that we're more likely to encounter much newer and much older commercial vehicles compared to private vehicles. It could be that we just got lucky and commercial vehicles averaged out to the same mean as private vehicles in our sample despite the typical age of commercial vehicles being wildly different. If we use Student's T-Test to compare means between groups that have very different variance, the value we calculate to help us decide whether to reject or fail to reject the null hypothesis becomes unreliable. This means we will be more likely to calculate a value that will lead us to reject the null hypothesis when we actually shouldn't reject it, thereby coming to an erroneous conclusion.

For cases where the group variances are not the same, we can use Welch's T-Test instead. Welch's T-Test is formulated slightly differently to help us avoid making the wrong conclusion. So, before we can decide to use Welch's T-Test or Student's T-Test to answer our question, we should check to see if the variance of private and commercial vehicles are the same or not. Fortunately, statistical hypothesis tests can help us check this—we just have to pick the right one!

6.3.2   *Using custom aggregates to implement the Brown-Forsythe test*

The family of tests that help us check for equal variances also carry some assumptions with them. We can use a test called Bartlett's Test for Equal Variances if the data is normally distributed—that is, symmetrical and roughly "bell shaped." However, in section 6.1 we found that the skewness of vehicle ages is 1.012, meaning it's not symmetrically distributed, so we can't use Bartlett's Test without running the risk of making an incorrect conclusion. A good alternative test that doesn't have this assumption is called the Brown-Forsythe Test for Equal Variances. Since we can't use Bartlett's Test reliably on this data, we'll use the Brown-Forsythe test to help us decide whether to use Student's T-Test or Welch's T-Test. The whole testing process we will go through from start to finish can be seen in figure 6.11.

First, we'll start by declaring the null hypothesis and alternative hypothesis. The null hypothesis of the Brown-Forsythe test is that the variances among groups are equal. The alternative hypothesis is that the variances among groups are not equal. The test will help us decide if enough evidence exists to say that group variances are different, in which case we will need to use Welch's T-Test, or if not enough evidence exists, we will use Student's T-Test.

Figure 6.12 displays the Brown-Forsythe equation. While it may look complicated, we'll break the equation down into smaller, more manageable pieces; then we'll assemble the final result. Because the Brown-Forsythe test involves a lot of grouping and aggregate operations, this is a great opportunity to learn about Dask's custom aggregate functions! The overall approach we're going to take to calculate the Brown-Forsythe equation will be performed in five steps:

1 Calculate the left fraction.
2 Calculate the denominator of the right fraction.
3 Calculate the numerator of the right fraction.
4 Divide the numerator of the right fraction by the denominator of the right fraction to calculate the value of the right fraction.
5 Multiply the left fraction by the right fraction.

In section 6.1, you created a Parquet file that includes an additional column containing the calculated vehicle age. We'll start by reading this file in again.

Listing 6.11   Setting up the Vehicle Age dataset

```
nyc_data_with_vehicle_age = dd.read_parquet('nyc_data_vehicleAge',
    engine='pyarrow')

nyc_data_filtered = nyc_data_with_vehicle_age[nyc_data_with_vehicle_age
    ['Plate Type'].isin(['PAS','COM'])]
```
Filter out citations to look only at passenger- (privately owned) and commercial-type vehicles

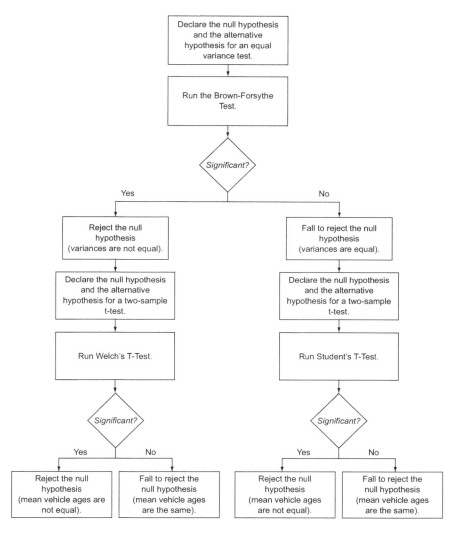

Figure 6.11   The process we will use to determine if mean vehicle age has any relationship with vehicle type

$$F = \frac{(N-p)}{(p-1)} \; \frac{\sum_{j=1}^{p} \; n_j(\bar{z}_j - \bar{z}_{..})^2}{\sum_{j=1}^{p} \sum_{i=1}^{n_j} \; (z_{ij} - \bar{z}_{.j})^2}$$

Where: $z_{ij} = |y_{ij} - \tilde{y}_j|$

N is the total number of observations.
p is the total number of groups.
n_j is the number of observations in group j.

$\tilde{y}_j$ is the median of group j.
$\bar{z}_{.j}$ is the mean of group j.
$\bar{z}_{..}$ is the mean of all z_{ij}.

Figure 6.12   The Brown-Forsythe Test for Equal Variances

The reason we want to filter the data to contain only vehicles with PAS-type plates or COM-type plates is because we previously recoded that column to also contain an Other value for vehicles that were neither PAS type nor COM type. Two-sample t-tests can only be used to test the difference in means between two groups, so we will filter out the Other category before proceeding. After applying the filter, we'll calculate the first part of the equation using simple aggregate functions you've learned before. Figure 6.13 shows what we'll be doing in the calculation.

The first part of the equation, called the *degrees of freedom*, is very simple to calculate. We will need to count the total number of citations that are in our filtered dataset, and also count the distinct groups we're testing (which for a two-sample t-test should always be 2!). We'll stash this value and multiply it by another value later to get the final result of the Brown-Forsythe test.

> **Listing 6.12   Calculating the left fraction of the Brown-Forsythe equation**

```
with ProgressBar():
    N = nyc_data_filtered['Vehicle Age'].count().compute()
    p = nyc_data_filtered['Plate Type'].unique().count().compute()
brownForsytheLeft = (N - p) / (p - 1)
```

Count the total number of observations.   **Calculate the left fraction.**   **Count the number of unique plate types.**

Everything in listing 6.12 should look familiar. The variable N represents the total number of observations in the dataset, and the variable p represents the number of groups. To find the values of N and p, we simply need to count the total number of observations and also count the number of unique groups. Then we'll use the values of N and p to calculate the left fraction of the equation.

CALCULATING A MEDIAN USING THE QUANTILE METHOD

Now we'll begin working on the right fraction by calculating the denominator (see figure 6.14). As you can see, we'll be calculating the same set of values for each group—private vehicles and commercial vehicles—in parallel, then summing the results. We'll start by calculating the median age for each vehicle type.

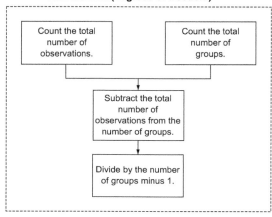

Figure 6.13   The first part of the Brown-Forsythe test

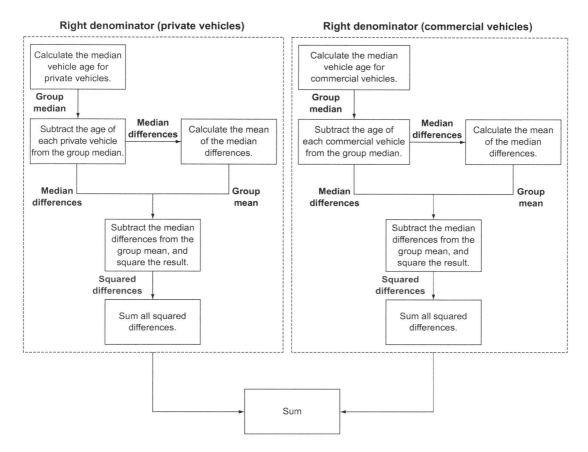

Figure 6.14   The process for calculating the right denominator

Split into two DataFrames based on Plate Type.　　　　　　　　**Calculate the medians for each Plate Type.**

```
with ProgressBar():
    passenger_vehicles = nyc_data_filtered[nyc_data_filtered['Plate Type'] ==
    'PAS']
    commercial_vehicles = nyc_data_filtered[nyc_data_filtered['Plate Type']
    == 'COM']

    median_PAS = passenger_vehicles['Vehicle Age'].quantile(0.5).compute()
    median_COM = commercial_vehicles['Vehicle Age'].quantile(0.5).compute()
```

Unlike Pandas and NumPy, Dask does not have an explicit median method on DataFrame
or Series objects. Instead, you must use the quantile method to calculate the 0.5 quantile
for the Vehicle Age column, which is equivalent to the 50th percentile, or median. Next,
we'll create a new column that uses these medians to subtract from the age of each vehicle
its corresponding group median. For privately owned (PAS) vehicles, we will subtract the

median age of all PAS vehicles from each vehicle's age. Similarly, for commercial (COM) vehicles, we will subtract the median age of all COM vehicles from each vehicle's age. To do this, we'll define a function to apply the conditional subtraction logic.

> **Listing 6.14 A function to calculate the absolute median deviation**

```
def absolute_deviation_from_median(row):
    if row['Plate Type'] == 'PAS':
        return abs(row['Vehicle Age'] - median_PAS)
    else:
        return abs(row['Vehicle Age'] - median_COM)
```

This function in listing 6.14 is very simple: if a vehicle is a PAS type, we subtract the median age of PAS vehicles from the vehicle's age. Otherwise, we subtract the the median of COM vehicles from the vehicle's age. We'll use this function with the same `apply` method you've used several times before, which will result in a column containing the absolute difference between the vehicle's age and its corresponding group median.

> **Listing 6.15 Creating a column to calculate the absolute median differences**

```
absolute_deviation = nyc_data_filtered.apply(absolute_deviation_from_median,
    axis=1, meta=('x', 'float32'))

nyc_data_age_type_test_stg1 = nyc_data_filtered.assign(MedianDifferences =
    absolute_deviation)
nyc_data_age_type_test = nyc_data_age_type_test_stg1.
    rename(columns={'MedianDifferences':'Median Difference'})
```

Apply the function to the DataFrame,   **Use the assign-rename pattern to add the Series object**
creating a new Series object.   **as a column of the original DataFrame.**

In listing 6.15, the `apply` function is used to create a new Series containing the result of the calculation; then we assign the column to our existing DataFrame and rename it. We're about halfway done with calculating the right denominator now. Let's check in with how we're doing. Figure 6.15 shows our progress so far.

All right! The next thing we'll need to do is to calculate the mean of the median differences for each group. We can do that simply with a `groupby/mean` call that we've seen a few times already.

> **Listing 6.16 Calculating the group means of the median differences**

```
with ProgressBar():
    group_means = nyc_data_age_type_test.groupby('Plate Type')['Median
    Difference'].mean().compute()
```

The result of this computation, `group_means`, is a Series containing the means of the Median Difference column grouped by Plate Type. We can access the mean of either group by using normal filter expressions. We'll use this in another conditional function that subtracts each Median Difference amount by the observation's corresponding Plate Type. This will result in a Group Mean Variance for each observation in the dataset.

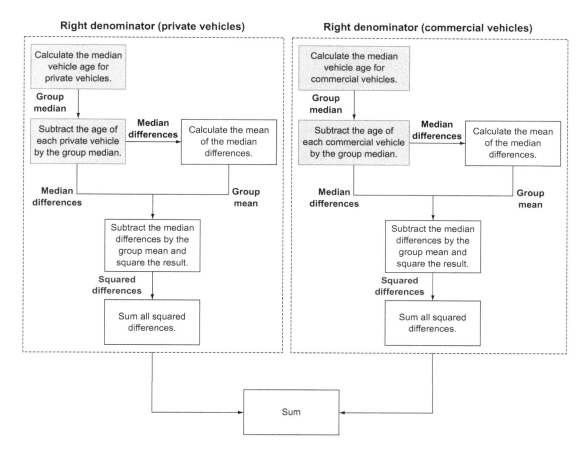

Figure 6.15 Our progress so far calculating the right denominator of the Brown-Forsythe equation

Listing 6.17 Calculating the Group Mean Variance

**Create a new Series using the
group_mean_variance function.**

**Create a function that subtracts each Median
Difference amount by the appropriate group
mean and squares the result.**

```
def group_mean_variance(row):
    if row['Plate Type'] == 'PAS':
        return (row['Median Difference'] - group_means['PAS'])**2
    else:
        return (row['Median Difference'] - group_means['COM'])**2

group_mean_variances = nyc_data_age_type_test.apply(group_mean_variance,
    axis=1, meta=('x', 'float32'))

nyc_data_age_type_test_gmv_stg1 = nyc_data_age_type_test.
    assign(GroupMeanVariances = groupMeanVariances)
nyc_data_age_type_test_gmv = nyc_data_age_type_test_gmv_stg1.
    rename(columns={'GroupMeanVariances':'Group Mean Variance'})
```

**Use the assign-rename
pattern to add the new
Series back to the original
DataFrame.**

Lastly, to finish calculating the right denominator of the Brown-Forsythe equation, all we need to do is sum up the Group Mean Variance column. We can do this with a simple call to the `sum` method.

Listing 6.18   Finishing calculating the right denominator

```
with ProgressBar():
    brown_forsythe_right_denominator = nyc_data_age_type_test_gmv['Group Mean
    Variance'].sum().compute()
```

Now that we've finished calculating the denominator, we'll finish by calculating the numerator. To do that, we'll follow the process outlined in figure 6.16.

We'll begin by calculating the *grand mean* of the Median Differences column. A grand mean is another way of saying "the mean of a column without any grouping." This is opposite of a *group mean*, which, as you may guess, is the mean of a group—for example, the mean vehicle age of PAS vehicles is a group mean, and the mean vehicle age of all vehicles is a grand mean.

Listing 6.19   Calculating the grand mean of the Median Difference column

```
with ProgressBar():
    grand_mean = nyc_data_ageTypeTest['Median Difference'].mean().compute()
```

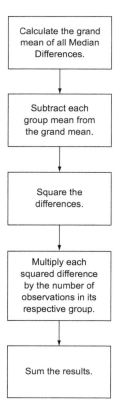

Figure 6.16   The process to calculate the right numerator of the Brown-Forsythe equation

CREATING A CUSTOM AGGREGATION OBJECT

Now that we have the grand mean calculated, we'll handle the next three steps in the process using a custom aggregation. As you can see in figure 6.16, we need both the group means and the count of observations in each group. Rather than calculating them separately, we can make use of the Aggregation object in the Dask DataFrame API to get both these values as part of the same computation. Let's see what this looks like.

Listing 6.20 A custom aggregation for calculating the right numerator

Give an internal name to the Aggregation.   **Define what to do at the partition/chunk level; here we want a count and a sum.**   **Further reduce the chunks by aggregating the chunk-level calculations.**

```
brown_forsythe_aggregation = dd.Aggregation(
    'Brown_Forsythe',
    lambda chunk: (chunk.count(), chunk.sum()),
    lambda chunk_count, chunk_sum: (chunk_count.sum(), chunk_sum.sum()),
    lambda group_count, group_sum: group_count * (((group_sum / group_count)
    - grand_mean)**2)
)
```

Apply a final transformation to the output.

Now things are starting to get interesting! In listing 6.20, we see an example of a custom aggregate function. Until this point, we've relied on Dask's built-in aggregate functions such as sum, count, mean, and so forth to perform aggregate calculations. But, it's necessary to define your own aggregate function if you have a more complex calculation that needs to be performed over a grouping.

Dask's facility for defining custom aggregate functions is the Aggregation class found in the dask.dataframe package. It has a minimum of three arguments with an optional fourth argument:

- An internal name for the aggregation
- A function to be applied to each partition
- A function to aggregate the results from each partition
- (Optional) A function to perform a final transformation on the aggregated values before outputting them

The first argument is simply an internal name for the aggregation. The second argument takes a function (which can either be a defined function or an anonymous lambda function) and applies it to each partition. This is called the *chunk step*. In listing 6.20, we're counting the number of observations in each chunk as well as summing up the values of each chunk, and returning a tuple containing these calculated values. Next, Dask will collect all the results of each chunk step and apply the function defined in the third argument to the collected chunk results. This is called the *aggregation step*. In listing 6.20, we're summing the values we calculated for each chunk, resulting in a grand total of the count of observations contained in the entire DataFrame and a grand total of the sum of Vehicle Ages in the entire DataFrame. But we're not quite done with this calculation. The fourth and final argument is called the *finalization step*, which gives us one last chance to transform the data before returning it to the user. In listing 6.20, we take the aggregated sum and divide by the aggregated count to get the group mean, subtract it from the grand mean, square the difference, and multiply by the count. This will yield the results we want to then sum up to get the final value for the right-hand numerator. Now that we've defined the aggregation, let's apply it to the data to calculate the value.

Listing 6.21   Using the custom aggregate function

```
with ProgressBar():
    group_variances = nyc_data_age_type_test.groupby('Plate Type').
    agg({'Median Differences': brown_forsythe_aggregation}).compute()
```

As you can see in listing 6.21, using custom aggregate functions is very similar to using any of the built-in aggregate functions. You can map custom aggregate functions to columns in a DataFrame using the agg method you learned previously, and you can also use them with the groupby method. Here we're using the custom aggregate function we defined to calculate the group variances for each Plate Type. The last thing we need to do to get the final value for the numerator is to sum the group variances. Since our custom aggregate function results in a Series object, we can simply use the sum method over it that you've seen several times before.

Listing 6.22   Finishing the right numerator calculation

```
brown_forsythe_right_numerator = group_variances.sum()[0]
```

Great! We now have all the pieces to finish calculating the Brown-Forsythe equation. All we need to do is divide the right numerator by the right denominator, and multiply by the left fraction we calculated first. This will yield a result called the *F statistic*. The F statistic will help guide us to a conclusion of whether or not to reject the null hypothesis. Let's calculate that now.

Listing 6.23   Calculating the F statistic

```
F_statistic = brown_forsythe_left * (brown_forsythe_right_numerator / brown_
    forsythe_right_denominator)
```

INTERPRETING THE RESULTS OF THE BROWN-FORSYTHE TEST

Since we've done all the hard work, calculating the F statistic is very simple and straightforward. If all goes well, you should receive an F statistic value of 27644.7165804. However, we're not quite done. Is this number good? Bad? The statistic by itself isn't really interpretable. In order for us to make a conclusion about our findings and either reject or fail to reject the null hypothesis, we have to compare this value with the *critical value* of the test's underlying distribution. The critical value provides a threshold that helps us interpret the meaning of the test statistic. If the test statistic is greater than the critical value, we can reject the null hypothesis. Otherwise, we fail to reject the null hypothesis. As the Brown-Forsythe test produces an F statistic, we must use the *F distribution* to find the critical value. To find the critical value from the F distribution, we need three parameters: two measures of the data's degrees of freedom and the confidence level we'd like to use.

The degrees of freedom for the Brown-Forsythe test are simply the number of groups we're testing minus one and the total number of observations minus the number of groups we're testing. This should look familiar—these were the two parts of the left fraction we calculated a while back. We can reuse the values we saved to the variables N and p to find the critical value.

The confidence level can be any value between 0 and 1 that you are free to choose. It essentially represents a probability that the result of the test will result in a correct conclusion. The higher the value, the stricter and more robust the result of the test becomes. For example, if we pick a confidence level of 0.95, there will be only about a 5% chance that the test might erroneously signify that you should reject the null hypothesis. You've likely heard of a *p-value* before; this is simply one minus the confidence level. A commonly accepted p-value in scientific research is 0.05, so to follow suit, we'll use a confidence level of 0.95 here. To calculate the F critical value, we'll use the F distribution from SciPy.

Listing 6.24 Calculating the F critical value

```
import scipy.stats as stats
alpha = 0.05
df1 = p - 1
df2 = N - p
F_critical = stats.f.ppf(q=1-alpha, dfn=df1, dfd=df2)
```

Listing 6.24 shows how to calculate the F critical value for our test. The `stats.f` class contains an implementation of the F distribution, and the `ppf` method calculates the value of an F distribution with the degrees of freedom `dfn` and `dfd` at point `q`. As you can see, point `q` is simply the confidence value we selected, and `dfn` and `dfd` use the two variables we computed at the beginning of the section. This calculation should result in an F critical value of 3.8414591786. Finally, we can report our findings and make a conclusion. The next listing will print out a nice statement summarizing our findings and highlighting the relevant numbers we used to come to our conclusion.

Listing 6.25 Reporting our findings of the Brown-Forsythe test

```
print("Using the Brown-Forsythe Test for Equal Variance")
print("The Null Hypothesis states: the variance is constant among groups")
print("The Alternative Hypothesis states: the variance is not constant among
     groups")
print("At a confidence level of " + str(alpha) + ", the F statistic was " +
     str(F_statistic) + " and the F critical value was " + str(F_critical) +
     ".")
if F_statistic > F_critical:
    print("We can reject the null hypothesis. Set equal_var to False.")
else:
    print("We fail to reject the null hypothesis. Set equal_var to True.")
```

In this particular case, we're told to reject the null hypothesis because the F statistic is larger than the F critical value. Therefore, when running a two-sample t-test to answer our original question, we should *not* assume equal variances among vehicle types. Now we can finally run the appropriate t-test and see if the average age of vehicles that received a parking ticket in New York City is significantly different based on the vehicle type! Before we move on, let's recap where we came from and what we're going to do next.

As you can see in figure 6.17, now that we've rejected the null hypothesis of the Brown-Forsythe test, we will want to run Welch's T-Test on the data to answer our original question of "Is the average age of privately owned vehicles the same as it is for commercially owned vehicles?" We're also presented with an important decision here: while Dask does have a handful of statistical hypothesis tests (including two-sample t-tests) built into the dask.array.stats package, you may recall from chapter 1 that when the data you're working with can comfortably fit into memory, it can be faster to pull the data out of Dask and work with it in memory. However, we will take a closer look at the statistical functions in the Dask Array library in chapter 9. For the two-sample t-test, we need only two one-dimensional numeric arrays: one containing all observations of PAS-type vehicle ages and one containing all observations of COM-type vehicle ages. Some quick "back-of-the-napkin" math suggests we should expect to have about 40,000,000 64-bit floating-point numbers, which equates to somewhere in the realm of 300 MB of data in memory. This should be easy to fit in memory, so we will opt to collect the arrays and perform our t-test computation locally.

Listing 6.26   Collecting an array of values

```
with ProgressBar():
    pas = passengerVehicles['Vehicle Age'].values.compute()
    com = commercialVehicles['Vehicle Age'].values.compute()
```

As you can see in listing 6.26, it's very easy to collect the values locally. The values attribute of a Dask Series will expose the underlying Dask Array and calling compute on a Dask Array will return a NumPy array containing the result.

> **CAUTION**   As a word of warning, don't get used to collecting an entire Series locally. Especially when working with a large dataset, you can easily fill up your local system's memory doing this, which will slow things down considerably as data will be paged to disk. Therefore, it's better to stay in the habit of using head unless you're absolutely sure the data you're selecting will fit in local memory, as we are here.

Now that we have the data down locally in NumPy arrays, we can run the t-test.

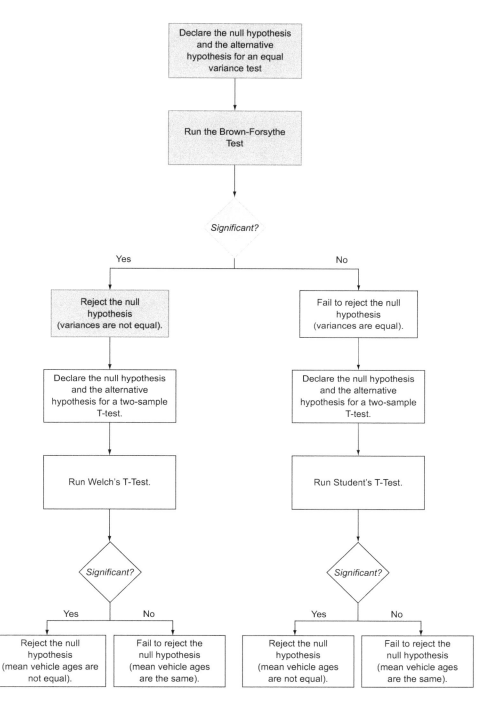

Figure 6.17 We've rejected the null hypothesis of the Brown-Forsythe test, so we will next run Welch's T-Test.

Listing 6.27   Running the two-sample t-test

```
stats.ttest_ind(pas, com, equal_var=False)

# Provides the following output:
# Ttest_indResult(statistic=-282.4101373587319, pvalue=0.0)
```

Very simple—SciPy does all the heavy lifting for us here. Notice that in listing 6.27, we set the `equal_var` argument to False. This lets SciPy know that we've run a test of equal variances and found that the group variances are not equal. With the parameter set this way, SciPy will run Welch's T-Test instead of Student's T-Test, avoiding the potential problems you learned about earlier in this section. SciPy also makes interpreting the result easy for us, because in addition to the test statistic, it's gone ahead and calculated the p-value as well. With p-values, we want it to be smaller than one minus the confidence level we've chosen. So if we choose a confidence level of 0.95 again, we're looking for a p-value of less than 0.05 to reject the null hypothesis. As a reminder, the null hypothesis of the t-test is that means are equal among groups. Since we see that the p-value of this test is less than 0.05, we can reject the null hypothesis and conclude that sufficient evidence exists to show that the average vehicle age is different based on vehicle plate type.

Null hypothesis	Condition	p-value	Reject?	Conclusion
PAS and COM vehicles have the same mean age.	$p < 0.05$	0.0	Yes	PAS and COM vehicles *do not* have the same mean age.

Now that we've walked through an example together, I hope you have a better idea of how to use your own custom aggregate functions in Dask, and you got some extra practice with other common Dask operations along the way. I also hope that you are starting to appreciate the power, simplicity, and flexibility Dask has to offer when it comes to implementing custom algorithms. We were able to implement a reasonably complex statistical calculation with a fairly small amount of code, and didn't even need to dive into the low-level guts of the framework to do what we needed to do! Pretty neat.

A Note on Welch's t-test and student's t-test

A number of recent publications by statisticians have shown that Welch's T-Test generally performs well enough on data where the two groups have equal variance. Statisticians are now recommending to always use Welch's T-Test and not bother with Student's T-Test, allowing you to shortcut checking the assumptions for Student's T-Test. However, the Brown-Forsythe Test for Equal Variances we discussed in this section is a great practical example for using custom aggregate functions in Dask, implementing statistics algorithms not currently in the Dask stats module, and the test itself is still inherently useful.

6.4 Rolling (window) functions

We'll close out this chapter on summarizing and analyzing DataFrames with something a bit less involved than the previous section, but equally important for many classes of analyses. No discussion on data analysis would be complete without talking about rolling functions. If you've worked with SQL, you may be familiar with window functions—rolling functions are just the name given to window functions in Dask.

If you're not familiar with the concept of windowing, it allows you to define calculations across a set of sequential data that incorporate variables which are positionally relative to another value. The most common application of windowing is analyzing data that has a time dimension, such as days or hours. For example, if we were analyzing sales revenue for an online store, we may want to know how many more (or fewer) items were sold today compared with yesterday. This could be mathematically expressed as $sales_t - sales_{t-1}$, where the subscript t indicates the time period that the sales were measured for. Since the difference equation refers to two time periods, we would say that it has a *two-period window*. If we applied this calculation across a sequence of sales observations, we would end up with a transformed sequence of differences between each day and the day prior. Hence, that simple equation is a window function! Of course, window functions can be far more complex and can span a much larger window as well. A 50-day simple moving average, which is commonly computed for describing the volatility and momentum of a publicly traded financial asset, is a good example of a more complicated window function with a larger window. In this section, we will use a rolling function to answer the following question:

Do the number of citations issued over time show any trends or cyclical patterns?

6.4.1 Preparing data for a rolling function

Rolling functions in Dask are fairly simple to use but take a bit of intelligent foresight to use properly due to the distributed nature of Dask DataFrames. Most importantly, Dask has some limitations around the size of the window that you can use: the size of the window can't be large enough to span more than one adjacent partition. As an example, if your data is partitioned by month, you could not specify a window size larger than two months (the month of data in focus and the month before/after the month). This makes sense when you consider that these operations can induce a lot of shuffling. Therefore, you should ensure that the partition sizes you choose are large enough to avoid this boundary issue, but keep in mind that larger partitions can begin to slow down your computations, especially if a lot of shuffling is necessary. Some common sense and experimentation are in order to find the best balance for each problem you want to solve. The data should also be index-aligned to ensure that it's sorted in the correct order. Dask uses the index to determine which rows are adjacent to one another, so ensuring proper sort order is critical for the correct execution of any calculations on the data. Let's have a look at an example of using a rolling function now!

Listing 6.28   Prepping data for a rolling function

```
nyc_data = dd.read_parquet('nyc_final', engine='pyarrow')

with ProgressBar():
    condition = ~nyc_data['monthYear'].isin(['201707','201708','201709','2017
    10','201711','201712'])
    nyc_data_filtered = nyc_data[condition]
    citations_by_month = nyc_data_filtered.groupby(nyc_data_filtered.index)
    ['Summons Number'].count()
```

To start, in listing 6.28, we'll prepare some data. We're going to go back to the NYC Parking Ticket dataset and look at a moving average of citations issued per month. What we're aiming to find out is if we can spot any discernable trend in the data after smoothing out some of the volatility. By averaging each month with a certain number of prior months, individual dips and spikes in a given month will be less prominent, which may reveal an underlying trend that would be difficult to see in the raw data.

In section 6.1, we noticed that the observations in our dataset tended to drop off dramatically after June 2017, and we opted to discard any observations after that month. We'll filter them out again here. Then, we'll count the number of citations per month.

6.4.2   *Using the rolling method to apply a window function*

With the `citationsByMonth` object representing a count of citations per month, we can apply the rolling function transformation before computing the result.

Listing 6.29   Computing a rolling mean of Citations per Month

```
with ProgressBar():
    three_month_SMA = citations_by_month.rolling(3).mean().compute()
```

In listing 6.29, you can see just how simple the built-in rolling functions are! Before applying what looks to be an aggregate function, we've chained a `rolling` method to tell Dask that we want to compute means in a three-period rolling window. Since the periods in this example are months, Dask will average together three-month rolling windows of monthly citation counts. For example, for the month of March 2017, Dask will compute the mean of the counts for March 2017, February 2017, and January 2017. This means that, by default, the number of periods you specify, n, will represent a window that includes the current period (March) and $n - 1$ periods before it (February and January). Let's take a look at what effect this has on the output, which can be seen in figure 6.18.

```
MonthYear
201401    NaN
201402    NaN
201403    7.497377e+05
201404    8.069723e+05
201405    9.068707e+05
201406    9.205720e+05
201407    9.478143e+05
...
201705    9.476880e+05
201706    9.114447e+05
Name: Summons Number, dtype: float64
```

Figure 6.18   Abbreviated output of the window function

Notice that the first two periods are NaN (missing) values. This is because the calculation for the month of February 2014 should include both January 2014 and December 2013, but our dataset doesn't have December 2013 in it. Instead of computing a partial value for periods with missing data, Dask will instead return a NaN value to signify that the true value is currently unknown. When using a rolling function, the result will always be *n – 1* number of rows smaller than the input dataset because of the nature of missing values in early windows.

If you would like to include both trailing and leading periods in your calculation, you can do that by setting the center parameter of the rolling method. This will cause Dask to compute a window that includes *n/2* periods before the current value and *n/2* periods after the current value. For example, if we used a three-period centered window, for the month of March 2017 our mean would include the count for February 2017, March 2017, and April 2017—one period in the past and one period in the future.

Listing 6.30 Using a centered window

```
citations_by_month.rolling(3, center=True).mean().head()
```

Listing 6.30 demonstrates centering, which will produce the output shown in figure 6.19.

As you can see in the figure, with centering we only lose the first row instead of the first two rows. Whether this is appropriate or not again depends on what problem you're trying to solve. You can also do much more than rolling means. In fact, every built-in aggregate function is also available as a rolling function, such as sum and count. You may also implement your own custom rolling functions by using either apply or map_overlap in the same way you would with a normal DataFrame or Series.

```
MonthYear

201401    NaN

201402    749737.666667

201403    806972.333333

201404    906870.666667

201405    920572.000000

Name: Summons Number, dtype: float64
```

Figure 6.19 Output of listing 6.30 showing MonthYear and the mean number of parking citations

Now that you have some tools for numerically describing and analyzing data in Dask, it's a good opportunity to turn our attention to another aspect of data analysis that's just as important: visualization. If you looked at the unabbreviated results of the code in listing 6.30, you could see that trends look numerically inconclusive. With some high points and some low points, the number of citations in June 2017 ends up not far off from the number of citations in June 2014. At times like these, it's much easier to spot trends and patterns visually than just staring at the numbers. It can also be more intuitive to understand descriptive statistics and correlations through visualization. So, in the next chapter, we'll pick up right where we left off by looking for trends in citations issued per month. However, we'll use the power of visualization to try to make our job easier!

Summary

- Dask DataFrames have a number of useful statistical methods such as `mean`, `min`, `max`, and so on. Even more statistical methods can be found in the dask.array.stats package.
- Basic descriptive statistics can be produced for a DataFrame or Series by using the `describe` method.
- Aggregate functions use the split-apply-combine algorithm to process data in parallel. Aggregating on a sorted column of a DataFrame will yield the best performance.
- Correlation analysis compares two continuous variables, whereas the t-test compares a continuous variable across a categorical variable.
- You can use the `Aggregate` object to define your own aggregate functions.
- You can use rolling functions to analyze trends across a time index, such as moving averages. You should partition the data by time period for the best performance.

Visualizing DataFrames
with Seaborn

This chapter covers

- Using the prepare-collect-plot-reduce pattern to overcome the challenges of visualizing large datasets

- Visualizing continuous relationships using `seaborn.scatterplot` and `seaborn.regplot`

- Visualizing groups of continuous data using Seaborn `seaborn.violinplot`

- Visualizing patterns in categorical data using `seaborn.heatmap`

In the previous chapter, we performed some basic analyses of the NYC Parking Ticket data by looking at descriptive statistics and some other numerical properties of the dataset. While describing data numerically is precise, the results can be somewhat difficult to interpret and are generally not intuitive. On the other hand, we humans are very good at detecting and understanding patterns in visual information. Incorporating visualization into our analyses can help us better understand the general makeup of our dataset as well as how different variables interact with one another.

For example, consider the relationship between average temperature and the number of citations issued that we explored in the previous chapter. We calculated a Pearson correlation coefficient of about 0.14. We concluded that the two variables have a weak positive correlation, meaning we should expect the number of citations issued to increase slightly as the average temperature rises. Given our findings, should we expect global climate change to become a lucrative phenomenon for the city of New York? Or does the nature of the relationship change depending on which range of values we're looking at? A simple correlation coefficient can't convey all that information. We'll come back to that question momentarily. For now, to really highlight why visualization is such an important part of data analysis, let's look at a classic problem in statistics known as *Anscombe's quartet*. Anscombe's quartet is a hypothetical dataset presented in 1973 by an English statistician named Francis Anscombe, who was frustrated by his field's lack of appreciation for visualization. He wanted to demonstrate that numerical methods alone don't always tell the full story: each of the four datasets that make up his quartet share the same mean, variance, correlation, regression line, and coefficient of determination. Figure 7.1 displays the four datasets that make up Anscombe's quartet.

If we relied on numerical methods alone, we might conclude that each of the four datasets is completely identical. However, graphically, they tell a different story. Two of the datasets, X_3 and X_4, have extreme outliers. Dataset X_4 appears to have an undefined

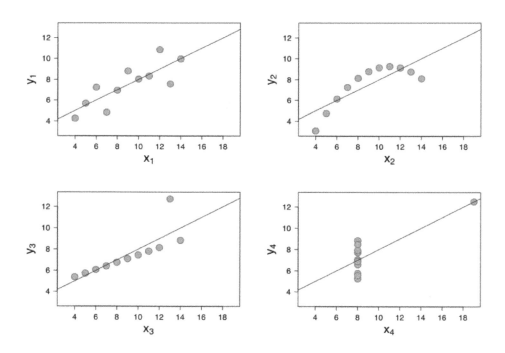

Figure 7.1   **Anscombe's quartet highlights the importance of using visualization for effective data analysis.**

slope, and dataset X_2 appears to be a nonlinear, perhaps parabolic function. Consequently, the appropriate methods we might use to numerically describe and analyze each of the four datasets would be completely different after learning more about the data through visualization.

Notice that Anscombe's quartet is a very small dataset, so visualizing it as a set of scatterplots is simple and straightforward. However, visualizing large datasets can be tricky due to both the volume and variety of data. Because there are many kinds of visualizations to choose from, for all different kinds of data, we can't possibly cover all kinds of visualizations in this book. Therefore, we will cover some general patterns and tactics that you can extend to produce many kinds of visualizations, and we will cover a few of the more common visualizations that are useful for analyzing structured data. As always, figure 7.2 shows what we've accomplished so far and where we'll turn our focus next.

In this chapter, we'll continue working on exploratory analysis and hypothesis formulation and testing, but with a focus on using visualizations to dig deeper into the analyses. We'll also blend some data-manipulation techniques you learned in previous chapters, such as aggregations, with new techniques like sampling. All the computations to prepare the data for visualization will be performed with Dask using the DataFrame API.

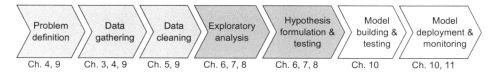

Figure 7.2 The *Data Science with Python and Dask* workflow

7.1 *The prepare-reduce-collect-plot pattern*

We face a few challenges when visualizing large datasets. From a technical perspective, plotting a large amount of data is, unsurprisingly, computationally intensive and can require a lot of memory. We've been able to cope with compute- and memory-hungry operations so far by distributing work across multiple workers using Dask, but we still need to eventually collect all the data we want to plot on the screen back to a single thread to render it on the screen. This means that if the size of the dataset we want to plot is bigger than the memory we have on the client machine, we won't be able to plot it. In the next chapter, we'll look at a library called Datashader that overcomes these challenges in a novel way. However, Datashader doesn't support some of the visualizations we'll discuss in this chapter, so we'll have to work around the technical issues.

The other thing we have to keep in mind when plotting large datasets is that the value of visualization comes from the ability to quickly and intuitively discern insights from the data. However, it can be quite easy to become overwhelmed when faced with a large amount of data. Take a look at the scatterplot in figure 7.3.

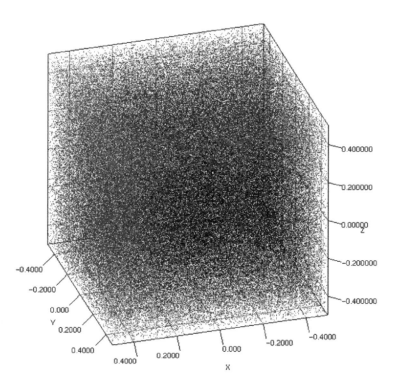

Figure 7.3   An example of a very dense scatterplot

It's really hard to tell what's going on at all in the scatterplot because so many individual points have been plotted on it. It simply looks like random noise! Applying some color coding could make it possible to see a few distinct regions in the data, but it would still be difficult to see where those regions begin and end and where they overlap with one another. This is a hallmark issue with visualizing large datasets: with so much data, individual data points stop being useful to analyze individually. Rather, we need to distill broad patterns and behaviors out of the data. We could do this in a number of ways, including clustering, aggregating, or sampling. Any of these three techniques can be used to make the data much easier to understand.

Figure 7.4 displays a different dataset, which still has a fairly large number of points, but it has also had a clustering technique applied to it. This results in a clear division of the data into three distinct regions. Even though a large number of points are still on this plot, it can be easier to interpret the data because it's possible to conceptually subdivide our analyses into explaining the behavior of three separate groups.

To overcome the technical and conceptual challenges with plotting large datasets, we'll use the prepare-reduce-collect-plot pattern for the remainder of the chapter to produce visualizations from Dask DataFrames. Ultimately, the objective of the pattern is

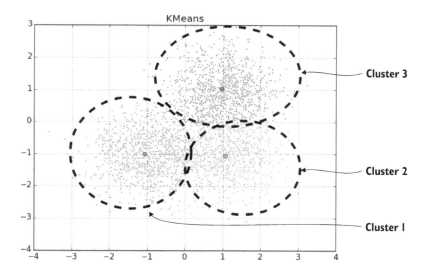

Figure 7.4 Applying a reduction technique like clustering can make data easier to interpret.

to transform the raw, large dataset down to a smaller subset specific to the needs of the visualization we want to produce, and to do as much of the work as possible with Dask.

Figure 7.5 shows the process step by step. We start the first step, Prepare, by identifying what kind of visualization would be appropriate for the question we'd like to answer. Are we interested in the relationship between two continuous variables? Choose a scatterplot. Interested in seeing counts of items by category? A bar chart works well. Once we've identified the type of visualization to produce, think about what you need to display on the axes. This will dictate the columns we need to select out of the DataFrame. Also we need to consider if it's necessary to filter the data at all. Perhaps we want to focus our analysis on a certain category. To do that, we will need to write a filter condition, which was covered in chapter 5, to select data only from that category.

The Reduce step is all about choosing an appropriate reduction method. Generally, you have two choices: aggregate the data into groups that make sense for the question we're trying to answer, such as summing or averaging all observations by month, or take a random sample of the data. Choosing to aggregate the data is normally a natural result of the question we're trying to answer. For example, in the NYC Parking Ticket dataset, we started with approximately 15 million citations. Since we wanted to know how many citations were issued per month, we were able to reduce 15 million data points down to less than 50 data points by grouping the data by month, then counting the number of

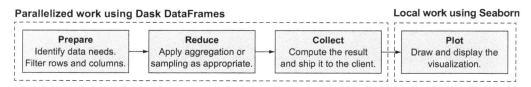

Figure 7.5 The prepare-reduce-collect-plot pattern for visualizing large datasets with Dask

citations. If we wanted to look at this data at the daily or hourly level instead, we would still be able to reduce the original 15 million citations to a much smaller number of data points. If it's not possible to aggregate the data in any meaningful way, or it's not appropriate for the question we're trying to answer, sampling can be used to focus in on a predetermined number of data points. However, since random sampling relies on random chance, it's possible that the randomly sampled data points won't form a realistic picture of the underlying behaviors in the data. This is especially likely to happen if we take a very small sample, so random sampling should be used with caution!

The third step in the process, Collect, is where the computation is executed and the result is turned into a single Pandas DataFrame. From there, we can use the reduced data with any plotting package. The final step, Plot, is where the visualization plotting methods are called and display options (such as plot titles, colors, size, and so on) are set. This step is not distributed since we've gathered all the data into one place during the Collect step.

Now let's take a look at a few examples of using this pattern to visualize some of the variables in the NYC Parking Ticket dataset. In these examples, we'll use Seaborn to produce the visualizations. Seaborn is part of the Python Open Data Science Stack and is a data visualization library based on Matplotlib, another popular visualization library. Seaborn provides a nice wrapper around Matplotlib that lets you easily produce common statistical data visualizations like regression plots, box plots, and scatterplots. If you haven't already installed Seaborn, you can find installation instructions in the appendix.

7.2 *Visualizing continuous relationships with scatterplot and regplot*

We'll now take a look at using the prepare-reduce-collect-plot pattern by returning to the correlation analysis between monthly average temperature and monthly citations issued that we looked at in the previous chapter. Given a Pearson correlation of 0.14, we wouldn't expect there to be much of a relationship, but let's see if Pearson correlation actually tells the whole story or not.

7.2.1 *Creating a scatterplot with Dask and Seaborn*

First, we'll begin as always by importing the relevant modules and loading in the data we saved at the end of chapter 5.

Listing 7.1 **Importing modules and data**

```
import dask.dataframe as dd
import pyarrow
from dask.diagnostics import ProgressBar
import os
import seaborn
import matplotlib.pyplot as plt

os.chdir('/Users/jesse/Documents')
nyc_data = dd.read_parquet('nyc_final', engine='pyarrow')
```

We'll go ahead and import Seaborn and Matplotlib as well here, since we will use it momentarily to set some display options for the final plot. A brief side note if this is your first time using Seaborn: you will frequently see calls to Matplotlib together with Seaborn code. Since Seaborn relies on Matplotlib's plotting engine (pyplot), controlling aspects of the rendered visualizationlike figure size and axis limits is done directly through the pyplot API.

To look at the relationship between monthly average temperature and number of citations, we'll need to get both the average monthly temperature and a count of citations grouped by month/year. Since the number of citations is likely to be several orders of magnitude larger than the average temperature, the temperature will be put on the x-axis and the number of citations will be put on the y-axis. We'll also filter out any data after June 2017, because those months were not completely reported in this dataset. Now that we've identified the necessary data, we'll produce the code to prepare and aggregate the data.

Listing 7.2   Preparing the reducing the data

```
row_filter = ~nyc_data['Citation Issued Month Year'].isin(['07-2017','08-
    2017','09-2017','10-2017','11-2017','12-2017'])

nyc_data_filtered = nyc_data[row_filter]

citationsAndTemps = nyc_data_filtered.groupby('Citation Issued Month Year').
    agg({'Summons Number': 'count', 'Temp': 'mean'})
```

Listing 7.2 should look familiar, because we produced this data before to calculate the correlation coefficient. As before, we simply filter the data and apply the agg method (aggregate) over it to calculate the count of citations and the mean of the temperature grouped by month. Now we're ready to collect and plot the data.

Listing 7.3   Collecting and plotting the data

```
seaborn.set(style="whitegrid")
f, ax = plt.subplots(figsize=(10, 10))
seaborn.despine(f, left=True, bottom=True)

with ProgressBar():
    seaborn.scatterplot(x="Temp", y="Summons Number",
                data=citationsAndTemps.compute(), ax=ax)
    plt.ylim(ymin=0)
    plt.xlim(xmin=0)
```

In listing 7.3, we start by setting the style settings for the scatterplot we're about to produce. The whitegrid style produces a clean-looking figure that has a white background with gray x and y grid lines. Next, we create a blank figure using the plt .subplots function and specify the size we want. This is done to override the default pyplot figure size, which can be a bit small when displayed on high resolution screens. The next call to seaborn.despine is another aesthetic modification to the figure we're about to produce. This simply removes the border box around the figure so all we can see are the gridlines in the plot area. Next, within the ProgressBar context (since we will be moving data from Dask to the local Python process), we call the `seaborn` `.scatterplot` function to plot the graph. Its required parameters are fairly simple: pass in a variable name each for the x and y axis as strings, and pass in a DataFrame to plot. In this example, we've also passed in our custom axes object we created to ensure the scatterplot will look the way it was configured to look. This parameter, however, is optional, and if you don't pass an axes object, it will plot using defaults. In the last two lines, we're setting the minimum of the y and x axes to 0 respectively. The reason these methods are called after the `seaborn.scatterplot` call is because Matplotlib will be able to calculate the maximum x and y size automatically. If you call these methods before plotting, Matplotlib won't have had a chance to see the data and calculate the maxima. Therefore, you would need to pass an explicit maximum or the plot wouldn't display correctly. After a bit of crunching, you should get a scatterplot that looks like figure 7.6.

Figure 7.6 indeed shows that a positive relationship exists between the two variables. As we move from 30 degrees to 60 degrees, the number of citations generally increases. The points are scattered fairly far apart from each other, hence the indication of a weak correlation.

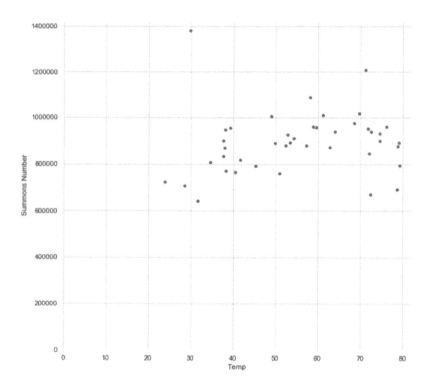

Figure 7.6   A scatterplot of average temperature vs. number of citations

7.2.2 *Adding a linear regression line to the scatterplot*

We can have Seaborn try to help us see the gradual pattern in the data better by plotting a regression plot instead of a scatterplot. To do that, we'll use the `regplot` function. Its required parameters are the same as the `scatterplot` function, so it's very easy to interchange the two.

> **Listing 7.4 Adding a regression line to a scatterplot using `regplot`**

```
seaborn.set(style="whitegrid")
f, ax = plt.subplots(figsize=(10, 10))
seaborn.despine(f, left=True, bottom=True)

with ProgressBar():
    seaborn.regplot(x="Temp", y="Summons Number",
                data=citationsAndTemps.compute(), ax=ax,
                robust=True)
    plt.ylim(ymin=0)
    plt.xlim(xmin=0)
```

In listing 7.4., you can see that the only thing that changed is the call to `regplot` instead of `scatterplot`. We also added the optional parameter, `robust`. This parameter tells Seaborn to produce a robust regression. A robust regression minimizes the influence of outliers on the regression equation. This means that points on the y axis that sit far away from other points won't pull the line we're trying to draw through the points up (or down) by very much. This is a good thing since these points are unlikely to occur on a regular basis, so we should treat them as anomalies instead of observations that are likely to happen again. For example, take a look at the point in figure 7.6 that represents roughly 1.4 million citations. This happened during a very cold month when the average temperature was only about 30 degrees Fahrenheit. We can see that all the other months that were just as cold accrued only around 700,000 citations. Some special circumstance must have happened during the month where 1.4 million citations were issued, since this seems to be unusual. If we allowed the anomalous data point to influence our regression line, it would cause us to overestimate the number of citations we can expect to be issued in cold months. There seem to be a few outliers in this dataset, so using a robust regression would be a good idea. When running the code, you will get a regression plot that looks like figure 7.7.

As you can see, a line has been plotted roughly through the center mass of the points. Keep in mind, however, that regression is a statistical estimation. Where the line was drawn could have been influenced by unusual observations (called *outliers*). The shaded area around the line represents the confidence interval, meaning that there is a 95% chance that the best-fitting line is somewhere inside that area. The line itself is the best "guess" given the data that was provided here.

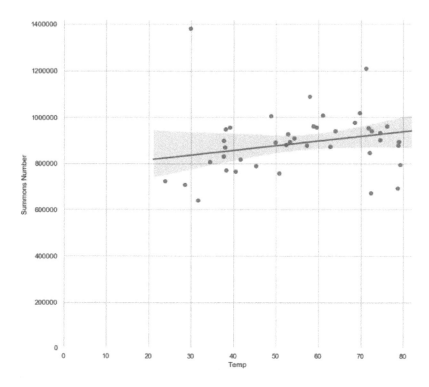

Figure 7.7　The scatterplot of average temperature vs. count of citations with an added regression line

7.2.3　*Adding a nonlinear regression line to a scatterplot*

However, it doesn't look like it fits particularly well. On closer examination of the scatterplot, it appears that the number of citations actually starts gradually decreasing past about 60 degrees. This makes intuitive sense: perhaps fewer enforcement officers are sent on patrol in more extreme weather. This would be a great opportunity to follow up with management to see if our hypothesis is true, or if another explanation exists for the drop off in citations. Regardless, the relationship does not appear to be linear. Instead, a nonlinear equation, such as a parabola, might fit the data better.

Figure 7.8 shows why fitting a parabola to the data might result in a more accurate fit. As you can see, moving from 20 degrees to about 60 degrees, the relationship seems to be positive: as the temperature increases, the number of citations written also increases. However, around the 60 degrees mark, the relationship seems to reverse direction. As temperature increases from 60 degrees, the number of citations seems to decrease overall. Seaborn supports nonlinear curve fitting in regression plots with a few parameter adjustments.

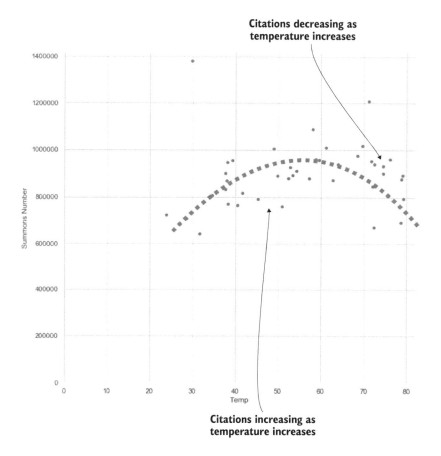

Figure 7.8   The relationship appears to be non-linear; the relationship changes direction around 60 degrees.

Listing 7.5   Fitting a nonlinear curve to a dataset

```
seaborn.set(style="whitegrid")
f, ax = plt.subplots(figsize=(10, 10))
seaborn.despine(f, left=True, bottom=True)

with ProgressBar():
    seaborn.regplot(x="Temp", y="Summons Number",
            data=citationsAndTemps.compute(), ax=ax,
            order=2)
    plt.ylim(ymin=0)
    plt.xlim(xmin=0)
```

In listing 7.5., the robust parameter was replaced with the order parameter. The order parameter determines how many terms to use in order to fit a nonlinear curve. Since the data looks roughly parabolic, an order of 2 is used (you might recall from high

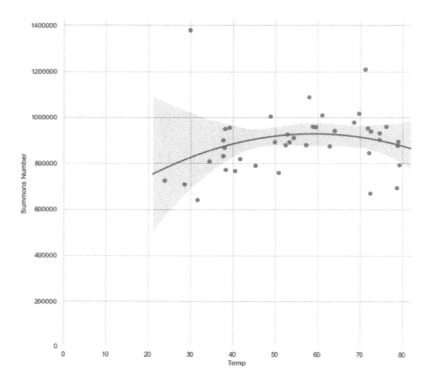

Figure 7.9   The scatterplot of average temperature vs. count of citations fit with a nonlinear curve

school algebra that a parabola has two terms: an x^2 term and an x term). This produces a regression plot that looks like figure 7.9.

Figure 7.9 appears to fit the data better than the previous linear regression. We've also learned something that we would have missed if we only looked at the Pearson correlation coefficient! Next, we'll have a look at visualizing relationships in categorical data.

7.3   *Visualizing categorical relationships with violinplot*

The NYC Parking Ticket data is full of many categorical variables, which presents an excellent opportunity to demonstrate a very useful visualization for analyzing categorical relationships: the violinplot. An example of a violinplot can be seen in figure 7.10. Violinplots are similar to boxplots in that they are a visual representation of several statistical properties of a variable including the mean, median, 25th percentile, 75th percentile, minimum, and maximum. But violionplots also incorporate a histogram into the plot, so you can determine what the distribution of the data looks like and where the most frequently occurring points are. Like boxplots, violinplots are used to compare behaviors of a continuous variable across groups. For example, we might want to know how the age of a vehicle relates to the color of a vehicle. Do black cars tend to be

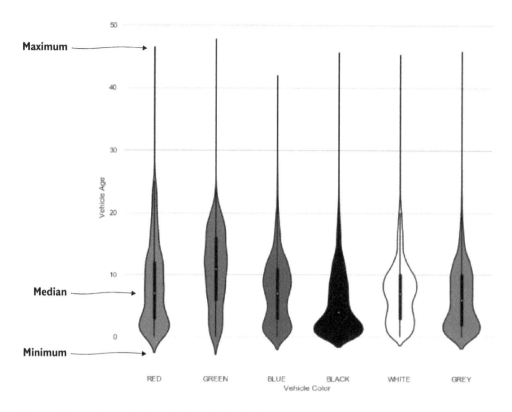

Figure 7.10   A violinplot showing the relative distributions of categorical data

newer or older? Would you be more likely to receive a ticket in a new red car or an old green car? A violinplot will help us investigate these questions.

7.3.1   Creating a violinplot with Dask and Seaborn

As we did in the previous example, we'll follow the prepare-reduce-collect-plot pattern to produce the violinplots. The data we need are the vehicle ages and vehicle colors recorded on each citation. However, in this case, there aren't any logical ways to pre-aggregate the data into smaller groups. To produce the descriptive statistics and histogram, we need the raw observations. Therefore, we will turn to sampling to help us reduce our dataset.

For the sake of example, we'll narrow our analysis to the top six most common vehicle colors: black, white, grey, red, blue, and green. This will allow us to produce a violinplot without using sampling first, so we can compare what the violinplot looks like using the entire dataset and what the violinplot looks like using a random sample of the data.

Listing 7.6   Reading in and filtering the data

```
nyc_data_withVehicleAge = dd.read_parquet('nyc_data_vehicleAge',
    engine='pyarrow')

row_filter = nyc_data_withVehicleAge['Vehicle Color'].isin(['BLACK','WHITE','
    GREY','RED','GREEN','BLUE'])
column_filter = ['Vehicle Age','Vehicle Color']

ages_and_colors = nyc_data_withVehicleAge[row_filter][column_filter]
```

For this example, we're also reusing some data we produced in chapter 6. This was the example where we calculated the difference between the Vehicle Year and the Citation Date for each citation to determine how old the vehicle was when it received a citation. In listing 7.6, we read in the data, select the relevant columns, and filter for the top vehicle colors. Next, we'll take a quick count to determine how many observations we have.

Listing 7.7   Counting the observations

```
with ProgressBar():
    print(ages_and_colors.count().compute())

# Produces the output:
# Vehicle Age      4972085
# Vehicle Color    4972085
# dtype: int64
```

With 4,972,085 observations, we should be able to get a decently representative sample by randomly sampling 1% of the observations without replacement. First, we'll see what the violinplot for all 4.97 million points looks like.

Listing 7.8   Creating the violinplot

```
seaborn.set(style="whitegrid")
f, ax = plt.subplots(figsize=(10, 10))
seaborn.despine(f, left=True, bottom=True)

group_order = ["RED", "GREEN", "BLUE", "BLACK", "WHITE", "GREY"]

with ProgressBar():
    seaborn.violinplot(x="Vehicle Color", y="Vehicle Age", data=ages_and_
    colors.compute(), order=group_order, palette=group_order, ax=ax)
```

Once again, we start by setting up the figure and axes as before. We then put the colors in a list so we can tell Seaborn how to arrange the groups on the violinplot. Then, inside the `ProgressBar` context, we call the `seaborn.violinplot` function to produce the violinplot. The parameters should look familiar, because they are the same as both `scatterplot` and `regplot`. You can also see where we pass in the list of colors we defined. The `order` parameter allows you to specify a custom order to display the groups in from left to right. Otherwise, the choice is random. It's good to use a consistent sort order if you plan to compare multiple instances of violinplots over the same groups. We also use the same list in the `palette` parameter to ensure the colors of the violinplot match the vehicle colors they represent (the red violinplot will be colored red, and so forth) After a bit of crunching, you will get a plot that looks like figure 7.11.

By looking at the violinplot in figure 7.11, we can see that red, blue, white, and grey vehicles have roughly the same median age (denoted by the white dot), whereas black vehicles tend to be newer and green vehicles tend to be older. All vehicle colors have roughly the same maximum age, but there are more instances of old red and green vehicles than other colors, which is denoted by a thicker line in the upper regions of the red and green plots. Wider areas indicate a higher number of observations, and narrower regions indicate fewer observations. The spikiness of the white plot looks particularly interesting, because it looks like white vehicles with an odd age are less common that vehicles with an even age. This might be worth looking into further to understand why.

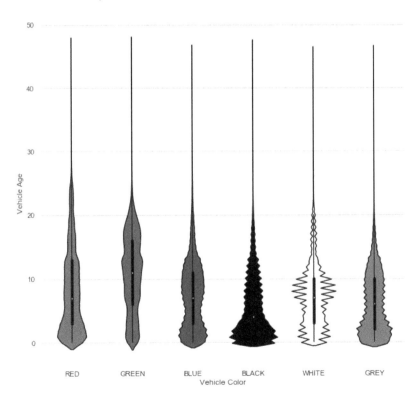

Figure 7.11 **A violinplot of vehicle color vs. vehicle age**

7.3.2   *Randomly sampling data from a Dask DataFrame*

Now let's compare this plot to a plot of a random sample of the data. We'll keep the plotting code the same, but we'll grab a 1% random sample from our filtered DataFrame.

Listing 7.9   Sampling the filtered DataFrame

```
sample = ages_and_colors.sample(frac=0.01)

seaborn.set(style="whitegrid")
f, ax = plt.subplots(figsize=(10, 10))
seaborn.despine(f, left=True, bottom=True)

with ProgressBar():
    seaborn.violinplot(x="Vehicle Color", y="Vehicle Age", data=sample.
    compute(), order=group_order, palette=group_order, ax=ax)
```

Sampling from a Dask DataFrame is quite simple; use the `sample` method on any Data-Frame and specify the percentage of the data you want to sample, and you will get a filtered DataFrame roughly the size of the percentage you specify. By default, sampling is performed *without* replacement. This means once a vehicle record is selected out of the DataFrame, that same vehicle record can't be selected again in the same sample.

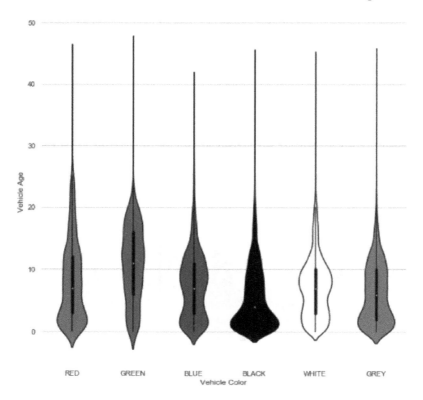

Figure 7.12   A violinplot of the random sample

This ensures that all the observations in your sample are unique. If you want to sample *with* replacement, you can specify that using the Boolean `replace` parameter. Take note, you can only specify the sample size in percentage terms—it's not possible to specify the exact number of items in the returned sample. Therefore, you'll need to count the population size and calculate the percentage of the population that will give you the sample size you want. 49,000 is plenty large for our purposes in this example, so we've taken a 1% sample without replacement. This will result in a plot that looks like figure 7.12.

Compared with figure 7.11, figure 7.12 looks very similar. We see the general patterns persist: black vehicles tend to be newer, green vehicles tend to be older, and more red and green older vehicles are on the road than other colors. The distributions are roughly the same shape, but they've lost some of their detail. The shape of the white and red distributions is much less jagged than they were in the population. However, overall, sampling has given us the ability to draw similar insights from the data without working with the entire set.

7.4 *Visualizing two categorical relationships with heatmap*

As you can see, violinplots are useful for understanding the behavior of your data when you have one categorical variable. However, it's not uncommon to have many categorical variables as we do in the NYC Parking Ticket dataset. If we want to see how categorical variables interact with each other, heatmaps are a very useful way to do so. While you can use a heatmap to visualize the relationship between any two categorical variables, it's quite common to use heatmaps across dimensions of time. For example, we looked at the trend in citations issued by month in the previous chapter and found that more citations tend to be issued in warmer months than colder months, but perhaps there's another time dimension that has a pattern as well. Day of the week could be interesting to explore: perhaps more citations are issued on weekdays than weekends (or vice versa).

Let's see if the day of week effect interacts with the month-of-year effect. To do this, we'll want to get the day of the week and month of the year each citation was written in. Then, we'll want to aggregate the citations by both month of year and day of week. That should naturally reduce the number of data points for the visualization to 84 (12 months by 7 days).

Listing 7.10 **Extracting the day of week and month of year**

```
from datetime import datetime
nyc_data_filtered = nyc_data[nyc_data['Issue Date'] < datetime(2017,1,1)]

day_of_week = nyc_data['Issue Date'].apply(lambda x: x.strftime("%A"),
    meta=str)    ◄

month_of_year = nyc_data['Issue Date'].apply(lambda x: x.strftime("%B"),
    meta=str)
```

Extract the day of week name and month of year name from the issue Date column.

First, we'll apply the `strftime` function over the Issue Date column to extract the day of week and month of year, respectively, in the same way we've applied functions over the data before in chapter 5.

Listing 7.11   Adding the columns back to the DataFrame

```
nyc_data_with_dates_raw = nyc_data_filtered.assign(DayOfWeek = day_of_week).
    assign(MonthOfYear = month_of_year)
column_map = {'DayOfWeek': 'Day of Week', 'MonthOfYear': 'Month of Year'}
nyc_data_with_dates = nyc_data_with_dates_raw.rename(columns=column_map)
```

Next, we add the columns back into the DataFrame using the assign-rename part of the drop-assign-rename pattern you learned previously.

Listing 7.12   Counting the citations by Month of Year and Day of Week

```
with ProgressBar():
    summons_by_mydw = nyc_data_with_dates.groupby(['Day of Week', 'Month of
    Year'])['Summons Number'].count().compute()
```

Now we use the `groupby` method to count the citations by Day of Week and Month of Year.

Listing 7.13   Transforming the result into a pivot table

```
heatmap_data = summons_by_mydw.reset_index().pivot("Month of Year", "Day of
    Week", "Summons Number")
```

After Dask finishes computing the aggregation, we need to pivot the data so we have 12 rows (one for each month) and 7 columns (one for each day of the week) in the DataFrame. To do that, we'll use the `pivot` method. The index must be reset first because Month of Year and Day of Week will initially be the index of the resulting DataFrame, so they need to be moved back into separate columns, so we can reference them in the call to `pivot`. Finally, we can produce the heatmap.

Listing 7.14   Creating the heatmap

```
months = ['January','February','March','April','May','June','July',
    'August','September','October','November','December']
weekdays =
    ['Monday','Tuesday','Wednesday','Thursday','Friday','Saturday','Sunday']

f, ax = plt.subplots(figsize=(10, 10))
seaborn.heatmap(heatmap_data.loc[months,weekdays], annot=True, fmt="d",
    linewidths=1, ax=ax)
```

Before calling the `heatmap` function, we'll stick the months and weekdays into separate lists in the appropriate order. As we've seen in previous examples, any sorting based on named time dimensions will result in alphabetical sorting as Pandas isn't aware that months or weekdays have any special meaning. In the call to `heatmap`, we use the `loc` method on the DataFrame to select the rows and columns in the correct order. Alternatively, we could sort the DataFrame using one of the previously demonstrated date-sorting methods. The `annot` parameter tells Seaborn to put the actual values in each cell, so we can see exactly how many citations were issued on Wednesdays in July. The `fmt` parameter tells Seaborn to format the contents as numbers rather than strings, and the `linewidths` parameter adjusts how much spacing should be placed between each cell in the heatmap. This function call should produce a heatmap that looks like figure 7.13. Heatmaps are very simple to read. The light areas indicate few citations, and the dark areas indicate many citations. We've also annotated the heatmap with the actual counts of citations by month/weekday.

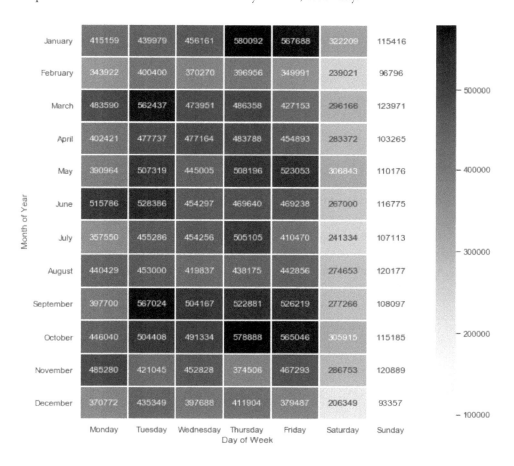

Figure 7.13   A heatmap of citations issued by day of week and month of year

The heatmap in figure 7.13 immediately shows that weekends tend to see fewer citations issued than weekdays, with Sundays especially lower. We're likely seeing the effect of fewer enforcement officers working weekend shifts. It appears that Sundays in December sees the fewest citations issued of any month/weekday combination, and Thursdays in January seem to have the highest number of citations issued. These might be outliers that would be worth exploring further.

Hopefully you now have a good understanding of how to apply the prepare-reduce-collect-plot pattern to produce visualizations for data analysis. As stated earlier in the chapter, this pattern can be extended to other libraries as well. While Seaborn can create a wide variety of useful and attractive visualizations, any plotting library that can accept Pandas DataFrames or NumPy arrays as input can be easily interchanged within this pattern.

In the next chapter, we'll explore how to produce interactive visualizations and dashboards that can be useful both for data exploration and reporting to end users.

Summary

- There may be "more to the story" than numerical analysis can explain—it's always worth it to visualize data.
- The prepare-reduce-collect-plot pattern can be used to create visualizations from large datasets. You can use any data visualization library that supports Pandas with this method.
- If it makes sense for the question you're trying to answer, your data can be reduced using aggregation (e.g. citations per month).
- Random sampling can also be a good method to visually approximate the shape of your data, given a sufficiently large sample size.
- The relationship between two continuous variables can be visualized using a scatterplot.
- Regplots can be used to plot linear regression as well as nonlinear regression.
- The distribution of a continuous variable across a categorical variable can be visualized using a violinplot.
- Two categorical variables can be visualized using a heatmap.

Visualizing location data with Datashader

This chapter covers

- Using Datashader to visualize many datapoints when downsampling isn't appropriate

- Plotting interactive heatmaps using Datashader and Bokeh

In the previous chapter, we looked at a few ways to gain insights from data using visualization. However, every method we looked at relied on finding workarounds to reduce the size of the data we used for plotting. Whether by randomly sampling, filtering, or aggregating the data, we used these *downsampling* techniques to overcome the inherent limitations of Seaborn and Matplotlib. Although we've shown that these techniques can be useful, downsampling can cause us to miss patterns in the data because we're throwing data away. This issue becomes the most evident when dealing with high-dimensional data, such as location.

Imagine for a moment that we wanted to use the NYC Parking Ticket dataset to find the areas of New York City where drivers are most likely to get parking tickets. One way we could do this is by finding the mean location by latitude and longitude of all issued citations. However, this would only tell us the "average" location of a parking ticket, which might not even be located on a city street! There may be many hotspots throughout the city, but we wouldn't be able to tell that by using only the mean. We could try to use some sort of clustering algorithm, such as k-Means, to identify multiple hotspots, but this would still be troublesome for a few reasons: the center points might again not be on any city streets, and we would have to manually choose the number of clusters to feed into the clustering algorithm. How would we know how many clusters to use if we don't have a good understanding of the data? The only way to get a true and accurate understanding of the data in this case is to use all of it. But if plotting libraries like Seaborn and Matplotlib don't work well with datasets stretching into the millions and billions of datapoints, how could we visualize datasets of this size without using any kind of downsampling? This is precisely where Datashader shines. Before we start, take a brief look at figure 8.1, which shows the progress we've made through our workflow.

We'll round out the Exploratory Analysis and Hypothesis Formulation & Testing steps of our workflow in this chapter with a look at another way to analyze data visually. Unlike in the previous chapter where we used the prepare-reduce-collect-plot pattern to downsample the data before plotting it with Seaborn, we'll look at how Datashader can be used to plot data stored in Dask DataFrames directly. Specifically, we'll look at how Datashader can be used to plot geographic-based data on a map.

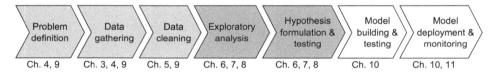

Figure 8.1   The *Data Science with Python and Dask* workflow

8.1   *What is Datashader and how does it work?*

Datashader is a relatively new library in the Python Open Data Science Stack that was created to produce meaningful visualizations of very large datasets. Unlike our work with Seaborn where we needed Dask to materialize a downsampled Pandas DataFrame before plotting, Datashader's plotting methods accept Dask objects directly and can take full advantage of distributed computing. Datashader can produce any grid-based visualization: scatterplots, line charts, heatmaps, and so on. Let's walk through the five-step pipeline that Datashader uses to render images to understand how it works.

Before we jump in, let's get some data to work with. Unfortunately, NYC OpenData does not publish the exact latitude/longitude coordinates of where each parking citation is issued in the NYC Parking Ticket dataset. Therefore, we'll turn to another medium-sized dataset available on NYC OpenData that does have detailed location data: New York City's database of 311 service calls. A 311 service call is an issue that a citizen reports to one of New York City's non-emergency services, such as when a streetlight is out or a pothole has formed on a road. The dataset contains a record of all reported issues from the beginning of 2010 to the present time and is updated regularly. As a motivating scenario for this chapter, we'll use this data to answer the following question:

> *Using the NYC 311 Service Call dataset, how can we show the frequency of service calls based on location and plot this data on a map to find common problem areas?*

The link to download the data can be found here: https://data.cityofnewyork.us/Social-Services/311-Service-Requests-from-2010-to-Present/erm2-nwe9. To export the data in CSV format, click the Export button in the top-right corner and select CSV. Also, please make sure you've installed the datashader, holoviews, and geoviews packages before continuing. Holoviews and Geoviews are dependencies of Datashader and must be installed for the code in this chapter to work correctly. Both libraries are used by Datashader to make interactive map-type visualizations. Installation instructions can be found in the appendix. After you've downloaded the data, import the necessary packages and load the data.

Listing 8.1 Loading in the data and imports

```
import dask.dataframe as dd
from dask.diagnostics import ProgressBar
import os
import datashader
import datashader.transfer_functions
from datashader.utils import lnglat_to_meters
import holoviews
import geoviews
from holoviews.operation.datashader import datashade

os.chdir('/Users/jesse/Documents')      ◄──┤ Set the working directory.

nyc311_geo_data = dd.read_csv('311_Service_Requests_from_2010_to_Present.
    csv', usecols=['Latitude','Longitude'])   ◄──────
```

> Read in just the latitude and longitude data for the 311 service requests.

Listing 8.1 contains all the standard steps to get started: importing the packages we'll use in this chapter, setting up the working directory, and reading in the data. The only thing particularly noteworthy is that we'll only bring in the Latitude and Longitude columns for now. To do this, we'll use the usecols parameter that you learned about in chapter 4. We don't need any of the other columns right now.

8.1.1 The five stages of the Datashader rendering pipeline

With the data and packages in place, let's continue with walking through how Datashader works. The five stages that Datashader uses to render images are:

- Projection
- Aggregation
- Transformation
- Colormapping
- Embedding

The first step, *projection*, deals with establishing the *Canvas* that Datashader will plot the image on. This includes choosing the size of the image (for example, 800 pixels wide by 600 pixels high), the variables that will be plotted on the x and y axes, and the range of the variables, which is used to center the visualization on the Canvas. The anatomy of a Canvas object can be seen in figure 8.2.

To create the Canvas object, we'll call the Canvas constructor and pass in the relevant arguments, as is shown next. This listing does not have any output, because the Canvas object we're creating is simply a container to hold our visualization.

Listing 8.2   Creating a Canvas object

```
x_range = (-74.3, -73.6)
y_range = (40.4, 41)
scene = datashader.Canvas(plot_width=600, plot_height=600, x_range=x_range,
    y_range=y_range)
```

The parameters should be all self-explanatory for the constructor: the plot width and height dictate the size of the image that will be produced (in pixels), and the x and y range parameters set the bounds for the grid. Here we've picked some map coordinates that roughly correspond to the area around New York City. Keep in mind that longitude is normally plotted along the x axis and latitude is normally plotted along the y axis. If you ever work with a dataset and you're unsure which range of coordinates to use, you can compute the min/max of each column using the aggregate functions you learned in chapter 6.

The second step in Datashader's plotting pipeline is *aggregation*. But wait a moment—didn't we just establish a few pages ago that Datashader is supposed to use all the data without downsampling? Then why would Datashader aggregate the data? Datashader uses the term *aggregation* a bit differently than how we've talked about aggregation in the past. When we talked about aggregation, we were referring to domain-specific aggregation, such as grouping parking citations by vehicle year. In all cases, the aggregations we performed were along a specific dimension contained in the data. On the

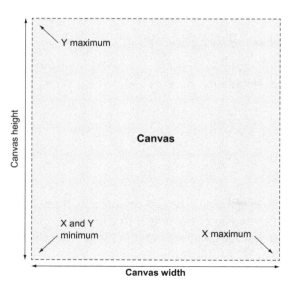

Figure 8.2   A visual representation of a Canvas object

other hand, Datashader aggregates data into buckets that represent pixels on your screen. The coordinate system used by your data is mapped to the pixel area of the image and all datapoints residing within one of those buckets will have an aggregate function (such as sum or mean) applied to them. For example, if each pixel happened to represent 1/100th of a degree latitude/longitude, a 100 x 100 image would cover the area of 1 square degree. At 40 degrees north, 1 degree of longitude is equivalent to 53 miles, and a degree of latitude is equivalent to 69 miles. This means that if we produced a 100 x 100 image of the area around New York City, each pixel on your screen would represent approximately 36.5 square miles. This is a pretty low resolution, since all 311 service calls in a 36.5 square mile area would be aggregated together. Figure 8.3 demonstrates how Datashader performs aggregation.

Fortunately, Datashader performs all this mapping and aggregation for you based on the width/height and range options you specified in the Projection step. A small range and a large image will result in a high-resolution image of the space, whereas a large range and a small image will result in a low-resolution image of the space. Given the range and size we specified in listing 8.2, we can expect each pixel of our image to represent about 120,000 square feet, which is about half the area of a standard city block in New York City. So, all we need to do now is tell Datashader which data we want it to use.

Listing 8.3   Defining the aggregation

```
aggregation  = scene.points(nyc311_geo_data, 'Longitude', 'Latitude')
```

This call is pretty simple since we don't need to apply any further transformation to the data. We're simply telling Datashader to take the data in the `nyc311_geo_data` Data-Frame, plot the Longitude column on the x axis, and plot the Latitude column on the y axis. Since we haven't specified another method of aggregation, such as sum, mean,

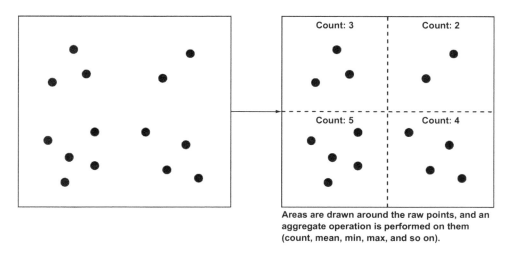

Areas are drawn around the raw points, and an aggregate operation is performed on them (count, mean, min, max, and so on).

Figure 8.3   Aggregation draws areas around the raw points and performs an aggregate operation on the areas; each of these areas resembles a single pixel in the final visualization.

and so forth, Datashader will simply count the number of points that fall into each pixel. So, for our example here, Datashader will be counting the number of 311 service calls that happen within each 120,000 square foot chunk of New York City.

The third step of the Datashader pipeline is *transformation*. We don't have any need to apply any transformations to our data in this example, since we're taking a simple count, but it's important to note that the aggregation object we just created in the previous listing is a simple xarray object that represents the pixel space defined in the Canvas object. This means we could perform any kind of array transformation we'd like on it, such as filtering out pixels that are in a certain percentile, multiplying the array by another array, or performing any sort of linear algebra transformation. In this particular example, the array is 600 x 600 and contains both a value related to the service calls that occurred in that specific area as well as the mapping back to the original latitude/longitude coordinates.

In figure 8.4, you can see the value at pixel 300, 300. The value of 140 is not a count of the number of service calls in that area. Instead, the value represents a relative rank of how many service calls occurred in that area compared to all other areas on the map. A value of 0 signifies no service calls in the area, and the value increases in areas where service calls occurred more frequently. This number is very important in the next step.

The fourth step is *colormapping*. In this step, Datashader will take the relative values computed in the Aggregation step and map them to a given color palette. In this example, we're using the default color palette, which ranges from white to dark blue. The higher the value in the underlying array, the darker the shade of blue. This colormapping is what ultimately conveys the information that we want to know. Figure 8.5 demonstrates how Datashader performs the colormapping step.

The fifth and final step is *embedding*. This is where Datashader renders the final image using the information computed in the aggregation step along with the colormap. To trigger the final rendering, we use the shade method on the aggregation object. If we want to use a different colormap (for example, red to blue), you can specify that with the cmap parameter. Embedding is demonstrated in figure 8.6.

Listing 8.4   Rendering the final image

```
image = datashader.transfer_functions.shade(aggregation)
```

The call to the shade method in listing 8.4 transforms the data into an image, which can then be displayed using IPython.

```
<xarray.DataArray ()>
array(140, dtype=int32)  ◄─────── Count of service calls
Coordinates:
    Latitude    float64 40.7   ◄───────  Latitude/longitude
    Longitude   float64 -73.95            represented by this pixel
```

Figure 8.4   The contents of the pixel located at 300, 300

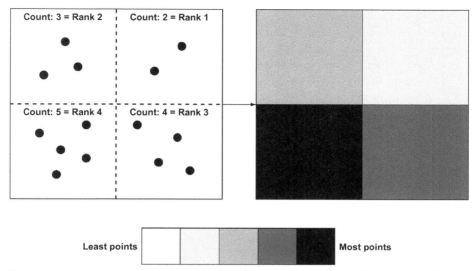

The aggregate values are ranked by lowest to highest, and are assigned a color based on the colormap.

Figure 8.5   Colormapping translates ranked values into colors.

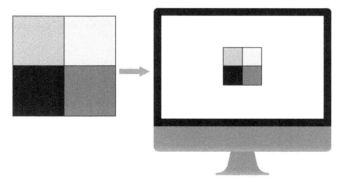

Figure 8.6   Embedding renders the final image on the screen.

8.1.2   Creating a Datashader Visualization

To recap, here's the complete code.

Listing 8.5   Complete code to produce our first Datashader visualization

Create a Canvas object for the plot.

Colormap and render the complete image.

Project and aggregate the data into the grid.

```
with ProgressBar():
    x_range = (-74.3, -73.6)
    y_range = (40.4, 41)
    scene = datashader.Canvas(plot_width=600, plot_height=600, x_range=x_
    range, y_range=y_range)
    aggregation  = scene.points(nyc311_geo_data, 'Longitude', 'Latitude')
    image = datashader.transfer_functions.shade(aggregation)
```

Notice that we've wrapped the code in the `ProgressBar` context as per usual with Dask-related code. Datashader is actually using Dask to produce the aggregation for us, so we can watch the progress of that aggregation! If you inspect the `image` object we're left with, you should see something similar to figure 8.7.

This is pretty exciting! We just plotted about 16 million datapoints in a matter of a few seconds. If you're familiar with the geography of New York City, you should immediately recognize the shape of the city. If you're not, that's all right too—since we have location data in a coordinate system, we can overlay this visualization on a map to help figure out where we are, which we'll be doing in the next section. You might also be curious as to how we can focus in on a specific part of the city. The top-leftmost island in the image is the island of Manhattan, one of the most densely populated parts of New York City. It makes sense that just about the entire island is darkly shaded: more people correlate with more requests for city services.

Figure 8.7   The output of the Datashader image

In fact, the only area that isn't darkly shaded is the white rectangle in the middle of the island, which is New York City's famous Central Park. Perhaps we want to only focus on Lower Manhattan and find where the problem areas are in that specific part of the city. In the next section, we'll cover how to make our visualization interactive, allowing us to pan and zoom around the city. We'll also add some map tiles so we have a better idea of where we're looking. Before we move on, let's recap the five plotting stages of Datashader. A summary of each stage can be seen in table 8.1.

Table 8.1   The five plotting stages of Datashader

Stage	Explanation
Projection	Creating a container (Canvas) to plot the visualization onto
Aggregation	Grouping data within the same "area" (coordinates/location)
Transformation	Applying mathematical transformation(s) on the aggregated values
Colormapping	Converting raw values into shades of colors to plot on the screen
Embedding	Rendering the final image on the Canvas

8.2 *Plotting location data as an interactive heatmap*

Before we make our visualization interactive, we should consider the time it will take to render each image. Any panning or zooming will dynamically change the x range and y range values that you set manually in the previous section. This will require the entire image to be re-rendered. The longer it takes to render a new image, the less useful the interactive feature becomes, so we'll want to do everything we can to minimize processing time. It's recommended that data used by Datashader is stored in Parquet format with Snappy compression—both of which we already covered in chapter 5! We'll convert the data from CSV to Parquet before we continue.

However, we have one more thing to consider. We also want to overlay our original heatmap on top of a map, so we can tell which parts of the city we're looking at. Another library called Geoviews allows you to do this. Geoviews uses the coordinate data to fetch *map tiles* from a third-party mapping service.

8.2.1 *Preparing geographic data for map tiling*

Map tiles are chunks of a map that are projected on a grid. For example, a tile might represent one square mile of Manhattan and contain all the roads and terrain features in that square mile. Just like with our data in Datashader, the size and area of the tile is based on the range and size of the Canvas. These tiles are provided by mapping services that use web APIs to deliver the necessary tiles. However, most mapping services don't index map tiles by latitude/longitude coordinates. Instead, they use a different coordinate system called Web Mercator. Web Mercator is just another grid coordinate system, but to produce the correct images, we'll need to convert our latitude/longitude coordinates into Web Mercator coordinates. Fortunately, Geoviews has a utility method that will do this conversion for us. We'll run the conversion on our coordinates, then save the converted coordinates to Parquet.

Listing 8.6   Preparing the data for map tiling

Combine the two series into a DataFrame by concatenating along the columns axis; you'll get a warning here, but it's ok because the two Series we're concatenating are index-aligned.

Convert the latitude/longitude coordinates to Web Mercator coordinates; this results in two separate series, one with x coordinates and one with y coordinates.

```
with ProgressBar():
    web_mercator_x, web_mercator_y = lnglat_to_meters(nyc311_geo_
     data['Longitude'], nyc311_geo_data['Latitude'])
    projected_coordinates = dd.concat([web_mercator_x, web_mercator_y],
     axis=1).dropna()
    transformed = projected_coordinates.rename(columns={'Longitude':'x',
     'Latitude': 'y'})
    dd.to_parquet(path='nyc311_webmercator_coords', df=transformed,
     compression="SNAPPY")
```

Rename the series to X and Y.

Save the results as a parquet to speed up data access with datashader.

In listing 8.6, we use the `lnglat_to_meters` method to convert the latitude/longitude coordinates into Web Mercator coordinates. This particular method takes two input objects (an X and a Y) and spits out the transformed X and Y as two separate objects. It can accept Dask Series objects without having to first collect and materialize it into a Pandas Series, so we simply have to pass in the Longitude column of our original DataFrame for the X value, and the Latitude column of our original DataFrame for the Y value.

We want to keep these values together in a single DataFrame, so we'll use the `concat` method that you learned about in chapter 5. However, this time, instead of using it to union two DataFrames, we'll use it to concatenate along the columns axis (axis 1). You'll receive a warning telling you that Dask is assuming the indexes are aligned between both Series, but you can ignore it in this case because `web_mercator_x` and `web_mercator_y` were created in the same order, making their indexes naturally aligned. We'll also use the `dropna` method that we've used before in chapter 4 to drop any rows that do not have valid coordinates. Finally, we'll rename the columns for convenience's sake to `x` and `y` appropriately and save the result to a Parquet file.

8.2.2 Creating the interactive heatmap

Now we'll read the Parquet file in and create the interactive visualization.

Listing 8.7   Creating the interactive visualization

Create a new Web Mercator tile provider using the specified API url.

Set a URL to the Stamen map tile API; {Z} represents zoom level, {X} is the Web Mercator X coordinate, and {Y} is the Web Mercator Y coordinate.

```
nyc311_geo_data = dd.read_parquet('nyc311_webmercator_coords')
```
Read the parquet data back in.

```
holoviews.extension('bokeh')
```
Enable the bokeh extension in HoloViews.

```
stamen_api_url = 'http://tile.stamen.com/terrain/{Z}/{X}/{Y}.jpg'

plot_options = dict(width=900, height=700, show_grid=False)

tile_provider = geoviews.WMTS(stamen_api_url).opts(style=dict(alpha=0.8),
    plot=plot_options)

points = holoviews.Points(nyc311_geo_data, ['x', 'y'])
service_calls = datashade(points, x_sampling=1, y_sampling=1, width=900,
    height=700)
```
Set the display options for the visualization.

```
tile_provider * service_calls
```
Overlay the map tiles with the heatmap.

Plot the X and Y points on a grid.

In listing 8.7, we begin by reading the Parquet data that we just saved back into our session. Next, we need to activate the Bokeh extension in Holoviews. These two packages manage the interactive part of the visualization, but we don't need to change anything to get everything to work out of the box. The map tile provider we'll be using is from a company called Stamen that maintains a repository of open source street map data created under the OpenStreetMap project. We'll store the URL for the API in a variable so the map tile provider object can use it later. Next, we'll define some display parameters for the visualization, specifying the width and height of the image area. Then, we create the tile provider object using the `geoviews.WMTS` constructor. This object is used to call the API URL and get the correct map tiles whenever the image needs to be updated. All we need to do is pass in the URL variable. We've chained this call with the `opts` method to set the display options. We then create the heatmap by using the `holoviews.Points` function, which is very similar to the `scene.points` method you used in the previous section. Also, instead of using `datashader.transfer_functions` `.shade` to produce the image, the `datashade` function from Holoviews is used instead. This allows Holoviews to continuously update the image as we pan/zoom with the Bokeh widget. The final line ties everything together. While the multiplication operator seems a bit odd, this is how the two layers are folded together to produce the final image. This will also fire up the Bokeh widget and render the first image. You should see something similar to figure 8.8.

As you can see, we've overlaid the heatmap on top of a map of New York City, and everything lines up perfectly! Also notice we have the Latitude and Longitude along the

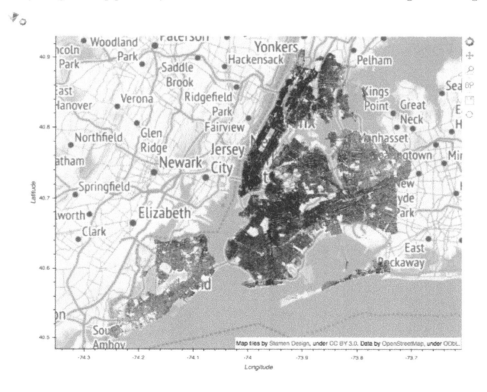

Figure 8.8   The interactive heatmap

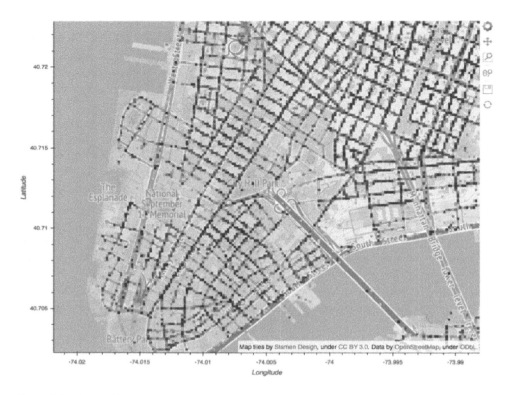

Figure 8.9   Zoomed into the southern tip of Manhattan

outside edge of the map, and controls in the upper right to enable panning and zooming. Figure 8.9 shows a zoomed-in image of the southernmost tip of Manhattan.

You can see that as we zoom in, the image updates along with the map tiles. It should take less than one second to re-render the image at the new zoom level. You can also see that relative to the area we've zoomed in on, there are some areas where more service calls happen than in other areas. For example, many service calls are occurring along Broadway, but fewer have occurred along some of the side streets, such as around the National September 11th Memorial. You can pan and zoom all around the city to explore problem areas.

Summary

- Datashader can be used to produce accurate images of large datasets without downsampling.
- Every DataShader object consists of a Canvas, an aggregation, and a transfer function.
- DataShader visualizations aggregate based on the number of pixels in the canvas area, and their resolution is dynamic, allowing you to "zoom in" to a particular area on a graph.

- Holoviews, Geoviews, and Bokeh can be used with Datashader to produce interactive visualizations with map tiles.
- Map tiles are overlaid on a grid using a tile provider. If your data has latitude/longitude coordinates, they should be translated to Web Mercator coordinates first.

Part 3

Extending and deploying Dask

In part 3, we round out our exploration of Dask by covering some advanced topics: unstructured data, machine learning, and deploying Dask to the cloud. These are good topics to end on, because you should be fairly comfortable with the Dask paradigm by now. Once again, all the chapters are anchored on real-world datasets and common tasks you may encounter in any data science project.

Chapter 9 discusses how to use Dask Bags—a parallelized implementation of standard Python Lists—and Dask Arrays—a parallelized implementation of NumPy Arrays—to work with more complicated, unstructured datasets. We'll cover some advanced collections topics such as mapping, folding, and reducing by parsing text data stored in JSON format.

Chapter 10 demonstrates how to use the Dask ML API to build parallelized scikit-learn models. This is extremely useful for building models from huge datasets where training time may be prohibitive and scaling the work out to many different machines effectively speeds up the training process.

Last but not least, chapter 11 covers two things: how to run Dask in the cloud using Docker and AWS, and how to run Dask in cluster mode. The chapter walks through a step-by-step configuration of an AWS environment, and then demonstrates how easy it is to execute and monitor code introduced in previous chapters in the cluster.

Working with
Bags and Arrays

9

This chapter covers

- Reading, transforming, and analyzing unstructured data using Bags

- Creating Arrays and DataFrames from Bags

- Extracting and filtering data from Bags

- Combining and grouping elements of Bags using fold and reduce functions

- Using NLTK (Natural Language Toolkit) with Bags for text mining on large text datasets

The majority of this book focuses on using DataFrames for analyzing structured data, but our exploration of Dask would not be complete without mentioning the two other high-level Dask APIs: Bags and Arrays. When your data doesn't fit neatly in a tabular model, Bags and Arrays offer additional flexibility. DataFrames are limited to only two dimensions (rows and columns), but Arrays can have many more. The Array API also offers additional functionality for certain linear algebra, advanced mathematics, and statistics operations. However, much of what's been covered already through working with DataFrames also applies to working with Arrays— just as Pandas and NumPy have many similarities. In fact, you might recall from chapter 1 that Dask DataFrames are parallelized Pandas DataFrames and Dask Arrays are parallelized NumPy arrays.

Bags, on the other hand, are unlike any of the other Dask data structures. Bags are very powerful and flexible because they are parallelized general collections, most like Python's built-in List object. Unlike Arrays and DataFrames, which have predetermined shapes and datatypes, Bags can hold any Python objects, whether they are custom classes or built-in types. This makes it possible to contain very complicated data structures, like raw text or nested JSON data, and navigate them with ease.

Working with unstructured data is becoming more commonplace for data scientists, especially data scientists who are working independently or in small teams without a dedicated data engineer. Take the following, for example.

In figure 9.1, the same data is presented two different ways: the upper half shows some examples of product reviews as structured data with rows and columns, and the lower half shows the raw review text as unstructured data. If the only information we care about is the customer's name, the product they purchased, and whether or not they were satisfied, the structured data gives us this information at a glance without any ambiguity. Every value in the Customer Name column is always the customer's name. Conversely, the varying length, writing style, and free-form nature of the raw text makes it unclear what data is relevant for analysis and requires some sort of parsing and interpretation to extract the relevant data. In the first review, the reviewer's name (Mary) is the fourth word of the review. However, the second reviewer put his name (Bob) at the very end of his review. These inconsistencies make it difficult to use a rigid data structure like a DataFrame or an Array to organize the information. Instead, the flexibility of Bags really shines here: whereas a DataFrame or Array always has a fixed number of columns, a Bag can contain strings, lists, or any other element of varying length.

Structured data

Customer name	Product	Satisfied?
Bob	Dog food	Yes
Mary	Chocolate	No
Joe	Chocolate	Yes

Unstructured data

```
My name is Mary, and I made my first
purchase with your store last week.
I bought some chocolate and did not
like the flavor. It was too sweet
for me. Shipping was fast and
convenient, so I would be willing to
buy again if more types of chocolate
were available.

I bought some food for my dog
Patches, and she really seemed to
enjoy it. Thanks, Bob.
```

Figure 9.1   An example comparison of structured and unstructured data

In fact, the typical use case that involves working with unstructured data comes from analyzing text data scraped from web APIs, such as product reviews, tweets from Twitter, or ratings from services like Yelp and Google Reviews. Therefore, we'll walk through an example of using Bags to parse and prepare unstructured text data; then we'll look at how to map and derive structured data from Bags to Arrays.

Figure 9.2 is our familiar workflow diagram, but it might be a bit surprising because we've stepped back to the first three tasks! Since we're starting with a new problem and dataset, rather than progressing onward from chapter 8, we'll be revisiting the first three elements of our workflow, this time with the focus on unstructured data. Many of the concepts that were covered in chapters 4 and 5 are the same, but we will look at how to technically achieve the same results when the data doesn't come in a tabular format such as CSV.

As a motivating example for this chapter, we'll look at a set of product reviews from Amazon.com sourced by Stanford University's Network Analysis Project. You can download the data from here: https://goo.gl/yDQgfH. To learn more about how the dataset was created, see McAuley and Leskovec's paper "From Amateurs to Connoisseurs: Modeling the Evolution of User Expertise through Online Reviews" (Stanford, 2013).

Figure 9.2   The *Data Science with Python and Dask* workflow

9.1   *Reading and parsing unstructured data with Bags*

After you've downloaded the data, the first thing you need to do is properly read and parse the data so you can easily manipulate it. The first scenario we'll walk through is

> *Using the Amazon Fine Foods Reviews dataset, determine its format and parse the data into a Bag of dictionaries.*

This particular dataset is a plain text file. You can open it with any text editor and start to make sense of the layout of the file. The Bag API offers a few convenience methods for reading text files. In addition to plain text, the Bag API is also equipped to read files in the Apache Avro format, which is a popular binary format for JSON data and is usually denoted by a file ending in .avro. The function used to read plain text files is `read_text`, and has only a few parameters. In its simplest form, all it needs is a filename. If you want to read multiple files into one Bag, you can alternatively pass a list of filenames or a string with a wildcard (such as *.txt). In this instance, all the files in the list of filenames should have the same kind of information; for example, log data collected over time where one file represents a single day of logged events. The `read_text` function also natively supports most compression schemes (such as GZip and

BZip), so you can leave the data compressed on disk. Leaving your data compressed can, in some cases, offer significant performance gains by reducing the load on your machine's input/output subsystem, so it's generally a good idea. Let's take a look at what the read_text function will produce.

Listing 9.1   Reading text data into a Bag

```
import dask.bag as bag
import os

os.chdir('/Users/jesse/Documents')
raw_data = bag.read_text('foods.txt')
raw_data

# Produces the following output:
# dask.bag<bag-fro..., npartitions=1>
```

As you've probably come to expect by now, the read_text operation produces a lazy object that won't get evaluated until we actually perform a compute-type operation on it. The Bag's metadata indicates that it will read the entire data in as one partition. Since the size of this file is rather small, that's probably OK. However, if we wanted to manually increase parallelism, read_text also takes an optional blocksize parameter that allows you to specify how large each partition should be in bytes. For instance, to split the roughly 400 MB file into four partitions, we could specify a blocksize of 100,000,000 bytes, which equates to 100 MB. This will cause Dask to divide the file into four partitions.

9.1.1 *Selecting and viewing data from a Bag*

Now that we've created a Bag from the data, let's see how the data looks. The take method allows us to look at a small subset of the items in the Bag, just as the head method allows us to do the same with DataFrames. Simply specify the number of items you want to view, and Dask prints the result.

Listing 9.2   Viewing items in a Bag

```
raw_data.take(10)

# Produces the following output:
'''('product/productId: B001E4KFG0\n',
 'review/userId: A3SGXH7AUHU8GW\n',
 'review/profileName: delmartian\n',
 'review/helpfulness: 1/1\n',
 'review/score: 5.0\n',
 'review/time: 1303862400\n',
 'review/summary: Good Quality Dog Food\n',
 'review/text: I have bought several of the Vitality canned dog food products
    and have found them all to be of good quality. The product looks more
```

```
     like a stew than a processed meat and it smells better. My Labrador is
     finicky and she appreciates this product better than  most.\n',
 '\n',
 'product/productId: B00813GRG4\n')'''
```

As you can see from the result of listing 9.2, each element of the Bag currently represents a line in the file. However, this structure will prove to be problematic for our analysis. There is an obvious relationship between some of the elements. For example, the review/score element being displayed is the review score for the product ID preceding it (B001E4KFG0). But since there is nothing structurally relating these elements, it would be difficult to do something like calculate the mean review score for item B001E4KFG0. Therefore, we should add a bit of structure to this data by grouping the elements that are associated together into a single object.

9.1.2 Common parsing issues and how to overcome them

A common issue that arises when working with text data is making sure the data is being read using the same character encoding as it was written in. Character encoding is used to map raw data stored as binary into symbols that we humans can identify as letters. For example, the capital letter J is represented in binary as 01001010 using the UTF-8 encoding. If you open a text file in a text editor using UTF-8 to decode the file, everywhere 01001010 is encountered in the file, it will be translated to a J before it is displayed on the screen.

Using the correct character encoding makes sure the data will be read correctly and you won't see any garbled text. By default, the read_text function assumes that the data is encoded using UTF-8. Since Bags are inherently lazy, the validity of this assumption isn't checked ahead of time, meaning you'll be tipped off that there's a problem only when you perform a function over the entire dataset. For example, if we want to count the number of items in the Bag, we could use the count function.

> **Listing 9.3 Exposing an encoding error while counting the items in the Bag**

```
raw_data.count().compute()

# Raises the following exception:
# UnicodeDecodeError: 'utf-8' codec can't decode byte 0xce in position 2620:
    invalid continuation byte
```

The count function, which looks exactly like the count function from the DataFrame API, fails with a UnicodeDecodeError exception. This tells us that the file is probably not encoded in UTF-8 since it can't be parsed. These issues typically arise if the text uses any kind of characters that aren't used in the English alphabet (such as accent marks, Hanzi, Hiragana, and Abjads). If you are able to ask the producer of the file which encoding was used, you can simply add the encoding to the read_text function using the encoding parameter. If you're not able to find out the encoding that the file was saved in, a bit of trial and error is necessary to determine which encoding to use. A good place to start is trying the cp1252 encoding, which is the standard encoding used by Windows. In fact, this example dataset was encoded using cp1252, so we can modify the read_text function to use cp1252 and try our count operation again.

Listing 9.4   Changing the encoding of the `read_text` function

```
raw_data = bag.read_text('foods.txt', encoding='cp1252')
raw_data.count().compute()

# Produces the following output:
# 5116093
```

This time, the file is able to be parsed completely and we're shown that the file contains 5.11 million lines.

9.1.3   *Working with delimiters*

With the encoding problem solved, let's look at how we can add the structure we need to group the attributes of each review together. Since the file we're working with is just one long string of text data, we can look for patterns in the text that might be useful for dividing the text into logical chunks. Figure 9.3 shows a few hints as to where some useful patterns in the text are.

In this particular example, the author of the dataset has put two newline characters (which show up as \n) between each review. We can use this pattern as a delimiter to split the text into chunks, where each chunk of text contains all attributes of the review, such as the product ID, the rating, the review text, and so on. We will need to manually parse the text file using some functions from the Python standard library. What we want to avoid doing, however, is reading the entire file into memory in order to do this. Although this file could comfortably fit into memory, an example that reads the entire file into memory would not work once you start working with datasets that exceed the limits of your machine (and it would defeat the whole purpose of parallelism to boot!). Therefore, we will use Python's file iterator to stream the file a small chunk at a time, search the text in the buffer for our desired delimiter, mark the position in the file where a review starts and ends, and then advance the buffer to find the position of the next review. We'll end up with a list of Delayed objects that have pointers to the start and end of each review, which can further be parsed into a dictionary of key-value pairs. The full process from start to finish is outlined in the flowchart in figure 9.4.

Figure 9.3   A pattern enables us to split the text into individual reviews.

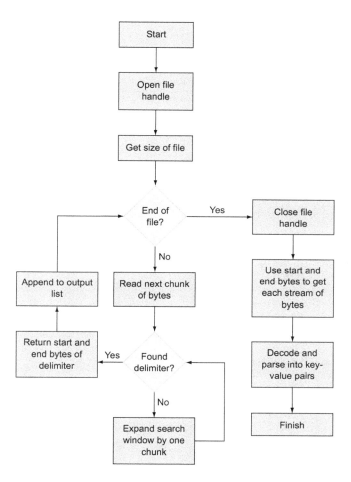

Figure 9.4   Our custom text-parsing algorithm to implement using Dask Delayed

First, we'll define a function that searches a part of a file for our specified delimiter. With Python's file handle system, it's possible to stream data in from a file starting at a specific byte number and stopping at a specific byte number. For instance, the beginning of the file is byte 0. The next character is byte 1, and so forth. Rather than load the whole file into memory, we can load chunks in at a time. For instance, we could load 1000 bytes of data starting at byte 5000. The space in memory we're loading the 1000 bytes of data into is called a *buffer*. We can *decode* the buffer from raw bytes to a string object, and then use all the string manipulation functions available to us in Python, such as `find`, `strip`, `split`, and so on. And, since the buffer space is only 1000 bytes in this example, that's approximately all the memory we will use.

We need a function that will

1 Accept a file handle, a starting position (such as byte 5000), and a buffer size.
2 Then read the data into a buffer and search the buffer for the delimiter.

> 3 If it's found, it should return the position of the delimiter relative to the starting position.
>
> > a However, we also need to cope with the possibility that a review is longer than our buffer size, which will result in the delimiter not being found.
> >
> > b If this happens, the code should keep expanding the search space of the buffer by reading the next 1000 bytes again and again until the delimiter is found.

Here's a function that will do that.

Listing 9.5   A function to find the next occurrence of a delimiter in a file handle

```
from dask.delayed import delayed

def get_next_part(file, start_index, span_index=0, blocksize=1000):
    file.seek(start_index)
    buffer = file.read(blocksize + span_index).decode('cp1252')
    delimiter_position = buffer.find('\n\n')
    if delimiter_position == -1:
        return get_next_part(file, start_index, span_index + blocksize)
    else:
        file.seek(start_index)
        return start_index, delimiter_position
```

Make sure the file handle is currently pointing at the correct starting position.

Read the next chunk of bytes, decode into a string, and search for the delimiter.

If the delimiter isn't found (find returns −1), recursively call the get_next_part function to search the next chunk of bytes; otherwise, return the position of the found delimiter.

Given a file handle and a starting position, this function will find the next occurrence of the delimiter. The recursive function call that occurs if the delimiter isn't found in the current buffer adds the current buffer size to the span_index parameter. This is how the window continues to expand if the delimiter search fails. The first time the function is called, the span_index will be 0. With a default blocksize of 1000, this means the function will read the next 1000 bytes after the starting position (1000 blocksize + 0 span_index). If the find fails, the function is called again after incrementing the span_index by 1000. Then it will then try again by searching the next 2000 bytes after the starting position (1000 blocksize + 1000 span_index). If the find continues to fail, the search window will keep expanding by 1000 bytes until a delimiter is finally found or the end of the file is reached. A visual example of this process can be seen in figure 9.5.

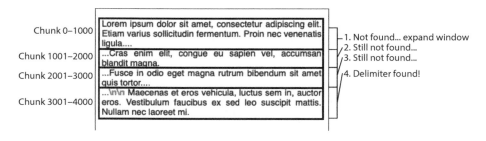

Figure 9.5   A visual representation of the recursive delimiter search function

To find all instances of the delimiter in the file, we can call this function inside a loop that will iterate chunk by chunk until the end of the file is reached. To do this, we'll use a while loop.

Listing 9.6 Finding all instances of the delimiter

```
with open('foods.txt', 'rb') as file_handle:
    size = file_handle.seek(0,2) - 1          Get the total size of the file in bytes.
    more_data = True
    output = []                               Initialize a few variables to control the loop
    current_position = next_position = 0      and store the output, starting at byte 0.
    while more_data:
        if current_position >= size:
            more_data = False
        else:
            current_position, next_position = get_next_part(file_handle,
    current_position, 0)
            output.append((current_position, next_position))
            current_position = current_position + next_position + 2
```

If the end of the file has been reached, terminate the loop; otherwise, find the next instance of the delimiter starting at the current position; append the results to the output list, and update the current position to after the delimiter.

Essentially this code accomplishes four things:

- Find the start position and bytes to delimiter for each review.
- Save all these positions to a list.
- Distribute the byte positions of reviews to the workers.
- Workers process the data for the reviews at the byte positions they receive.

After initializing a few variables, we enter the loop starting at byte 0. Every time a delimiter is found, the current position is advanced to just after the position of the delimiter. For instance, if the first delimiter starts at byte 627, the first review is made up of bytes 0 through 626. Bytes 0 and 626 would be appended to the output list, and the current position would be advanced to 628. We add two to the next_position variable because the delimiter is two bytes (each '\n' is one byte). Therefore, since we don't really care about keeping the delimiters as part of the final review objects, we'll skip over them. The search for the next delimiter will pick up at byte 629, which should be the first character of the next review. This continues until the end of the file is reached. By then we have a list of tuples. The first element in each tuple represents the starting byte, and the second element in each tuple represents the number of bytes to read after the starting byte. The list of tuples looks like this:

```
[(0, 471),
 (473, 390),
 (865, 737),
 (1604, 414),
 (2020, 357),
 ...]
```

Context managers

When working with file handles in Python, it's good practice to use the context manager pattern, `with open(…) as file_handle:`, which can be seen in the first line of listing 9.6. The `open` function in Python requires explicit cleanup once you're done reading/writing to the file by using the `.close()` method on the file handle. By wrapping code in the context manager, Python will close the open file handle automatically once the block of code is finished executing.

Before moving on, check the length of the `output` list using the `len` function. The list should contain 568,454 elements.

Now that we have a list containing all the byte positions of the reviews, we need to create some instructions to transform the list of addresses into a list of actual reviews. To do that, we'll need to create a function that takes a starting position and a number of bytes as input, reads the file at the specified byte location, and returns a parsed review object. Because there are thousands of reviews to be parsed, we can speed up this process using Dask. Figure 9.6 demonstrates how we can divide up the work across multiple workers.

Effectively, the list of addresses will be divided up among the workers; each worker will open the file and parse the reviews at the byte positions it receives. Since the reviews are stored as JSON, we will create a dictionary object for each review to store its attributes. Each attribute of the review looks something like this: `'review/userId: A3SGXH7AUHU8GW\n'`, so we can exploit the pattern of each key ending in `': '` to split the data into key-value pairs for the dictionaries. The next listing shows a function that will do that.

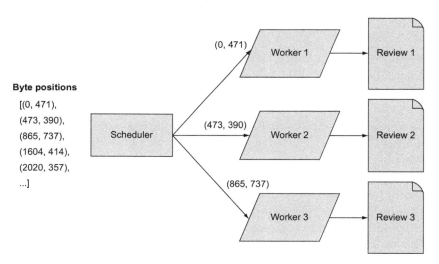

Figure 9.6   Mapping the parsing code to the review data

Listing 9.7 Parsing each byte stream into a dictionary of key-value pairs

Create a file handle using the passed-in filename.

Advance to the passed-in starting position and buffer the specified number of bytes.

```
def get_item(filename, start_index, delimiter_position, encoding='cp1252'):
    with open(filename, 'rb') as file_handle:
        file_handle.seek(start_index)
        text = file_handle.read(delimiter_position).decode(encoding)
        elements = text.strip().split('\n')
        key_value_pairs = [(element.split(': ')[0], element.split(': ')[1])
                           if len(element.split(': ')) > 1
                           else ('unknown', element)
                           for element in elements]
    return dict(key_value_pairs)
```

Split the string into a list of strings using the newline character as a delimiter; the list will have one element per attribute.

Parse each raw attribute into a key-value pair using the ':' pattern as a delimiter; cast the list of key-value pairs to a dictionary.

Now that we have a function that will parse a specified part of the file, we need to actually send those instructions out to the workers so they can apply the parsing code to the data. We'll now bring everything together and create a Bag that contains the parsed reviews.

Listing 9.8 Producing the Bag of reviews

```
reviews = bag.from_sequence(output).map(lambda x: get_item('foods.txt', x[0],
    x[1]))
```

The code in listing 9.8 does two things: first, we turn the list of byte addresses into a Bag using the `from_sequence` function of the Bag array. This creates a Bag that holds the same list of byte addresses as our original list, but now allows Dask to distribute the contents of the Bag to the workers. Next, the `map` function is called to transform each byte address tuple into its respective review object. Map effectively hands out the Bag of byte addresses and the instructions contained in the `get_item` function to the workers (remember that when Dask is running in local mode, the workers are independent threads on your machine). A new Bag called `reviews` is created, and when it is computed, it will output the parsed reviews. In listing 9.8, we pass in the `get_item` function inside of a `lambda` expression so we can keep the filename parameter fixed while dynamically inputting the start and end byte address from each item in the Bag. As before, this entire process is lazy. The result of listing 9.8 will show that a Bag has been created with 101 partitions. However, taking elements from the Bag will now result in a very different output!

Listing 9.9 Taking elements from the transformed Bag

```
reviews.take(2)

# Produces the following output:
'''({'product/productId': 'B001E4KFG0',
```

```
'review/userId': 'A3SGXH7AUHU8GW',
'review/profileName': 'delmartian',
'review/helpfulness': '1/1',
'review/score': '5.0',
'review/time': '1303862400',
'review/summary': 'Good Quality Dog Food',
'review/text': 'I have bought several of the Vitality canned dog food
   products and have found them all to be of good quality. The product
   looks more like a stew than a processed meat and it smells better.
   My Labrador is finicky and she appreciates this product better than
   most.'},
{'product/productId': 'B00813GRG4',
'review/userId': 'A1D87F6ZCVE5NK',
'review/profileName': 'dll pa',
'review/helpfulness': '0/0',
'review/score': '1.0',
'review/time': '1346976000',
'review/summary': 'Not as Advertised',
'review/text': 'Product arrived labeled as Jumbo Salted Peanuts...
   the peanuts were actually small sized unsalted. Not sure if this
   was an error or if the vendor intended to represent the product as
   "Jumbo".'})'''
```

Each element in the transformed Bag is now a dictionary that contains all attributes of the review! This will make analysis a lot easier for us. Additionally, if we count the items in the transformed Bag, we also get a far different result.

> **Listing 9.10   Counting items in the transformed Bag**

```
from dask.diagnostics import ProgressBar

with ProgressBar():
    count = reviews.count().compute()
count

# Produces the following output:
'''
[########################################] | 100% Completed |  8.5s
568454
'''
```

The number of elements in the Bag has been greatly reduced because we've assembled the raw text into logical reviews. This count also matches the number of reviews stated by Stanford on the dataset's webpage, so we can be sure that we've correctly parsed the data without running into any more encoding issues! Now that our data is a bit easier to work with, we'll look at some other ways we can manipulate data using Bags.

9.2   *Transforming, filtering, and folding elements*

Unlike lists and other generic collections in Python, Bags are not subscript-able, meaning it's not possible to access a specific element of a Bag in a straightforward way. This can make data manipulation slightly more challenging until you become comfortable with thinking about data manipulation in terms of transformations. If you are familiar with functional programming or MapReduce style programming, this line of thinking comes naturally. However, it can seem a bit counterintuitive at first if you have a background of SQL, spreadsheets, and Pandas. If this is the case, don't worry. With a bit of practice, you too will be able to start thinking of data manipulation in terms of transformations!

The next scenario we'll use for motivation is the following:

Using the Amazon Fine Foods Reviews dataset, tag the review as being positive or negative by using the review score as a threshold.

9.2.1 Transforming elements with the map method

Let's start easy—first, we'll simply get all the review scores for the entire dataset. To do this, we'll use the map function again. Rather than thinking about what we're trying to do as getting the review scores, think about what we're trying to do as transforming our Bag of reviews to a Bag of review scores. We need some kind of function that will take a review (dictionary) object in as an input and spit out the review score. A function that does that looks like this.

Listing 9.11   Extracting a value from a dictionary

```
def get_score(element):
    score_numeric = float(element['review/score'])
    return score_numeric
```

This is just plain old Python. We could pass any dictionary into this function, and if it contained a key of review/score, this function would cast the value to a float and return the value. If we map over our Bag of dictionaries using this function, it will transform each dictionary into a float containing the relevant review score. This is quite simple.

Listing 9.12   Getting the review scores

```
review_scores = reviews.map(get_score)
review_scores.take(10)

# Produces the following output:
# (5.0, 1.0, 4.0, 2.0, 5.0, 4.0, 5.0, 5.0, 5.0, 5.0)
```

The review_scores Bag now contains all the raw review scores. The transformations you create can be any valid Python function. For instance, if we wanted to tag the reviews as being positive or negative based on the review score, we could use a function like this.

Listing 9.13   Tagging reviews as positive or negative

```
def tag_positive_negative_by_score(element):
    if float(element['review/score']) > 3:
        element['review/sentiment'] = 'positive'
    else:
        element['review/sentiment'] = 'negative'
```

```
        return element

reviews.map(tag_positive_negative_by_score).take(2)

'''
Produces the following output:

({'product/productId': 'B001E4KFG0',
  'review/userId': 'A3SGXH7AUHU8GW',
  'review/profileName': 'delmartian',
  'review/helpfulness': '1/1',
  'review/score': '5.0',
  'review/time': '1303862400',
  'review/summary': 'Good Quality Dog Food',
  'review/text': 'I have bought several of the Vitality canned dog food
     products and have found them all to be of good quality. The product
     looks more like a stew than a processed meat and it smells better. My
     Labrador is finicky and she appreciates this product better than most.',
  'review/sentiment': 'positive'},
 {'product/productId': 'B00813GRG4',
  'review/userId': 'A1D87F6ZCVE5NK',
  'review/profileName': 'dll pa',
  'review/helpfulness': '0/0',
  'review/score': '1.0',
  'review/time': '1346976000',
  'review/summary': 'Not as Advertised',
  'review/text': 'Product arrived labeled as Jumbo Salted Peanuts...the
     peanuts were actually small sized unsalted. Not sure if this was an
     error or if the vendor intended to represent the product as "Jumbo".',
  'review/sentiment': 'negative'})'''
```

This review is more than 3 (5.0), so it is a positive review.

This review is less than 3 (1.0), so it is a negative review.

In listing 9.13, we mark a review as being positive if its score is greater than three stars; otherwise, we mark it as negative. You can see the new review/sentiment elements are displayed when we take some elements from the transformed Bag. However, be careful: while it may look like we've modified the original data since we're assigning new key-value pairs to each dictionary, the original data actually remains the same. Bags, like DataFrames and Arrays, are immutable objects. What happens behind the scenes is each old dictionary being transformed to a copy of itself with the additional key-value pairs, leaving the original data intact. We can confirm this by looking at the original reviews Bag.

Listing 9.14 Demonstrating the immutability of Bags

```
reviews.take(1)

'''
Produces the following output:

({'product/productId': 'B001E4KFG0',
  'review/userId': 'A3SGXH7AUHU8GW',
  'review/profileName': 'delmartian',
```

```
'review/helpfulness': '1/1',
'review/score': '5.0',
'review/time': '1303862400',
'review/summary': 'Good Quality Dog Food',
'review/text': 'I have bought several of the Vitality canned dog food
    products and have found them all to be of good quality. The product
    looks more like a stew than a processed meat and it smells better.
    My Labrador is finicky and she appreciates this product better than
    most.'},)
'''
```

As you can see, the review/sentiment key is nowhere to be found. Just as when working with DataFrames, be aware of immutability to ensure you don't run into any issues with disappearing data.

9.2.2 Filtering Bags with the filter method

The second important data manipulation operation with Bags is filtering. Although Bags don't offer a way to easily access a specific element, say the 45th element in the Bag, they do offer an easy way to search for specific data. Filter expressions are Python functions that return True or False. The filter method maps the filter expression over the Bag, and any element that returns True when the filter expression is evaluated is retained. Conversely, any element that returns False when the filter expression is evaluated is discarded. For example, if we want to find all reviews of product B001E4KFG0, we can create a filter expression to return that data.

Listing 9.15 Searching for a specific product

```
specific_item = reviews.filter(lambda element: element['product/productId']
    == 'B001E4KFG0')
specific_item.take(5)

'''
Produces the following output:

/anaconda3/lib/python3.6/site-packages/dask/bag/core.py:2081: UserWarning:
    Insufficient elements for `take`. 5 elements requested, only 1 elements
    available. Try passing larger `npartitions` to `take`.
  "larger `npartitions` to `take`.".format(n, len(r)))

({'product/productId': 'B001E4KFG0',
 'review/userId': 'A3SGXH7AUHU8GW',
 'review/profileName': 'delmartian',
 'review/helpfulness': '1/1',
 'review/score': '5.0',
 'review/time': '1303862400',
 'review/summary': 'Good Quality Dog Food',
 'review/text': 'I have bought several of the Vitality canned dog food
    products and have found them all to be of good quality. The product
    looks more like a stew than a processed meat and it smells better.
    My Labrador is finicky and she appreciates this product better than
    most.'},)
'''
```

Listing 9.15 returns the data we requested, as well as a warning letting us know that there were fewer elements in the Bag than we asked for indicating there was only one review for the product we specified. We can also easily do fuzzy-matching searches. For example, we could find all reviews that mention "dog" in the review text.

Listing 9.16   Looking for all reviews that mention "dog"

```
keyword = reviews.filter(lambda element: 'dog' in element['review/text'])
keyword.take(5)

'''
Produces the following output:
({'product/productId': 'B001E4KFG0',
  'review/userId': 'A3SGXH7AUHU8GW',
  'review/profileName': 'delmartian',
  'review/helpfulness': '1/1',
  'review/score': '5.0',
  'review/time': '1303862400',
  'review/summary': 'Good Quality Dog Food',
  'review/text': 'I have bought several of the Vitality canned dog food
      products and have found them all to be of good quality. The product
      looks more like a stew than a processed meat and it smells better.
      My Labrador is finicky and she appreciates this product better than
      most.'},
...)
'''
```

And, just as with mapping operations, it's possible to make filtering expressions more complex as well. To demonstrate, let's use the following scenario for motivation:

> *Using the Amazon Fine Foods Reviews dataset, write a filter function that removes reviews that were not deemed "helpful" by other Amazon customers.*

Amazon gives users the ability to rate reviews for their helpfulness. The review/ helpfulness attribute represents the number of times a user said the review was helpful over the number of times users voted for the review. A helpfulness of 1/3 indicates that three users evaluated the review and only one found the review helpful (meaning the other two did not find the review helpful). Reviews that are unhelpful are likely to either be reviews where the reviewer unfairly gave a very low score or a very high score without justifying it in the review. It might be a good idea to eliminate unhelpful reviews from the dataset because they may not fairly represent the quality or value of a product. Let's have a look at how unhelpful reviews are influencing the data by comparing the mean review score with and without unhelpful reviews. First, we'll create a filter expression that will return True if more than 75% of users who voted found the review to be helpful, thereby removing any reviews below that threshold.

If no one has voted the review to be helpful, discard it; otherwise, if the review has been voted on and more than 75% of reviewers found it helpful, keep it.

Parse the helpfulness score into a numerator and denominator by splitting on the / and casting each number to a float.

```python
def is_helpful(element):
    helpfulness = element['review/helpfulness'].strip().split('/')
    number_of_helpful_votes = float(helpfulness[0])
    number_of_total_votes = float(helpfulness[1])
    # Watch for divide by 0 errors
    if number_of_total_votes > 1:
        return number_of_helpful_votes / number_of_total_votes > 0.75
    else:
        return False
```

Unlike the simple filter expressions defined inline using `lambda` expressions in listings 9.15 and 9.16, we'll define a function for this filter expression. Before we can evaluate the percentage of users that found the review helpful, we first have to calculate the percentage by parsing and transforming the raw helpfulness score. Again, we can do this in plain old Python using local scoped variables. We add some guards around the calculation to catch any potential divide-by-zero errors in the event no users voted on the review (note: practically, this means we assume reviews that haven't been voted on are deemed unhelpful). If it's had at least one vote, we return a Boolean expression that will evaluate to True if more than 75% of users found the review helpful. Now we can apply it to the data to see what happens.

```python
helpful_reviews = reviews.filter(is_helpful)
helpful_reviews.take(2)

'''
Produces the following output:

({'product/productId': 'B000UA0QIQ',
  'review/userId': 'A395BORC6FGVXV',
  'review/profileName': 'Karl',
  'review/helpfulness': '3/3',
  'review/score': '2.0',
  'review/time': '1307923200',
  'review/summary': 'Cough Medicine',
  'review/text': 'If you are looking for the secret ingredient in Robitussin
    I believe I have found it.  I got this in addition to the Root Beer
    Extract I ordered (which was good) and made some cherry soda.  The
    flavor is very medicinal.'},
 {'product/productId': 'B0009XLVG0',
  'review/userId': 'A2725IB4YY9JEB',
  'review/profileName': 'A Poeng "SparkyGoHome"',
  'review/helpfulness': '4/4',
  'review/score': '5.0',
  'review/time': '1282867200',
```

This is a helpful review.

```
'review/summary': 'My cats LOVE this "diet" food better than their regular
    food',
'review/text': "One of my boys needed to lose some weight and the other
    didn't.  I put this food on the floor for the chubby guy, and the
    protein-rich, no by-product food up higher where only my skinny boy can
    jump.  The higher food sits going stale.  They both really go for this
    food.  And my chubby boy has been losing about an ounce a week."})
'''
```

9.2.3 *Calculating descriptive statistics on Bags*

As expected, all of the reviews in the filtered Bag are "helpful." Now let's take a look at how that affects the review scores.

Listing 9.19   Comparing mean review scores

```
helpful_review_scores = helpful_reviews.map(get_score)

with ProgressBar():
    all_mean = review_scores.mean().compute()
    helpful_mean = helpful_review_scores.mean().compute()
print(f"Mean Score of All Reviews: {round(all_mean, 2)}\nMean Score of
    Helpful Reviews: {round(helpful_mean,2)}")

# Produces the following output:
# Mean Score of All Reviews: 4.18
# Mean Score of Helpful Reviews: 4.37
```

In listing 9.19, we first extract the scores from the filtered Bag by mapping the get_score function over it. Then, we can call the mean method on each of the Bags that contain the review scores. After the means are computed, the output will display. Comparing the mean scores allows us to see if there's any relationship between the helpfulness of reviews and the sentiment of the reviews. Are negative reviews typically seen as helpful? Unhelpful? Comparing the means allows us to answer this question. As can be seen, if we filter out the unhelpful reviews, the mean review score is actually a bit higher than the mean score for all reviews. This is most likely explained by the tendency of negative reviews to get downvoted if the reviewers don't do a good job of justifying the negative score. We can confirm our suspicions by looking at the mean length of reviews that are helpful or unhelpful.

Listing 9.20   Comparing mean review lengths based on helpfulness

```
def get_length(element):
    return len(element['review/text'])

with ProgressBar():
    review_length_helpful = helpful_reviews.map(get_length).mean().compute()
    review_length_unhelpful = reviews.filter(lambda review: not is_
     helpful(review)).map(get_length).mean().compute()
```

```
print(f"Mean Length of Helpful Reviews: {round(review_length_helpful, 2)}\
    nMean Length of Unhelpful Reviews: {round(review_length_unhelpful,2)}")

# Produces the following output:
# Mean Length of Helpful Reviews: 459.36
# Mean Length of Unhelpful Reviews: 379.32
```

In listing 9.20, we've chained both map and filter operations together to produce our result. Since we already filtered out the helpful reviews, we can simply map the get_length function over the Bag of helpful reviews to extract the length of each review. However, we hadn't isolated the unhelpful reviews before, so we did the following:

1 Filtered the Bag of reviews by using the remove_unhelpful_reviews filter expression
2 Used the not operator to invert the behavior of the filter expression (unhelpful reviews are retained, helpful reviews are discarded)
3 Used map with the get_length function to count the length of each unhelpful review
4 Finally, calculated the mean of all review lengths

It looks like unhelpful reviews are indeed shorter than helpful reviews on average. This means that the longer a review is, the more likely it will be voted by the community to be helpful.

9.2.4 Creating aggregate functions using the foldby method

The last important data manipulation operation with Bags is *folding*. Folding is a special kind of reduce operation. While reduce operations have not been explicitly called out in this chapter, we've already seen a number of reduce operations throughout the book, as well as even in the previous code listing. Reduce operations, as you may guess by the name, reduce a collection of items in a Bag to a single value. For example, the mean method in the previous code listing reduces the Bag of raw review scores to a single value: the mean. Reduce operations typically involve some sort of aggregation over the Bag of values, such as summing, counting, and so on. Regardless of what the reduce operation does, it always results in a single value. Folding, on the other hand, allows us to add a grouping to the aggregation. A good example is counting the number of reviews by review score. Rather than count all the items in the Bag using a reduce operation, using a fold operation will allow us to count the number of items in each group. This means a fold operation reduces the number of elements in a Bag to the number of distinct groups that exist within the specified grouping. In the example of counting reviews by review score, this would result in reducing our original Bag down to five elements as there are five distinct review scores possible. Figure 9.7 shows an example of folding.

First, we need to define two functions to feed to the foldby method. These are called the binop and combine functions.

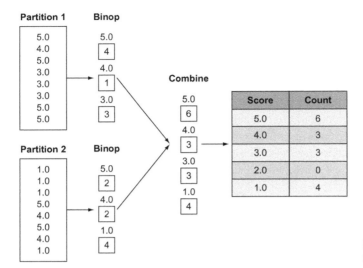

Figure 9.7   An example of a fold operation

The binop function defines what should be done with the elements of each group, and always has two parameters: one for the accumulator and one for the element. The accumulator is used to hold the intermediate result across calls to the binop function. In this example, since our binop function is a counting function, it simply adds one to the accumulator each time the binop function is called. Since the binop function is called for every element in a group, this results in a count of items in each group. If the value of each element needs to be accessed, for instance if we wanted to sum the review scores, it can be accessed through the element parameter of the binop function. A sum function would simply add the element to the accumulator.

The combine function defines what should be done with the results of the binop function across the Bag's partitions. For example, we might have reviews with a score of three in several partitions. We want to count the total number of three-star reviews across the entire Bag, so intermediate results from each partition should be summed together. Just like the binop function, the first argument of the combine function is an accumulator, and the second argument is an element. Constructing these two functions can be challenging, but you can effectively think of it as a "group by" operation. The binop function specifies what should be done to the grouped data, and the combine function defines what should be done with groups that exist across partitions.

Now let's take a look at what this looks like in code.

Listing 9.21   Using foldby to count the reviews by review score

```
def count(accumulator, element):
    return accumulator + 1

def combine(total1, total2):
    return total1 + total2
```

◄— Define a function to count items by increasing an accumulator variable by 1 for each element.

◄— Define a function to reduce the counts per group across partitions.

```
with ProgressBar():
    count_of_reviews_by_score = reviews.foldby(get_score, count, 0, combine,
      0).compute()
count_of_reviews_by_score
```

**Put everything together using the foldby method,
using 0 as the initial value for each accumulator.**

The five required arguments of the `foldby` method, in order from left to right, are the `key` function, the `binop` function, an initial value for the `binop` accumulator, the `combine` function, and an initial value for the `combine` accumulator. The `key` function defines what the values should be grouped by. Generally, the `key` function will just return a value that's used as a grouping key. In the previous example, it simply returns the value of the review score using the `get_score` function defined earlier in the chapter. The output of listing 9.21 looks like this.

Listing 9.22   The output of the `foldby` operation

```
# [(5.0, 363122), (1.0, 52268), (4.0, 80655), (2.0, 29769), (3.0, 42640)]
```

What we're left with after the code runs is a list of tuples, where the first element is the key and the second element is the result of the `binop` function. For example, there were 363,122 reviews that were given a five-star rating. Given the high mean review score, it shouldn't come as any surprise that most of the reviews gave a five-star rating. It's also interesting that there were more one-star reviews than there were two-star or three-star reviews. Nearly 75% of all reviews in this dataset were either five stars or one star—it seems most of our reviewers either absolutely loved their purchase or absolutely hated it. To get a better feel for the data, let's dig a little bit deeper into the statistics of both the review scores and the helpfulness of reviews.

9.3   *Building Arrays and DataFrames from Bags*

Because the tabular format lends itself so well to numerical analysis, it's likely that even if you begin a project by working with an unstructured dataset, as you clean and massage the data, you might have a need to put some of your transformed data into a more structured format. Therefore, it's good to know how to build other kinds of data structures using data that begins in a Bag. In the Amazon Fine Foods dataset we've been looking at in this chapter, we have some numeric data, such as the review scores and the helpfulness percentage that was calculated earlier. To get a better understanding of what information these values tell us about the reviews, it would be helpful to produce descriptive statistics for these values. As we touched on in chapter 6, Dask provides a wide range of statistical functions in the `stats` module of the Dask Array API. We'll now look at how to convert the Bag data we want to analyze into a Dask Array so we can use some of those statistics functions. First, we'll start by creating a function that will isolate the review score and calculate the helpfulness percentage for each review.

> **Listing 9.23   A function to get the review score and helpfulness rating of each review**

Get the review score and cast it to a float.

Calculate the helpfulness rating.

```
def get_score_and_helpfulness(element):
    score_numeric = float(element['review/score'])
    helpfulness = element['review/helpfulness'].strip().split('/')
    number_of_helpful_votes = float(helpfulness[0])
    number_of_total_votes = float(helpfulness[1])
    # Watch for divide by 0 errors
    if number_of_total_votes > 0:
        helpfulness_percent = number_of_helpful_votes / number_of_total_votes
    else:
        helpfulness_percent = 0.
    return (score_numeric, helpfulness_percent)
```

Return the two values as a tuple.

The code in listing 9.23 should look familiar. It essentially combines the get_score function and the calculation of the helpfulness score from the filter function used to remove unhelpful reviews. Since this function returns a tuple of the two values, mapping over the Bag of reviews using this function will result in a Bag of tuples. This effectively mimics the row-column format of tabular data, since each tuple in the Bag will be the same length, and each tuple's values have the same meaning.

To easily convert a Bag with the proper structure to a DataFrame, Dask Bags have a to_dataframe method. Now we'll create a DataFrame holding the review score and helpfulness values.

> **Listing 9.24   Creating a DataFrame from a Bag**

```
scores_and_helpfulness = reviews.map(get_score_and_helpfulness).to_
    dataframe(meta={'Review Scores': float, 'Helpfulness Percent': float})
```

The to_dataframe method takes a single argument that specifies the name and datatype for each column. This is essentially the same meta argument that we saw many times with the drop-assign-rename pattern introduced in chapter 5. The argument accepts a dictionary where the key is the column name and the value is the datatype for the column. With the data in a DataFrame, all the previous things you've learned about DataFrames can now be used to analyze and visualize the data! For example, calculating the descriptive statistics is the same as before.

> **Listing 9.25   Calculating descriptive statistics**

```
with ProgressBar():
    scores_and_helpfulness_stats = scores_and_helpfulness.describe().compute()
scores_and_helpfulness_stats
```

Listing 9.25 produces the output shown in figure 9.8.

The descriptive statistics of the review scores give us a little more insight, but generally tell us what we already knew: reviews are overwhelmingly positive. The helpfulness percentage, however, is a bit more interesting. The mean helpfulness score is only about 41%, indicating that more often than not, reviewers didn't find reviews to be helpful. However, this is likely influenced by the high number of reviews that didn't have any votes. This might indicate that either Amazon shoppers are generally apathetic to reviews of food products and therefore don't go out of their way to say something when a review was helpful—which may be the case since tastes are so variable—or that the typical Amazon shopper truly didn't find these reviews very helpful. It might be interesting to compare these findings with reviews of other types of items that aren't food to see if that makes a difference in engagement with reviews.

	Review Scores	Helpfulness Percent
count	568454.000000	568454.000000
mean	4.183199	0.407862
std	1.310436	0.462068
min	1.000000	0.000000
25%	4.000000	0.000000
50%	5.000000	0.360390
75%	5.000000	1.000000
max	5.000000	3.000000

Figure 9.8 The descriptive statistics of the Review Scores and Helpfulness Percent

9.4 *Using Bags for parallel text analysis with NLTK*

As we've looked at how to transform and filter elements in Bags, something may have become apparent to you: if all the transformation functions are just plain old Python, we should be able to use any Python library that works with generic collections—and that's precisely what makes Bags so powerful and versatile! In this section, we'll walk through some typical tasks for preparing and analyzing text data using the popular text analysis library NLTK (Natural Language Toolkit). As motivation for this example, we'll use the following scenario:

> *Using NLTK and Dask Bags, find the most commonly mentioned phrases in the text of both positive and negative reviews for Amazon products to see what reviewers frequently discuss in their reviews.*

9.4.1 *The basics of bigram analysis*

To find out more of what the reviewers in this dataset are writing about, we will perform a *bigram analysis* of the review text. Bigrams are pairs of adjacent words in text. The reason bigrams tend to be more useful than simply counting the frequency of individual words is they typically add more context. For example, we might expect positive reviews to contain the word "good" very frequently, but that doesn't really help us understand *what* is good. The bigram "good flavor" or "good packaging" tells us a lot more about what the reviewers find positive about the products. Another thing that we need to do in order to better understand the true subject or sentiment of the reviews is to remove words that don't help convey that information. Many words in the English language add structure to a sentence but don't convey information. For example, articles like "the," "a," and "an" do not provide any context or information. Because these words are so common (and necessary for proper sentence formation), we're just as likely to find these words in positive reviews as we are negative reviews. Since they don't add any information, we will remove them. These are known as *stopwords*, and one of the most important data preparation tasks when doing text analysis is detecting and removing stopwords. Figure 9.9 shows examples of a few common stopwords.

The process we'll follow for performing the bigram analysis consists of the following steps:

1 Extract the text data.
2 Remove stopwords.
3 Create bigrams.
4 Count the frequency of the bigrams.
5 Find the top 10 bigrams.

"This food tastes so good!"

"A terrible experience"

"A great experience"

Stopwords are words that don't add any information about the subject or meaning of a sentence.

Figure 9.9   Example of stopwords

9.4.2 *Extracting tokens and filtering stopwords*

Before we jump in, make sure you have NLTK set up properly in your Python environment. See the appendix for instructions on installing and configuring NLTK. With NLTK installed, we need to import the relevant modules into our current workspace; then we'll create a few functions to help us along with the data prep.

Listing 9.26   Extract and filter functions

Create a tokenizer using a regex expression that will extract only words; this means punctuation, numbers, and so forth will be discarded.

```
from nltk.corpus import stopwords
from nltk.tokenize import RegexpTokenizer
from functools import partial

tokenizer = RegexpTokenizer(r'\w+')

def extract_reviews(element):
    return element['review/text'].lower()

def filter_stopword(word, stopwords):
    return word not in stopwords

def filter_stopwords(tokens, stopwords):
    return list(filter(partial(filter_stopword, stopwords=stopwords), tokens))

stopword_set = set(stopwords.words('english'))
```

This function takes an element from the Bag, gets the review text, and changes all letters to lowercase; this is important because Python is case-sensitive.

This function uses the filter function above it to check every word in a list of words (tokens) and discard the word if it is a stopword.

Get the list of English stopwords from NLTK and cast it from a list to a set; using a set is faster than a list in this comparison.

This function returns True if the word is not in the list of stopwords.

In listing 9.26, we're defining a few functions to help grab the review text from the original Bag and filter out the stopwords. One thing to point out is the use of the `partial` function inside the `filter_stopwords` function. Using `partial` allows us to freeze the value of the `stopwords` argument while keeping the value of the `word` argument dynamic. Since we want to compare every word to the same list of stopwords, the value of the `stopwords` argument should remain static. With our data preparation functions defined, we'll now map over the Bag of reviews to extract and clean the review text.

Listing 9.27 Extracting, tokenizing, and cleaning the review text

```
review_text = reviews.map(extract_reviews)
review_text_tokens = review_text.map(tokenizer.tokenize)
review_text_clean = review_text_tokens.map(partial(filter_stopwords,
    stopwords=stopword_set))

review_text_clean.take(1)

# Produces the following output:
'''
(['bought',
  'several',
  'vitality',
  'canned',
  'dog',
  'food',
  'products',
  'found',
  'good',
  'quality',
  'product',
  'looks',
  'like',
  'stew',
  'processed',
  'meat',
  'smells',
  'better',
  'labrador',
  'finicky',
  'appreciates',
  'product',
  'better'],)
'''
```

Removes the stopwords from each list of tokens in the Bag

Transforms the Bag of review strings to a Bag of lists of tokens

Transforms the Bag of review objects to a Bag of review strings

The code in listing 9.27 should be pretty straightforward. We simply use the `map` function to apply the extracting, tokenizing, and filtering functions to the Bag of reviews. As you can see, we're left with a Bag of lists, and each list contains all the unique non-stopwords found in the text of each review. If we take one element from this new Bag, we're returned a list of all words in the first review (except for stopwords, that is). This is important to note: currently our Bag is a nested collection. We'll come back to that momentarily. However, now that we have the cleaned list of words for each review, we'll transform our Bag of lists of tokens into a Bag of lists of bigrams.

Listing 9.28 Creating bigrams

```
def make_bigrams(tokens):
    return set(nltk.bigrams(tokens))

review_bigrams = review_text_clean.map(make_bigrams)
review_bigrams.take(2)

# Produces the following (abbreviated) output:
'''
({('appreciates', 'product'),
  ('better', 'labrador'),
  ('bought', 'several'),
  ('canned', 'dog'),
   ...
  ('vitality', 'canned')},
 {('actually', 'small'),
  ('arrived', 'labeled'),
  ...
  ('unsalted', 'sure'),
  ('vendor', 'intended')})

'''
```

In listing 9.28, we simply have another function to map over the previously created Bag. Again, this is pretty exciting because this process is completely parallelized using Dask. This means we could use the exact same code to analyze billions or trillions of reviews! As you can see, we now have a list of bigrams. However, we still have the nested data structure. Taking two elements results in two lists of bigrams. We're going to want to find the most frequent bigrams across the entire Bag, so we need to get rid of the nested structure. This is called *flattening* a Bag. Flattening removes one level of nesting; for example, a list of two lists containing 5 elements each becomes a single list containing all 10 elements.

Listing 9.29 Flattening the Bag of bigrams

```
all_bigrams = review_bigrams.flatten()
all_bigrams.take(10)

# Produces the following output:
'''
(('product', 'better'),
 ('finicky', 'appreciates'),
 ('meat', 'smells'),
 ('looks', 'like'),
 ('good', 'quality'),
 ('vitality', 'canned'),
 ('like', 'stew'),
 ('processed', 'meat'),
 ('labrador', 'finicky'),
 ('several', 'vitality'))
'''
```

After flattening the Bag in listing 9.29, we're now left with a Bag that contains all bigrams without any nesting by review. It's now no longer possible to figure out which bigram came from which review, but that's OK because that's not important for our analysis. What we want to do is fold this Bag using the bigram as the key, and counting the number of times each bigram appears in the dataset. We can reuse the `count` and `compute` functions we defined earlier in the chapter.

Listing 9.30   Counting the bigrams and finding the top 10 most common bigrams

```
with ProgressBar():
    top10_bigrams = all_bigrams.foldby(lambda x: x, count, 0, combine,
        0).topk(10, key=lambda x: x[1]).compute()
top10_bigrams

# Produces the following output:
'''
[########################################] | 100% Completed | 11min  7.6s
 [(('br', 'br'), 103258),
  (('amazon', 'com'), 15142),
  (('highly', 'recommend'), 14017),
  (('taste', 'like'), 13251),
  (('gluten', 'free'), 11641),
  (('grocery', 'store'), 11627),
  (('k', 'cups'), 11102),
  (('much', 'better'), 10681),
  (('http', 'www'), 10575),
  (('www', 'amazon'), 10517)]
'''
```

The `foldby` function in listing 9.30 looks exactly like the `foldby` function you saw earlier in the chapter. However, we've chained a new method to it, `topk`, which gets the top *k* number of elements when the Bag is sorted in descending order. In the previous example, we get the top 10 elements as denoted by the first parameter of the method. The second parameter, the `key` parameter, defines what the Bag should be sorted by. The folding function returns a Bag of tuples where the first element is the key and the second element is the frequency. We want to find the top 10 most frequent bigrams, so the Bag should be sorted by the second element of each tuple. Therefore, the `key` function simply returns the frequency element of each tuple. This has been shortened by using a `lambda` expression since the `key` function is so simple. Taking a look at the most common bigrams, it looks like we have some unhelpful entries. For example, "amazon com" is the second most frequent bigram. This makes sense, since the reviews are from Amazon. It looks like some HTML may have also leaked into the reviews, because "br br" is the most common bigram. This is in reference to the HTML tag, `<br>`, which denotes whitespace. These words aren't helpful or descriptive at all, so we should add them to our list of stopwords and rerun the bigram analysis.

Listing 9.31   Adding more stopwords and rerunning the analysis

```
more_stopwords = {'br', 'amazon', 'com', 'http', 'www', 'href', 'gp'}
all_stopwords = stopword_set.union(more_stopwords)          ◄─┐

filtered_bigrams = review_text_tokens.map(partial(filter_stopwords,
    stopwords=all_stopwords)).map(make_bigrams).flatten()

with ProgressBar():
    top10_bigrams = filtered_bigrams.foldby(lambda x: x, count, 0, combine,
        0).topk(10, key=lambda x: x[1]).compute()
top10_bigrams
```

> Create a new list of stopwords that is a union of the old stopword set and the new stopwords we want to add.

```
# Produces the following output:
'''
[########################################] | 100% Completed | 11min 19.9s
[(('highly', 'recommend'), 14024),
 (('taste', 'like'), 13343),
 (('gluten', 'free'), 11641),
 (('grocery', 'store'), 11630),
 (('k', 'cups'), 11102),
 (('much', 'better'), 10695),
 (('tastes', 'like'), 10471),
 (('great', 'product'), 9192),
 (('cup', 'coffee'), 8988),
 (('really', 'good'), 8897)]
'''
```

9.4.3   *Analyzing the bigrams*

Now that we've removed the additional stopwords, we can see some clear topics. For example, "k cups" and "coffee" were mentioned a large number of times. This is probably because many of the reviews are for coffee pods for Keurig coffee machines. The most common bigram is "highly recommend," which also makes sense because a lot of the reviews were positive. We could continue iterating over our list of stopwords to see what new patterns emerge (perhaps we could remove the words such as "like" and "store" because they don't add much information), but it would also be interesting to see how the list of bigrams look for reviews that are negative. To close out the chapter, we'll filter our original set of reviews to those that got only one or two stars, and then see what bigrams are the most common.

Listing 9.32   Finding the most common bigrams for negative reviews

> Use a filter expression to find all reviews where the review score was less than 3.

> Since we've started with a new set of reviews, we have to tokenize it.

```
negative_review_text = reviews.filter(lambda review: float(review['review/
    score']) < 3).map(extract_reviews)

negative_review_text_tokens = negative_review_text.map(tokenizer.tokenize)   ◄─
```

```
negative_review_text_clean = negative_review_text_tokens.map(partial(filter_
    stopwords,
stopwords=all_stopwords))

negative_review_bigrams = negative_review_text_clean.map(make_bigrams)
negative_bigrams = negative_review_bigrams.flatten()

with ProgressBar():
    top10_negative_bigrams = negative_bigrams.foldby(lambda x: x, count, 0,
        combine, 0).topk(10, key=lambda x: x[1]).compute()
top10_negative_bigrams

# Produces the following output:
'''
[######################################] | 100% Completed |  2min 25.9s
 [(('taste', 'like'), 3352),
  (('tastes', 'like'), 2858),
  (('waste', 'money'), 2262),
  (('k', 'cups'), 1892),
  (('much', 'better'), 1659),
  (('thought', 'would'), 1604),
  (('tasted', 'like'), 1515),
  (('grocery', 'store'), 1489),
  (('would', 'recommend'), 1445),
  (('taste', 'good'), 1408)]
'''
```

The list of bigrams we get from listing 9.32 shares some similarities with the bigrams from all reviews, but also has some distinct bigrams that show frustration or disappointment with the product ("thought would," "waste money," and so forth). Interestingly, "taste good" is a bigram for the negative reviews. This might be because reviewers would say something like "I thought it would taste good" or "It didn't taste good." This shows that the dataset needs a bit more work—perhaps more stopwords—but now you have all the tools you need to do it! We'll come back to this dataset in the next chapter, when we'll use Dask's machine learning pipelines to build a sentiment classifier that will try to predict whether a review is positive or negative based on its text. In the meantime, hopefully you've come to appreciate how powerful and flexible Dask Bags are for unstructured data analysis.

Summary

- Unstructured data, such as text, doesn't lend itself well to being analyzed using DataFrames. Dask Bags are a more flexible solution and are useful for manipulating unstructured data.
- Bags are unordered and do not have any concept of an index (unlike DataFrames). To access elements of a Bag, the take method can be used.
- The map method is used to transform each element of a Bag using a user-defined function.

- The `foldby` function makes it possible to aggregate elements of a Bag before mapping a function over them. This can be used for all sorts of aggregate-type functions.
- When analyzing text data, tokenizing the text and removing stopwords helps extract the underlying meaning of the text.
- Bigrams are used to extract phrases from text that may have more meaning than their constituent words (for example, "not good" versus "not" and "good" in isolation).

Machine learning
with Dask-ML

This chapter covers

- Building machine learning models using the Dask-ML API

- Using the Dask-ML API to extend scikit-learn

- Validating models and tuning hyperparameters using cross-validated gridsearch

- Using serialization to save and publish trained models

A common admission by data scientists is that the 80/20 rule definitely applies to data science: that is, 80% of time spent on data science projects is preparing data for machine learning and the other 20% is actually building and testing the machine learning models. This book is no exception! By now, we've been through the gathering, cleaning, and exploration process for two different datasets in two different "flavors"—using DataFrames and using Bags. It's now time to move on and build some machine learning models of our own! For a point of reference, figure 10.1 shows how we're progressing through our workflow. We've almost arrived at the end!

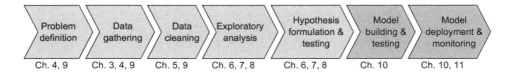

Figure 10.1   Having thoroughly covered data preparation, it's time to move on to model building.

In this chapter, we'll have a look at the last major API of Dask: Dask-ML. Just as we've seen how Dask DataFrames parallelize Pandas and Dask Arrays parallelize NumPy, Dask-ML is a parallel implementation of scikit-learn. Figure 10.2 shows the relationship between the Dask APIs and the underlying functionality they provide.

If you have prior experience with scikit-learn, you will find the API very familiar; if not, what you learn here should give you enough of an introduction to scikit-learn for you to be able to continue exploring it on your own! Dask-ML is a relatively recent addition to Dask and therefore has not had as much time to mature compared to Dask's other APIs. However, it still offers a wide variety of functionality and was designed with flexibility that allows it to solve most problems where scikit-learn would normally be used. We'll pick up where we left off in the previous chapter with the Amazon Fine Foods reviews and use the following scenario as a backdrop to exploring Dask-ML:

> *Using the Amazon Fine Foods Reviews dataset, train a sentiment classifier model with Dask-ML that can interpret whether a review is positive or negative without knowing the review score.*

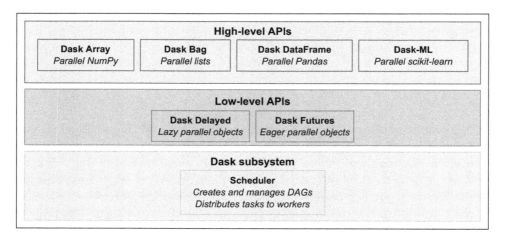

Figure 10.2   A review of the API components of Dask

10.1   Building linear models with Dask-ML

Before we jump in to model building, we'll need to take care of a few things:

1 We'll need to tag the reviews as positive or negative using the code from chapter 9.

2 Then we'll need to convert the data into a format that our machine learning model can understand.

3 Finally, we'll need to set aside a small chunk of the data to use for testing and validating the accuracy of our model.

First, the reviews need to be tagged as either positive or negative. We went through some code in chapter 9 to do that based on the review score that the reviewer provided. If the review received three stars or more, we tagged the review as positive. If the review received two stars or fewer, we tagged the review as negative. To recap, here's the code we used to do that.

Listing 10.1   Tagging the review data based on the review score

```
import dask.bag as bag
import os
from dask.diagnostics import ProgressBar

os.chdir('/Users/jesse/Documents')
raw_data = bag.read_text('foods.txt')

def get_next_part(file, start_index, span_index=0, blocksize=1024):
    file.seek(start_index)
    buffer = file.read(blocksize + span_index).decode('cp1252')
    delimiter_position = buffer.find('\n\n')
    if delimiter_position == -1:
        return get_next_part(file, start_index, span_index + blocksize)
    else:
        file.seek(start_index)
        return start_index, delimiter_position

def get_item(filename, start_index, delimiter_position, encoding='cp1252'):
    with open(filename, 'rb') as file_handle:
        file_handle.seek(start_index)
        text = file_handle.read(delimiter_position).decode(encoding)
        elements = text.strip().split('\n')
        key_value_pairs = [(element.split(': ')[0], element.split(': ')[1])
                                if len(element.split(': ')) > 1
                                else ('unknown', element)
                                for element in elements]
        return dict(key_value_pairs)

with open('foods.txt', 'rb') as file_handle:
    size = file_handle.seek(0,2) - 1
    more_data = True
    output = []
    current_position = next_position = 0
    while more_data:
```

Open the raw text file for processing.

Helper function to find the next review based on the current byte position in the file handle

Helper function to read the data and parse at a given byte position

Create a list of byte ranges for each complete review object.

```
            if current_position >= size:
                more_data = False
            else:
                current_position, next_position = get_next_part(file_handle,
        current_position, 0)
                output.append((current_position, next_position))
                current_position = current_position + next_position + 2

reviews = bag.from_sequence(output).map(lambda x: get_item('foods.txt', x[0],
    x[1]))   ◄─────────────────────────────────────┐
                                              **Turn the Bag of byte ranges
def tag_positive_negative_by_score(element):  ◄──  into a Bag of review objects.**
    if float(element['review/score']) > 3:
        element['review/sentiment'] = 'positive'   **Tag each review as
    else:                                          positive or negative
        element['review/sentiment'] = 'negative'   using the review score.**
    return element

tagged_reviews = reviews.map(tag_positive_negative_by_score)
```

10.1.1   *Preparing the data with binary vectorization*

Now that we've tagged the reviews again, we need to turn the review text into a format that the machine learning algorithm can understand. We humans can intuitively understand that if someone says a product is "great," that person likely has a positive sentiment toward the product. Computers, on the other hand, don't generally share the same grasp of language that humans do—a computer doesn't intrinsically understand what "great" means or how it translates to sentiments about a product. However, think about what was just said: if a person says a product is "great," they probably feel positively toward the product. This is a pattern we can search for in our data. Were reviews that used the word "great" more likely to be positive than reviews that didn't? If so, we could state that the presence of the word "great" in a review makes it some amount more likely to be positive. This is the whole idea behind one common way to transform text data to a machine-understandable format called *binary vectorization*. Using binary vectorization, we take a *corpus*, or a unique list of all words that show up in our review data, and generate a vector of 1s and 0s, where a 1 indicates the presence of a word and a 0 indicates the absence of a word.

In figure 10.3, you can see that the words that appear in the raw text such as "lots" and "fun" are assigned a 1 in the binary vector, whereas words that do not appear in the raw text (but appear in other text samples) are marked with a 0. Once the text has been transformed with binary vectorization, we can use any of the standard classification algorithms, such as logistic regression, to find correlations between the presence

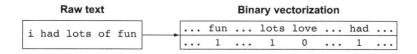

Figure 10.3   An example of binary vectorization

of words and the sentiment. This in turn will help us build a model to classify reviews as positive or negative where we don't have the actual review score. Let's take a look at how to transform our raw reviews into an array of binary vectors.

First, we'll apply some of the transformations we applied in chapter 9 to tokenize the text and remove stopwords (if this is your first time running this code, make sure you've followed the instructions in the appendix to set up NLTK correctly).

Listing 10.2 Tokenizing text and Removing stopwords

```
from nltk.corpus import stopwords
from nltk.tokenize import RegexpTokenizer
from functools import partial

tokenizer = RegexpTokenizer(r'\w+')

def extract_reviews(element):          ◄── Helper function to isolate the review text from
    element['review/tokens'] = element['review/text'].lower()    each review and change all letters to lowercase
    return element
                                       Helper function to break long strings of text into
def tokenize_reviews(element):     ◄── individual words (tokens) using the NLTK tokenizer
    element['review/tokens'] = tokenizer.tokenize(element['review/tokens'])
    return element
                                       Filter function to check if a
def filter_stopword(word, stopwords):  ◄── token is in the list of stopwords
    return word not in stopwords
                                       Helper function to drop all stopwords
def filter_stopwords(element, stopwords):  ◄── from each set of review tokens
    element['review/tokens'] = list(filter(partial(filter_stopword,
      stopwords=stopwords), element['review/tokens']))
    return element
                                       Add a few more stopwords to
                                       the base stopword collection.
stopword_set = set(stopwords.words('english'))
more_stopwords = {'br', 'amazon', 'com', 'http', 'www', 'href', 'gp'}  ◄──
all_stopwords = stopword_set.union(more_stopwords)

review_extracted_text = tagged_reviews.map(extract_reviews)   ◄──

review_tokens = review_extracted_text.map(tokenize_reviews)
review_text_clean = review_tokens.map(partial(filter_stopwords,
    stopwords=all_stopwords))
                                 Map the helper functions to the data, producing
                                 a cleaned set of tokens for each review.
```

As you've already seen the code from listing 10.2 in chapter 9, we'll move on. With the cleaned and tokenized review data, let's get a quick count of the number of unique words that show up in the reviews. To do this, we'll revisit a few built-in functions from the Bag API.

Listing 10.3   Counting the unique words in the Amazon Fine Foods review set

```
def extract_tokens(element):
    return element['review/tokens']          ◄──┐  Isolate the review tokens
                                                 │  from each review.
extracted_tokens = review_text_clean.map(extract_tokens)
unique_tokens = extracted_tokens.flatten().distinct()     ◄──────────────┐

with ProgressBar():
    number_of_tokens = unique_tokens.count().compute()    ◄──┐
number_of_tokens
                                      Count the number of unique tokens.

#Produces the following output:      Flatten the data so we have a single list of all non-
# 114290                             unique tokens, then uniqueify the list with distinct.
```

This code should look mostly familiar. The only thing noteworthy is that the extracted
tokens must be flattened to get a distinct list of all words. Because the extract_tokens
function returns a list of lists of strings, we need to use flatten to concatenate all the
inner lists before applying distinct. According to our code, 114,290 unique words
appear in our 568,454 reviews. This means the array we would produce with binary vectorization would be 568,454 rows by 114,290 columns or 64.9 billion ones and zeros. At
one byte per Boolean value, by way of NumPy's data sizes, this is ~64 GB of data. While
Dask is certainly up to the task of dealing with such large arrays, we'll scale down the
exercise a bit to make it easier to run this solution quickly. Instead of using the entire
corpus of 114,290 unique words, we'll use a corpus of the top 100 most frequently used
words in the review dataset. If you'd like to use a larger or smaller corpus, you can easily
modify the code to use the top 1,000 or top 10 words instead. You can also modify the
code to use the entire corpus if you'd like. All the code will work regardless of the size
of the corpus you select. Of course, in practice, it would be best to start with the entire
corpus—by selecting only the top 100 words, we may be leaving out some important
patterns that occur infrequently but are strong predictors of the target variable. Again,
I'm only suggesting scaling down here for the sake of a fast-running example. Let's
take a look at how to get the top 100 most common words in our corpus.

Listing 10.4   Finding the top 100 most common words in the reviews dataset

Helper function to add 1 to the counter for each
instance of a given word found in the corpus

```
def count(accumulator, element):       Helper function to combine results for
    return accumulator + 1             the same word across partitions

def combine(total_1, total_2):    ◄──  Groups the data by word and counts the
    return total_1 + total_2           occurrences using folding

with ProgressBar():    ◄──────────────
    token_counts = extracted_tokens.flatten().foldby(lambda x: x, count, 0,
      combine, 0).compute()
```

```
top_tokens = sorted(token_counts, key=lambda x: x[1], reverse=True)   ◄────
top_100_tokens = list(map(lambda x: x[0], top_tokens[:100]))
```

Slice the list of words to the first 100 records; then produce a list of the words isolated from the counts.   **Sort the results descending by count.**

Again, this code should look familiar since we've looked at a few examples of folding in the previous chapter. As before, we use the count and combine functions to count the occurrences of each word in the corpus. The result of the fold gives us a list of tuples where element 0 of each tuple is the word and element 1 of each tuple is the count of occurrences. Using Python's built-in sorted method, we sort along element 1 of each tuple (the frequency counts) to return a list of tuples sorted in descending order. Finally, we use the map function to peel the words out of the sorted tuples to return a list of the top 100 most commonly used words. Now that we have our final corpus, we can apply binary vectorization across the review tokens. We'll do this by searching each review to see if it contains the words in the corpus.

Listing 10.5   Generating training data by applying binary vectorization

Change the positive/negative sentiment tag into a binary value; 1 represents positive and 0 represents negative.   **Compare the corpus to each review's list of tokens using np.where; return 1 if the word exists in the list of tokens and 0 if not.**

```
import numpy as np
def vectorize_tokens(element):   ◄────
    vectorized_tokens = np.where(np.isin(top_100_tokens, element['review/
     tokens']), 1, 0)
    element['review/token_vector'] = vectorized_tokens
    return element

def prep_model_data(element):
    return {'target': 1 if element['review/sentiment'] == 'positive' else 0,
            'features': element['review/token_vector']}

model_data = review_text_clean.map(vectorize_tokens).map(prep_model_data)   ◄────

model_data.take(5)
                                           Map both functions on the data to
'''                                        produce a dictionary with the target and
Produces the following output:            feature vector for each review.
({'target': 1,
  'features': array([1, 1, 0, 0, 0, 0, 1, 0, 0, 0, 1, 0, 0, 0, 0, 0, 0, 0, 0,
     0, 0, 0, 0,
        0, 0, 0, 0, 1, 1, 0, 0, 0, 0, 0, 0, 0, 0, 0, 1, 0, 0, 1, 0, 0, 0, 0,
        0, 0, 0, 0, 0, 0, 0, 0, 0, 0, 0, 0, 0, 0, 0, 0, 0, 0, 0, 0, 0, 0, 0,
        0, 0, 0, 0, 0, 0, 0, 0, 0, 0, 0, 0, 0, 0, 0, 0, 0, 0, 0, 0, 0, 0, 1,
        0, 0, 0, 0, 0, 0, 0, 0])},
  ...
  {'target': 1,
  'features': array([0, 0, 0, 0, 1, 0, 0, 0, 0, 0, 0, 0, 0, 0, 0, 0, 0, 0, 0,
     0, 0, 0, 1,
        0, 0, 0, 0, 0, 0, 0, 0, 0, 0, 0, 0, 0, 0, 0, 0, 0, 0, 0, 0, 0, 0, 0,
        0, 0, 0, 0, 0, 0, 0, 0, 0, 0, 0, 0, 0, 0, 0, 0, 0, 0, 0, 0, 0, 0, 0,
```

```
      0, 0, 0, 0, 0, 0, 0, 0, 0, 0, 0, 0, 0, 0, 0, 0, 0, 0, 0, 0, 0, 0, 0,
      0, 0, 0, 0, 0, 0, 0, 0])})
```

'''

The code in listing 10.5 shows another good example of how we can mix other libraries like NumPy into Dask. Here, we use the `where` function in NumPy to compare the list of words from the corpus to the list of tokens for each review. This results in a vector of 100 ones and zeros for each review, as you can see in the sample output. We also apply binary vectorization to the sentiment tag, which is what we want to predict—also known as our *target*. The result of the code returns a Bag of dictionaries, where each dictionary object represents a review and contains its respective binarized values. We're getting very close to building our model, but one important thing stands in the way: our data is still in a Bag, and it needs to be in an Array for Dask-ML to read it. Previously, we converted data from a Bag to an Array by first converting it to a DataFrame and then using the `values` attribute of the DataFrame to directly access the underlying Array. We could do that here, but DataFrames tend to not perform very well with a large number of columns. Instead, we'll take the existing NumPy arrays that we produced in the binary vectorization step and concatenate them into one large Dask Array. Put another way, we'll *reduce* a list of arrays to a single array using concatenation. Figure 10.4 shows a visual representation of what we want to accomplish.

Effectively, we're building a Dask Array from scratch one row at a time. This is actually fairly quick and efficient, because Dask's lazy evaluation means we're largely dealing with metadata until we actually try to materialize the data in the final array. Let's take a look at how to do this in code.

Listing 10.6   Creating the feature array

Partition is an iterable object that has to be materialized before passing to dask_array.concatenate.

Extract the features element from each dictionary, convert each NumPy array to a Dask Array object, and then reduce all arrays together using concatenation.

```
from dask import array as dask_array
def stacker(partition):
    return dask_array.concatenate([element for element in partition])

with ProgressBar():
    feature_arrays = model_data.pluck('features').map(lambda x: dask_array.
     from_array(x, 1000).reshape(1,-1)).reduction(perpartition=stacker,
      aggregate=stacker)
    feature_array = feature_arrays.compute()
feature_array

#Produces the following output:
# dask.array<concatenate, shape=(568454, 100), dtype=int64, chunksize=(1,
     100)>
```

Listing 10.6 contains several new methods that we'll unpack. First is the `concatenate` function from the Dask Array API. It will concatenate, or combine, a list of Dask Arrays into a single Dask Array. Since we ultimately want to combine each of the 568,454

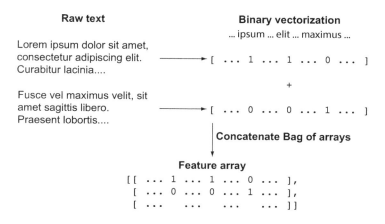

Figure 10.4 **Vectorizing the raw data into a Bag of arrays, then concatenating to a single array**

vectors into one large array, this is exactly the function we want to use. Since the data is spread out across roughly 100 partitions, we'll need to reduce each partition's list of arrays into a single array, and then combine the 100 partition-level arrays into one final large array. This can be done with the `reduction` method of Dask Array. This function works slightly differently from `map` in that the function passed to it should receive an entire partition instead of a single element. After mapping the `from_array` function to each element, each partition is essentially a lazy list of Dask Array objects. This is exactly what input `dask_array.concatenate` wants. However, the partition object passed into our `stacker` function happens to be a generator object, which `dask_array.concatenate` cannot cope with. Therefore, we have to materialize it into a list by using a list comprehension. You may think, at first, that this would be counterproductive, because materializing the partition into a list would bring the data with it. However, the partition happens to be a list of lazy Dask Array objects, so the only data that actually gets shuttled around is some metadata and the DAG tracking the computation that's occurred so far. We can see that we get the result we want because the new Array shape states it's 568,454 rows by 100 columns. The shape of the feature array can be seen in figure 10.5.

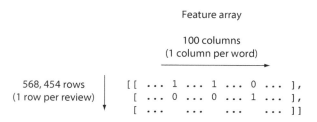

Figure 10.5 **The shape of the feature array**

Since we've done so much to the data already, now would be an opportune time to save our progress. Writing out the data before we train the model will also speed things up since the data will already be in the shape needed to build the model. The Array API contains a method to write Dask Arrays to disk using the ZARR format, which is a column-store format similar to Parquet. The specifics of the file format are irrelevant here—we're just using ZARR because the Array API makes it easy to read and write to that format. We'll quickly dump the prepared data to disk and read it back in for fast access.

Listing 10.7   Writing the data to ZARR and reading it back in

```
with ProgressBar():
    feature_array.rechunk(5000).to_zarr('sentiment_feature_array.zarr')
    feature_array = dask_array.from_zarr('sentiment_feature_array.zarr')

with ProgressBar():
    target_arrays = model_data.pluck('target').map(lambda x: dask_array.
     from_array(x, 1000).reshape(-1,1)).reduction(perpartition=stacker,
     aggregate=stacker)
    target_arrays.compute().rechunk(5000).to_zarr('sentiment_target_array.
     zarr')
    target_array = dask_array.from_zarr('sentiment_target_array.zarr')
```

Listing 10.7 is straightforward—since we've already gotten the feature array into the shape we want through the concatenating we did in listing 10.6, we just need to save it. We reuse the concatenating code on the target array data to follow the same process for the target data. The only new item worth pointing out is our decision to rechunk the data. You might have noticed after the concatenation, the array had a chunk size of (1,100). This means that each chunk contains one row and 100 columns. The ZARR format writes one file per chunk, meaning we would produce 568,454 individual files if we didn't rechunk the data. This would be extremely inefficient because of the overhead involved with getting data off a disk—this is the case regardless of if we're running Dask in local mode or on a large cluster. Typically, we'd want each chunk to be somewhere between 10 MB and 1 GB to minimize the IO overhead. I've selected a chunk size of 5,000 rows per chunk in this example, so we end up with around 100 files, similar to the 100 partitions that the raw data was broken into. We also follow the same process of converting the target variable to an array and writing it to disk. Now we're finally ready to build our model!

10.1.2   Building a logistic regression model with Dask-ML

We'll start by using an algorithm built in to Dask-ML's API: logistic regression. Logistic regression is an algorithm that can be used to predict binary (yes or no, good or bad, and so forth) outcomes. This perfectly fits our desire to build a model to predict the sentiment of a review, because sentiment is discrete: it's either positive or negative. But how can we know how good our model is at predicting sentiment? Or, put another way, how can we be sure that our model actually learned some useful patterns in the data? To do that, we'll want to set aside some reviews that the algorithm isn't allowed to look at and learn from. This is called a *holdout set* or a *test set*. If the model does a good job predicting the outcomes of the holdout set, we can be reasonably confident that the model has actually learned useful patterns that generalize to our problem well. Otherwise, if the model does not perform well on the holdout set, it's likely due to the algorithm picking up on strong patterns that are unique to the data that it was trained on. This is called *overfitting* to the training set and should be avoided. Dask-ML, like scikit-learn, has some tools to help randomly select a holdout set that we can use for validation. Let's take a look at how to split the data and build a logistic regression model.

Listing 10.8   Building the logistic regression

```
from dask_ml.linear_model import LogisticRegression
from dask_ml.model_selection import train_test_split

X = feature_array
y = target_array.flatten()

X_train, X_test, y_train, y_test = train_test_split(X, y, random_state=42)

lr = LogisticRegression()

with ProgressBar():
    lr.fit(X_train, y_train)
```

The train_test_split function divides the data into two pieces randomly; by default this is a 90/10 split, where 90% of the data is in train and 10% of the data is in test.

The fit method is not lazy, so we wrap it in a ProgressBar context to monitor execution.

In listing 10.8, now that we've done all the hard work for data prep, building the model itself is relatively easy. The `train_test_split` function will randomly split off a holdout set for us; then it's as simple as feeding the features (`X`) and targets (`y`) to the `fit` method of the `LogisticRegression` object. It's worth mentioning that we set the `random_state` parameter of the `train_test_split` function to 42, and you may be wondering why. The value of this parameter doesn't really matter—what's most important is that you set it. This ensures the data is split the same way every time the `train_test_split` function is called on the dataset. This is important when you're running and comparing many models against each other. Because of inherent variability in the data, you could, by random chance, test on a very easy or very hard-to-predict holdout set. In this case, the improvement (or worsening) of the model you'd witness wouldn't be because you did anything to affect the model. Therefore, we want to make sure the data is "randomly" split the same way every time the model is built. After a few minutes, the model will be trained and ready to make predictions. Then, it's time to score the model to see how good a job it does predicting reviews it hasn't seen before.

10.2   *Evaluating and tuning Dask-ML models*

While it may seem easy to build a model compared to all the hard work we've done preparing the data, we're hardly finished. The goal is always to produce the most accurate model possible, and you must make a number of considerations to achieve that goal. First, there's the sheer number of algorithms out there. For classification alone, there's logistic regression, support vector machines, decision trees, random forests, Bayesian models, and so on. And each of these models has several different *hyperparameters* that define things like how sensitive the algorithm is to outliers and highly influential points. With many combinations of models and parameters, how can we be sure we have the best model we can make? The answer is through methodical experimentation. If we have a way to score the accuracy of an arbitrary model, finding the best model can be done objectively and we can use automation to make the task easier. The highest scoring model is the *champion* model until a new *challenger* model comes along and beats it. Then, the challenger becomes the new champion and the cycle repeats. This champion-challenger model works quite well in practice, but we have to start somewhere. By definition, it doesn't really matter how good or bad the first champion model is—it simply serves as a baseline to compare with potential challengers. Therefore, it's perfectly fine to start with a simple model, such as logistic regression, and use all the default values.

10.2.1   *Evaluating Dask-ML models with the score method*

Once we've established a baseline, we can pit it against more sophisticated models that use different algorithms or different sets of hyperparameters. Fortunately, every scikit-learn algorithm, and by extension every Dask-ML algorithm, comes with a `score` method. The `score` method calculates a widely accepted scoring metric based on the type of algorithm. For example, classification algorithms calculate the classification accuracy score when the `score` method is called. This score represents the percent of correct classification predictions, and ranges between 0 and 1 with a higher score being more accurate. Some data scientists prefer to use other scores such as the F1 accuracy score, but the pros and cons of each scoring method are irrelevant for this exercise. You should always choose the scoring metric that best aligns to the needs of your solution, and it's a very good idea to learn about the different scoring methods out there. Since we've already trained a baseline logistic regression, let's take a look at how well it performs.

Listing 10.9   Scoring the logistic regression model

```
lr.score(X_test, y_test).compute()

#Produces the following output:
# 0.79629173556626676
```

As you can see the code to score a model is very simple. Where we passed the train versions of X and y to the `fit` method, we pass the test versions of X and y to the `score` method. In one line, this will generate predictions using the features contained in X_ test and compare the predictions to the actual values contained in y_test. Our baseline model correctly classified 79.6% of the reviews in the test set. Not a bad start! And now that we have a baseline, we can set off to try to beat it with a challenger model. As you work, keep in mind that a perfect classification score is not likely to be achievable. Our goal here isn't to find a model that's 100% perfect, but to make deliberate, measurable progress and use objective criteria to find the best model we can within the constraints of time, data quality, and so on.

10.2.2 Building a naïve Bayes classifier with Dask-ML

Let's see how our logistic regression model fares against a naïve Bayes classifier. Naïve Bayes is a commonly used algorithm in text classification because it's a simple algorithm and has reasonably good predictive power even with small datasets. There's just one problem here: there is no naïve Bayes classifier class in the Dask-ML API. However, we can still use Dask to train a naïve Bayes classifier! No, we're not going to build the algorithm from scratch. Instead, we can use one of Dask-ML's interfaces to scikit-learn called the Incremental wrapper. The Incremental wrapper allows us to use any scikit-learn algorithm with Dask so long as the algorithm implements the partial_fit interface.

> **scikit-learn and partial_fit**
>
> The partial_fit method is available on some models to allow for batch training. This allows you to effectively "update" a model with additional data rather than retraining from scratch every time your training data has been refreshed. It can also be used to train models from large datasets that can't be held in memory all at once. For example, a model could be trained by loading 1,000 rows of a DataFrame, training the model on those 1,000 rows, loading the next 1,000 rows, continuing to train, and so forth. Dask-ML uses this interface to train scikit-learn models with minimal configuration by the user.

A growing number of scikit-learn algorithms are supporting this interface because there's been a growing interest in batch learning for large datasets. The naïve Bayes algorithms fall into the group of algorithms that support batch learning, so they can easily be used with Dask to parallelize training. Let's see what this looks like.

Listing 10.10   Training a naïve Bayes classifier with the Incremental wrapper

```
from sklearn.naive_bayes import BernoulliNB          ◄──  Import a naïve Bayes
from dask_ml.wrappers import Incremental                   classifier from Scikit-learn.

nb = BernoulliNB()              Wrap the estimator in the
                                Incremental wrapper.
parallel_nb = Incremental(nb)   ◄──────────────          Call fit on the Incremental
                                                          wrapped estimator; note that
with ProgressBar():                                       the classes must be predefined.
    parallel_nb.fit(X_train, y_train, classes=[0,1])  ◄──
```

The code in listing 10.10 largely looks the same as the code in listing 10.8, except this time we've imported an algorithm from scikit-learn rather than Dask-ML. To use the algorithm with Dask, all we have to do is create the estimator object as normal, then wrap it in the Incremental wrapper. The Incremental wrapper is essentially a helper function that tells Dask about the estimator object so it can pass it off to the workers for training. Fitting the model continues as normal, with one key exception: we have to specify the valid target classes up front. Since we have only two potential outcomes in our dataset, positive and negative, which we've encoded as 1 and 0, respectively, we simply pass them in a list here. The code should take only a few seconds to run; then we can score the model to see if it beats the logistic regression.

Listing 10.11   Scoring the Incremental wrapped model

```
parallel_nb.score(X_test, y_test)

#Produces the following output: 0.78886817014389754
```

Curiously, unlike the `score` method for the Dask-ML algorithm, the `score` method for Incremental is not lazy, so we don't need a call to `compute`. It looks like the naïve Bayes model performs similar to logistic regression model, but its score is about 1% worse than the logistic regression—meaning the logistic regression is still our champion for now. We should continue trying other algorithms as potential challengers, but we will leave that for now to talk about the other element we should experiment with: hyperparameter tuning.

10.2.3   *Automatically tuning hyperparameters*

As stated previously, most algorithms have a few hyperparameters that control how the algorithm behaves. While the default values are typically selected by the algorithm's author to provide the best general performance, it's usually possible to eke out some additional accuracy gains by tuning the hyperparameters to fit the training data better. Tuning hyperparameters manually can be a highly repetitive and monotonous process, but thanks to the scikit-learn and Dask-ML APIs, we can automate a lot of that work. For example, we might want to evaluate the effect that changing a couple of the hyperparameters for logistic regression will have on the results. Using a "meta-estimator" called `GridSearchCV`, we can instruct Dask-ML to try many different combinations of hyperparameters and automatically pit the models against each other in champion-challenger fashion. It's quite easy to use, as you'll see in the next code listing.

Listing 10.12   Using `GridSearchCV` to tune hyperparameters

```
from dask_ml.model_selection import GridSearchCV

parameters = {'penalty': ['l1', 'l2'], 'C': [0.5, 1, 2]}     ◀——    Define a dictionary of
                                                                     parameters and their
lr = LogisticRegression()                                            values to try.
```

```
tuned_lr = GridSearchCV(lr, parameters)

with ProgressBar():
    tuned_lr.fit(X_train, y_train)
```

Wrap a normal estimator in the GridSearchCV wrapper along with the parameter dictionary.

The GridSearchCV object behaves like the Incremental wrapper. Just as before, we can take any algorithm, such as Dask-ML's logistic regression, and wrap it in GridSearchCV. The other element we need is a dictionary containing the parameters we want the grid search to try and the list of possible values to try. As can be seen in listing 10.12, we're having the grid search change two parameters: the penalty parameter and the C coefficient. The value associated with each parameter name is a list of the values to try.

The C coefficient and penalty parameter in logistic regression

Two important hyperparameters of a logistic regression model are the penalty type and the C coefficient. Both these hyperparameters deal with how the algorithm determines what a good fitting model for the data is. Specifically, they deal with techniques used to prevent a model from picking up on patterns that are unique to the subset of the data used for training but that are not generally found across the whole dataset.

L1 regularization, also called *lasso regression*, essentially eliminates less-important inputs from the model.

L2 regularization, also called *ridge regression*, doesn't eliminate less-important features from the model, but essentially tries to keep the model balanced by not letting any single feature affect the outcome of the model more than others.

The C coefficient is used to control how strong the regularization effect is. A lower value of C means regularization will be more aggressive, and a higher C means less regularization will be applied.

You can include any parameter in the grid search by including it in the dictionary. scikit-learn's API documentation lists all the parameters and example values for each algorithm, so you can use that as a reference for choosing parameters to tune. It's important to note that GridSearchCV is a "brute force" type algorithm—meaning it will try all combinations of parameters you pass into it. In listing 10.12, we provided two choices for the penalty parameter and three choices for the C coefficient. This means six models in total will be built, each representing a different combination of parameters. Be careful not to choose a search space that's too large, or the time it will take the grid search to complete may become prohibitively long. However, GridSearchCV scales quite well with Dask. Each model can be built on a separate worker, meaning it's not at all hard to cut down on grid search time by deploying to a cluster and/or scaling up the number of workers. Once the grid search is complete, you can see a report of what happened for each model, including its test scores and the time it took to train it. To see the results, we'll run the following code.

Listing 10.13   Seeing the results of the `GridSearchCV`

```
import pandas as pd
pd.DataFrame(tuned_lr.cv_results_)
```

The completed `GridSearchCV` object has an attribute called `cv_results_`, which is a dictionary of test metrics. It's much easier to read when displayed in a Pandas DataFrame, so we'll put it in a DataFrame and print the results. It should look like figure 10.6.

In figure 10.6 we get a whole bunch of metrics about what happened during the `GridSearchCV` process. The four columns of greatest interest are the test score columns. This shows how well each model performed on different splits of the data. Interestingly, the model with a C coefficient of `1` and a penalty of `L2` performed the best (tied with several other C coefficient combinations). These happen to be the default values for logistic regression, so in this case hyperparameter tuning didn't find a modification of the model that performed better than the baseline. If you're curious about the default values of each algorithm, they can be found in the scikit-learn documentation. The defaults generally do a good job of fitting in most cases, but it never hurts to check if hyperparameter tuning can eke out any improvement. To make our search exhaustive, we'd want to run hyperparameter tuning over each different algorithm we try as well (such as naïve Bayes). With the techniques and code snippets we covered in this section, you should be able to build an automated pipeline that will try many combinations of algorithms and hyperparameters! Another thing to keep in mind is that we can use the champion-challenger model to evaluate the value of new data and features. For example, if we increased our corpus from 100 words to 150 words, how much more accurate does the model get? With objective experimentation, we can answer all those questions and end up with the best model we can produce. However, at the moment, our original logistic regression does the best job of predicting the sentiment of a review. We should expect to be able to feed our model new reviews it hasn't seen before and, on average, correctly predict if they were positive or negative experiences with about 80% accuracy.

	params	mean_fit_time	std_fit_time	mean_score_time	std_score_time	split0_test_score	split1_test_score	split2_test_score	mean_test_score	std.
0	{'C': 0.1, 'penalty': 'l1'}	1191.207684	26.653346	1.321249	0.663898	0.785682	0.788338	0.791587	0.788535	
1	{'C': 0.1, 'penalty': 'l2'}	540.608969	10.821922	0.631223	0.099735	0.790801	0.793709	0.796981	0.793830	
2	{'C': 0.5, 'penalty': 'l1'}	1188.468648	30.724562	0.593868	0.160326	0.790291	0.793938	0.797087	0.793772	
3	{'C': 0.5, 'penalty': 'l2'}	143.983551	3.258577	0.600326	0.104046	0.790801	0.793715	0.796987	0.793834	
4	{'C': 1, 'penalty': 'l1'}	1054.391921	82.434235	0.332632	0.093776	0.790689	0.793551	0.796559	0.793600	
5	{'C': 1, 'penalty': 'l2'}	86.940994	7.386560	0.352932	0.029528	0.790801	0.793715	0.796987	0.793834	

Figure 10.6   The `GridSearchCV` results

10.3 Persisting Dask-ML models

The last thing we'll briefly touch on in this chapter is persisting a trained Dask-ML model so it can be published or deployed somewhere else. For many data science projects, the resulting model, such as our classification model, is intended to be used somewhere in an application to make predictions or recommendations. Although it can take an immense amount of computing power to produce a model, it generally takes much less power to produce predictions that can be surfaced in a user-facing application.

Many data science workflows consist of spinning up a large and powerful cluster to churn through data and produce a model, publish the model to a repository such as Amazon S3, shut down the cluster to save costs, and expose the model via inexpensive, less-powerful machines such as web servers. This makes sense, because the size of a predictive model tends to be only a few kilobytes to a few megabytes at most, compared to the terabytes or petabytes of training data that might be used to train the model. We can use a binary serialization library to help us take what we've learned from all the data—which is the resulting predictive model—and persist it to disk so it can be reused without having to rebuild from scratch the next time we want to use it.

Python has a built-in binary serialization library, called `pickle`, which allows us to take any Python object in memory and save it to disk. Deserializing that object later by reading it off disk and loading it back into memory can recreate the object faithfully to the state it was in when it was saved to disk. This also means that a Python object can be created on one machine, serialized, transmitted over the network, and deserialized and consumed by a different machine. In fact, that's how Dask sends data and tasks to different worker nodes in a cluster!

Fortunately, this process is also very easy. The only requirement is that the machine that loads the serialized object must have all the Python libraries used by that object. For example, if we serialized a Dask DataFrame, we couldn't load it on a machine that didn't have Dask installed; we would get an ImportError on trying to load the file. Other than that, it's very simple. For this example, we'll use a library called `dill`, which is a wrapper around the `pickle` library. Dill has better support for complex data structures such as JSON and nested dictionaries, whereas Python's built-in `pickle` library sometimes has issues. To write one of our models to disk is very simple. For example, here's how to write the naïve Bayes classifier to disk.

Listing 10.14   Writing the naïve Bayes classifier to disk

```
import dill
with open('naive_bayes_model.pkl', 'wb') as file:
    dill.dump(parallel_nb, file)
```

That's all there is to it. The `dump` function serializes the object you pass to it and writes it to the file handle you specify. Here we've opened a handle to a new file called naïve_bayes_model.pkl, so the data will be written into that file. Because pickle files are binary files, we need to always read and write with the b flag in the file handle to denote that the file should be opened in binary mode. To read in a model file is also very simple.

Listing 10.15   Reading the naïve Bayes classifier from disk

```
with open('naive_bayes_model.pkl', 'rb') as file:
  nb = dill.load(file)
nb.predict(np.random.randint(0, 2,(100, 100)))

#Produces the following output:
# array([0, 1, 1, 1, 1, 1, 1, 1, 1, 1, 1, 1, 1, 1, 1, 1, 1, 1, 1, 1, 1, 1, 1,
    1, 1, 1, 1, 1, 1, 1, 1, 1, 1, 1, 1, 0, 1, 1, 1, 1, 1, 1, 1, 0, 1, 1, 1,
    1, 1, 1, 1, 1, 1, 1, 1, 1, 1, 1, 1, 1, 1, 1, 1, 1, 1, 1, 1, 1, 1, 0, 1,
    1, 1, 1, 1, 1, 1, 1, 1, 1, 1, 1, 1, 1, 1, 1, 1, 1, 1, 1, 1, 0, 1, 1, 1,
    1, 1, 1, 1, 1])
```

As can be seen in listing 10.15, we simply read the file in using the load function. We don't have to have any of the data we used to train the model around—the model object is completely self-contained. To demonstrate its ability to produce predictions, we've fed in some dummy data by generating some random binary vectors. As expected, we get an array of predictions.

I hope you now have an appreciation for how easy it is to use Dask-ML once you've put in the hard work to prepare the data! In the next chapter, we'll finish our journey by exploring how to use Dask in cluster mode and how to deploy Dask on the cloud using AWS.

Summary

- Binary vectorization is used to relate the existence of a word in a chunk of text to some predictor (for example, sentiment).
- Machine learning uses statistical and mathematical methods to find patterns that relate features (inputs) to predictors (outputs).
- Data should be split into training and testing sets to avoid overfitting.
- When trying to decide which model to use, select some error metrics and use the champion-challenger approach to objectively find the best model based on your selected metrics.
- You can use GridSearchCV to automate the selection and tuning processes of your machine learning models.
- Trained machine learning models can be saved using the dill library to reuse later to generate predictions.

Scaling and deploying Dask

This chapter covers

- Creating a Dask Distributed cluster on Amazon AWS using Docker and Elastic Container Service

- Using a Jupyter Notebook server and Elastic File System to store and access data science notebooks and shared datasets in Amazon AWS

- Using the Distributed client object to submit jobs to a Dask cluster

- Monitoring execution of jobs on the cluster using the Distributed monitoring dashboard

Up to this point, we've been working with Dask in *local mode*. This means that everything we've asked Dask to do has all been executed on a single computer. Running Dask in local mode is very useful for prototyping, development, and ad-hoc exploration, but we can still quickly reach the performance limits of a single computer. Just as our hypothetical chef in chapter 1 needed to call in reinforcements to get her kitchen prepped in time for dinner service, we too can configure Dask to spread the work out across many computers to process large jobs more quickly. This becomes especially important in production systems when time constraints apply. Therefore, it's typical to scale out and run Dask in *cluster mode* in production.

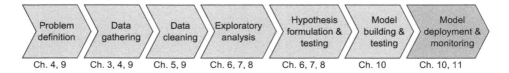

Figure 11.1   This chapter will cover the last elements of the workflow: deployment and monitoring.

Figure 11.1 shows that we've arrived at the final part of our workflow: deployment and monitoring. Although it's always good to be planning ahead when designing a solution, it's quite rare for the final version to closely represent how it was originally envisioned. This is why deployment and monitoring have been put last in our workflow. Once you have a good idea of what data is necessary to solve a problem, the volume of that data, and how quickly you or your applications must provide an answer to the problem, you can begin to plan out what resources will be needed to host your final solution. These considerations are typically settled during prototyping of the solution. Fortunately, Dask is intended to make the transition from a prototype on a laptop to a full-scale application on a cluster as seamless as possible. In fact, whether the scheduler is running in local mode or cluster mode is transparent to everything else. This means that any Dask code you write—and by association all the code we've covered in the past 10 chapters—will run both on your laptop and on any size cluster without modifications.

That said, it's still worth seeing firsthand how to set up, maintain, and monitor a Dask cluster. In this chapter, we'll walk through how to set up a cluster using Amazon AWS that you can use as a private sandbox. AWS was chosen for this exercise because it is a very popular cloud computing platform with a supportive community, lots of learning resources, and a generous account tier that allows you to experiment with AWS free of charge. Dask is just as suited to run on other cloud computing platforms such as Microsoft Azure or Google Cloud Platform, and, of course, can also be run on private server farms. While this exercise will also provide some good hands-on experience with elements of AWS and Docker, the focus will primarily be on Dask. We'll cover only the essentials of AWS and Docker that you need to know to get the cluster up and running. We'll also look at a few general troubleshooting steps you can take if you run into issues with AWS and Docker. However, they are both vast subjects in their own right, and it wouldn't be useful to cover them in depth here.

11.1   *Building a Dask cluster on Amazon AWS with Docker*

Before we get started, we'll cover some basic terminology and have a look at the architecture we're going to be creating in AWS.

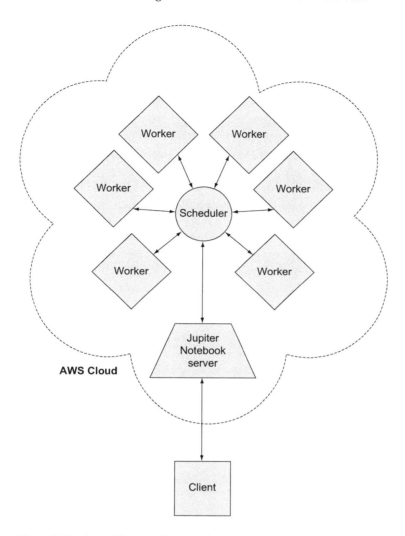

Figure 11.2   An architecture diagram of our Dask Distributed cluster

As you can see in figure 11.2, the system has four distinct elements: the client, the notebook server, the scheduler, and the workers. The four elements each serve different roles:

- *Scheduler*—Receives jobs from the client by way of the notebook server, divides up the work to be done, and coordinates the workers to complete the job
- *Worker*—Receives tasks from the scheduler and computes them
- *Jupyter Notebook server*—Provides a frontend to allow the user to run code and submit jobs to the cluster
- *Client*—Displays the results to the user

11.1.1 *Getting started*

In local mode, all elements run on the same computer, and the number of workers corresponds with the number of CPU cores by default. In cluster mode, we'll configure each of the elements to run on a separate computer. We'll also gain the freedom to increase or decrease the number of workers on the fly, which gives us the flexibility to scale the cluster as needed. But, since all these elements will reside on different computers, we must consider a few new things: the data must be in a shared place that can be accessed by all the workers, and all the workers must have the right Python packages installed. The first consideration is straightforward—we'll set up a shared filesystem that each of the workers can access, and then put the data there. The second consideration has, historically, been a bit trickier to handle. For instance, if we want to run the code from chapter 9 that filters out all of the stopwords using NLTK (Natural Language Toolkit) on a cluster, we have to make sure that every worker in the cluster has NLTK installed and also has the stopword data downloaded. This might not be a problem to do manually if we have a handful of workers in the cluster, but if we needed to scale the cluster to 10,000 workers, it would take a very long time to configure the workers one at a time. This is where Docker becomes incredibly useful. Docker essentially allows us to create a blueprint, called an *image*, that contains data and instructions to build an identical copy of a system. The image can be launched inside a *container* and becomes a fully functional self-contained system, much like a virtual machine. This image can be deployed to Amazon Elastic Container Service (ECS) to launch many hundreds or thousands of workers, all with the same identical configuration and software, at the press of a button. Later in the chapter, we'll build a Docker image that contains all the software we need to run the Dask worker alongside all the necessary Python packages. We'll also do the same for the scheduler and the notebook server. Our overall objective for this section is encompassed in this scenario:

> *Set up an Amazon AWS environment with eight Elastic Container Service instances and deploy a Dask cluster using the prebuilt Dask Docker images.*

To follow along with the examples, you will need to download and install the latest copy of Docker on your machine from www.docker.com/get-started. This will allow you to build the images that we will deploy to Amazon ECS. You will also need to create an AWS account by following the instructions at https://aws.amazon.com/free. Please note that this exercise was designed to stay within the limits of the AWS free tier; however, Amazon requires you to provide payment information up front to activate your account, and you must follow the cleanup instructions at the end of the exercise to avoid account charges. In the event you do exceed the limits of AWS Free Tier, the resources we're using are very inexpensive, so the costs you would incur are minimal. You'll also need an SSH client. If you're using macOS or a Unix/Linux-based OS, an SSH client should be preinstalled on your system. However, if you're running Windows, you will need to download an SSH client such as PuTTY (https://docs.aws.amazon .com/AWSEC2/latest/UserGuide/putty.html). Finally, install the AWS Command

Line Interface (CLI) tools by following the directions at https://aws.amazon.com/cli. Once you're finished getting set up, we'll follow a seven-step process to set up the cluster:

1 Create a security key.
2 Create the ECS cluster.
3 Configure the cluster's networking.
4 Create a shared data drive in Elastic File System (EFS).
5 Allocate space for Docker images in Elastic Container Repository (ECR).
6 Build and deploy the images for the scheduler, worker, and notebook server.
7 Connect to the cluster.

11.1.2 Creating a security key

To start, log in to the AWS console. You should be greeted by a screen that looks similar to figure 11.3.

Figure 11.3   The AWS Console home screen

The first thing we need to do is create a security key that we will use later to authenticate with AWS while deploying the Docker images. To do this, hover over your account name in the top-right corner next to the bell icon, as shown in figure 11.4.

Click My Security Credentials, and you will be brought to the Your Security Credentials page. If you receive a warning message popup, such as in figure 11.5, choose Continue to Security Credentials.

Figure 11.4   Account control menu

Figure 11.5   Security warning message

Click the Access Keys drop-down area. If you have any existing keys, you can select Delete to remove them. Then, click Create New Access Key. You should see a dialog box similar to figure 11.6 with your new access key and secret access key (the keys in figure 11.6 have been masked for security—you will see your actual generated keys in the dialog box on your screen). Click Download Key File to download a CSV file containing these two values. You can take a screenshot if you'd like, because we will use these keys later. It's important that you keep track of your secret access key and also keep it safe. It can't be recovered if you lose it (you'd have to create a new key), and it could be used to compromise your AWS account if it got into the wrong hands. Treat it like a password or a credit card number.

Now that you've created a security key, the next step in the process is to create the ECS cluster.

Figure 11.6   Create Access Key dialog box

11.1.3 *Creating the ECS cluster*

When working in the cloud, it's typical to talk about "compute resources" rather than physical computers. This is because when servers are requisitioned in the cloud, they are rarely dedicated physical machines solely for your personal use. Instead, they are virtual machines, called *instances*, that run on huge clusters of servers shared by many other cloud customers. For all intents and purposes, though, they appear to be separate physical machines. Each instance gets its own separate IP address, filesystem space, and so on. In AWS, compute resources are requisitioned through Elastic Compute Cloud (EC2)—this service allows you to create and tear down virtual servers that can be used to host anything you want. ECS allows you to run Docker images in containers on EC2 instances. Again, this is beneficial for us because we won't have to log in to each EC2 instance and configure it manually. We can simply use the EC2 instances to run copies of the preconfigured Docker images we'll build later in the chapter.

Since so many users have embraced the ease of using Docker for cloud deployments, Amazon has streamlined the process to requisition EC2 instances and configure them for Docker into a setup wizard. We'll step through that wizard in a moment. First, we need to create an SSH key that we will associate to the EC2 instances. This will allow you to log in to the EC2 instances using SSH, which we will need to do later in the process. To start, roll over the Services menu in the AWS Console, and under the Compute section, choose EC2. Figure 11.7 shows the area of the menu where you can find the link to EC2.

Once you arrive at the EC2 dashboard, click the area similar to figure 11.8 where it says 0 Key Pairs.

Next, click the Create Key Pair button, as shown in figure 11.9.

When prompted to give the key pair a name, type `dask-cluster-key` and click Create. This will create the key pair and download a copy of it to your Downloads folder. It should be named dask-cluster-key.pem.txt. Rename it to dask-cluster-key.pem and put it somewhere safe. This is also a private key file; you should protect it because it can be used to access your EC2 instances.

Now that we've created the key pair, we can create the ECS cluster. Go back to the Services menu in the top-left of the AWS Console and select ECS under the Compute menu. Once greeted by the welcome screen for ECS, click the Clusters menu option under the Amazon ECS menu on the left edge of the screen. You should now see a screen that looks similar to figure 11.10.

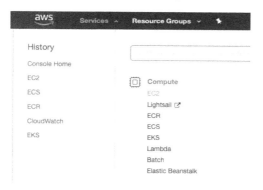

Figure 11.7   Navigate to the EC2 dashboard.

Figure 11.8   Navigating to the Key Pair view

Figure 11.9   Select Create Key Pair.

Figure 11.10   The Amazon ECS cluster management screen

Click the blue Create Cluster button in the upper-left area of the screen. This will start the ECS Create Cluster wizard. When prompted to select a cluster template, select EC2 Linux + Networking, as shown in figure 11.11.

Click Next Step to advance to the Configure Cluster screen. Enter a name for your cluster in the Cluster Name box, such as `dask-cluster`. The name cannot have any spaces, capital letters, or special characters other than hyphens. Select the t2.micro instance type in the EC2 Instance Type drop-down box. This is the Instance type that's eligible for the AWS Free Tier. Finally, enter 8 in the Number of Instances box and select the key pair you created earlier in the Key pair drop-down box. The rest of the options can be left to their default values. Verify your configuration looks similar to figure 11.12 before proceeding.

Once you've verified the configuration, click the Finish button at the bottom of the screen to create the cluster. If everything was entered successfully, you will see the Launch Status screen. This screen displays the progress while the cluster is requisitioned and built. Once the blue View Cluster button lights up, the cluster is finished being built. Click Clusters on the menu on the left side of the screen. This will bring you back to the Clusters screen, where you should see your newly built cluster. Your screen should look similar to figure 11.13.

Figure 11.11   ECS Create Cluster wizard step 1

Figure 11.12 Cluster configuration settings

Figure 11.13 Cluster status window showing the newly built cluster

The most important thing to note on this screen is the number of Container Instances on the far right-hand side of the screen. This shows you how many EC2 instances are currently running and joined to the cluster. Since we requisitioned eight EC2 instances, you should see eight container instances available. If you don't see eight container instances, wait a few minutes and refresh the page. Occasionally it will take several minutes for the EC2 instances to completely boot up and connect to the cluster.

11.1.4 *Configuring the cluster's networking*

Now that the cluster is up and running, we need to configure the cluster's firewall rules to allow us to connect to it. To do this, we'll need to go back to the EC2 Dashboard. Click the Services menu and select EC2 under the Compute section. Once on the EC2 Dashboard, select Security Groups from the menu on the left edge of the screen under the Network & Security heading, as shown in figure 11.14.

Figure 11.14   EC2 Dashboard menu showing Security Groups configuration

On the Security Groups page, locate the security group that corresponds with the cluster you just created. The group name should be something similar to EC2Container-Service-<cluster name>-EcsSecurityGroup-xxxxxxxx. Click the check box to the left of the security group to select it. Figure 11.15 shows an example of the security groups.

On the lower half of the screen, select the Inbound tab and click the Edit button. An example of this is shown in figure 11.16.

First, create a rule to allow inbound SSH connections from your IP address. This will allow you to log in to the EC2 instances that are part of the cluster. Under the Type column, choose SSH, and under the Source column, choose My IP. You can also type in an optional description for the firewall rule. Figure 11.17 shows an example of this configuration (note: your IP address will be different from the IP address listed in the figures).

Figure 11.15   An example security group for the ECS cluster

Figure 11.16   Inbound firewall rules

Figure 11.17 Example SSH firewall rule

The next rule to configure is to allow all the EC2 instances to talk to each other. For example, the Dask scheduler needs to be able to talk to the workers to hand out instructions. Click Add Rule again, select All TCP from the Type column, and choose Custom from the Source column. Next to the drop-down box where you selected Custom, start typing EC2 (with capital letters). A drop-down will appear with the security groups listed, as shown in figure 11.18.

From the drop-down list, choose the ECS cluster security group. Lastly, we need to open ports for the Jupyter Notebook server as well as the Dask diagnostics pages. Figure 11.19 shows the relevant configurations for the two additional rules to be created.

To create the inbound rule for the Jupyter Notebook server, click Add Rule, select Custom TCP Rule from the Type column, type `8888` into the Port Range column, and select My IP from the Source column. Then, create an identical rule for the Dask diagnostic ports. Instead of port 8888, type `8787 - 8789` into the Port Range column. Once all rules have been created, click the Save button.

Figure 11.18 Creating an inbound rule from a security group

Figure 11.19 Firewall rules for Jupyter and Dask diagnostics

Now that the rules have been saved, it's a good idea to test them to make sure everything is working as expected. To do this, we first need to look up the IP address or hostname of one of your running EC2 instances. From the EC2 Dashboard, click Instances on the left menu under the Instances heading. This will bring you to the EC2 Instances Manager. On the screen, you should see a list of all currently running EC2 instances. This should look similar to figure 11.20.

In the Public DNS (IPv4) column, copy one of the hostnames. It doesn't matter which one you select.

CONNECTING USING SSH ON MACOS/LINUX/UNIX

To connect to the EC2 instance, use the following directions based on the operating system you're using:

1   Open a Terminal window and navigate to the folder where you stored the dask-cluster-key.pem file.
2   If this is your first time connecting, make the PEM file read-only by typing `chmod 400 dask-cluster-key.pem`; otherwise, your SSH client may not allow you to use the key file to connect.
3   To connect, type `ssh -i dask-cluster-key.pem ec2-user@<hostname>`; fill the hostname you copied from the EC2 Instance Manager into <hostname> space.
4   If you are prompted to add a key fingerprint, type `yes`.
5   If your connection is successful, you should see a login screen similar to figure 11.21.
6   If your connection was unsuccessful, double-check that the SSH command was typed correctly. If connection problems persist, double-check the firewall rules to ensure the correct ports are open.

CONNECTING USING SSH ON WINDOWS

Windows does not have a built-in SSH client, unlike MacOS/Linux/Unix systems. Amazon recommends using a free SSH client called PuTTY to connect to EC2. You can find instructions for downloading and installing PuTTY and using it to connect to your EC2 instance at https://docs.aws.amazon.com/AWSEC2/latest/UserGuide/putty.html.

After you've connected successfully to your EC2 instance, you can go ahead and disconnect for now. You'll reconnect at the end of the next section to upload some data to the shared file system we're about to create. On that note, don't bother keeping the

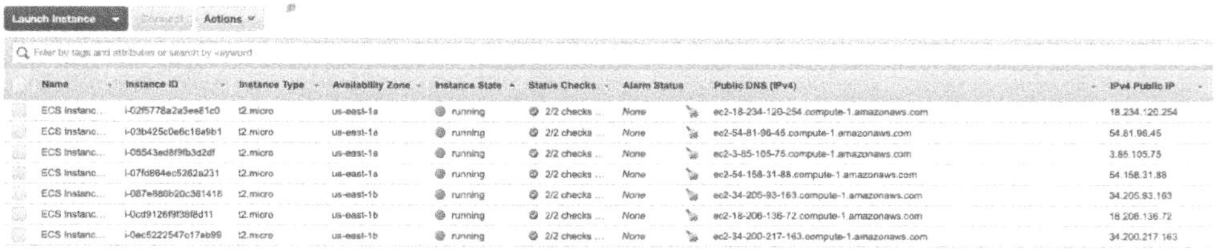

Figure 11.20   A list of all running EC2 instances

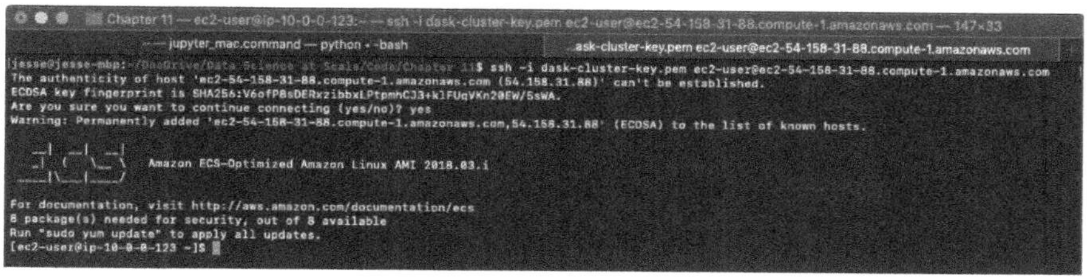

Figure 11.21   Successful connection to an EC2 instance

host name or IP address of your EC2 instance copied down anywhere. EC2 instances are *ephemeral*, meaning characteristics like their IP address and filesystem contents are only around for the life of the instance. When EC2 instances are terminated, they release their IP address allocations, and it's unlikely the instance will receive the same IP address when it's started back up. Generally, any time you need to connect to an EC2 instance, you should use the EC2 Instance Manager to look up its current IP address. Similarly, don't store any data you want long-term access to on an EC2 instance. Instead, put data that you want to be persistent on a persistent filesystem, such as the Elastic File System share that we will create in the next section.

11.1.5   Creating a shared data drive in Elastic File System

Before leaving the EC2 Instance Manager, you'll need to get the VPC ID from one of the EC2 instances. The VPC ID is used by EC2 to identify cloud resources that are part of your account. To get this value, select one of the instances in the EC2 Instance Manager and look at the lower half of the window for the VPC ID value. You should find this value below the Private IP value, as shown in figure 11.22.

Copy this value, then click the Services menu on the top-left corner of the screen. Choose EFS under the Storage heading. You'll be taken to a welcome screen for Amazon EFS. Click the blue Create File System button to start the EFS creation wizard. In the first step, select the VPC ID from the VPC drop-down box that matches the VPC ID you copied down from the EC2 instance. Under the Create Mount Targets section, leave the default

Figure 11.22   VPC ID in EC2 Instance Manager

values for the Subnet column. However, clear the Security Groups boxes. Then, start typing EC2 (with uppercase letters) and select the security group ID for the ECS cluster (it should look similar to EC2ContainerService-<cluster name>-EcsSecurityGroup-xxxxxxxxx). Your screen should look similar to figure 11.23.

Configure file system access

An Amazon EFS file system is accessed by EC2 instances running inside one of your VPCs. Instances connect to a file system by using a network interface called a mount target. Each mount target has an IP address, which we assign automatically or you can specify.

VPC   vpc-0a2df8e3dfc8fe3e4 ▾ ⓘ

Create mount targets

Instances connect to a file system by using mount targets you create. We recommend creating a mount target in each of your VPC's Availability Zones so that EC2 instances across your VPC can access the file system.

Availability Zone	Subnet	ⓘ	IP address	ⓘ	Security groups	ⓘ
✓ us-east-1a	subnet-0e05c14b916a3e8e6 ▾		Automatic ✎		sg-0a6779447dfbc9b22 - EC2ContainerService-dask-cluster-EcsSecurityGroup-19IMGAMH6D7RF ✕	
✓ us-east-1b	subnet-041fe56385013b421 ▾		Automatic ✎		sg-0a6779447dfbc9b22 - EC2ContainerService-dask-cluster-EcsSecurityGroup-19IMGAMH6D7RF ✕	

Figure 11.23   File system access configuration in EFS

Click the Next Step button. Accept the default values for step 2 and click the Next Step button again. Finally, on the review screen, click Create File System to finish. In a few minutes, you should see that the filesystem has been successfully created. Before moving away from the page, copy the DNS name of the filesystem we just created. This value is displayed under the File System Access header, as shown in figure 11.24.

Now that the filesystem is created, we need to tell the EC2 instances to mount the filesystem at boot time so you can use it for storage. To do this, navigate back to the EC2 Dashboard. On the left side menu, click Launch Configurations under the Auto Scaling heading. The Launch Configurations Manager should display and look similar to figure 11.25.

Select the launch configuration (there should only be one), click the Actions button, and select Copy Launch Configuration. The Copy Launch Configuration wizard will appear. At the top edge of the screen, click 3. Configure Details, and expand the Advanced Details section. Your screen should look similar to figure 11.26.

Give your new launch configuration a unique name in the Name field. Also, be sure ecsInstanceRole is selected in the IAM Role drop-down box. Otherwise, the EC2 instances will not be able to communicate with ECS after rebooting. In the User Data field, copy the contents of listing 11.1 into the text box.

File system access

DNS name   fs-56e07db7.efs.us-east-1.amazonaws.com ❓

Figure 11.24   DNS name of EFS

Figure 11.25   The Launch Configurations Manager

Figure 11.26 Launch configuration details

Listing 11.1 User data for launch configuration

```
Content-Type: multipart/mixed; boundary="==BOUNDARY=="
MIME-Version: 1.0

--==BOUNDARY==
Content-Type: text/cloud-boothook; charset="us-ascii"

# Install nfs-utils
cloud-init-per once yum_update yum update -y
cloud-init-per once install_nfs_utils yum install -y nfs-utils

# Create /efs folder
cloud-init-per once mkdir_efs mkdir /efs

# Mount /efs
cloud-init-per once mount_efs echo -e '<your filesystem DNS name>:/ /efs nfs4
    nfsvers=4.1,rsize=1048576,wsize=1048576,hard,timeo=600,retrans=2 0 0' >>
    /etc/fstab
mount -a

--==BOUNDARY==
Content-Type: text/x-shellscript; charset="us-ascii"
```

```
#!/bin/bash
echo ECS_CLUSTER=<your ecs cluster name> >> /etc/ecs/ecs.config
echo ECS_BACKEND_HOST= >> /etc/ecs/ecs.config
--==BOUNDARY==--
```

Fill in the filesystem DNS name you copied from the EFS confirmation screen where <your filesystem DNS name> appears, and fill in your ECS cluster name where <your ecs cluster name> appears (it should be dask-cluster unless you selected a different name). This data essentially tells the EC2 instances to configure themselves to mount the EFS filesystem you created earlier in the section at boot time. Once you've finished adding the User Data to the configuration, click Skip to Review, and then click Create Launch Configuration. When prompted to select a key pair, select the dask-cluster-key you previously generated. Check the check box and click Create Launch Configuration. Figure 11.27 displays this dialog box.

After the launch configuration has been created, click the Close button. Then, on the left-side menu, click Auto Scaling Groups under the Auto Scaling heading. We'll now need to configure the EC2 instances to use the new launch configuration. Select the auto scaling group that was created automatically when the ECS cluster was created (there should only be one), and click the Edit button. Your Auto Scaling Group Manager screen should look similar to figure 11.28.

In the Edit Details dialog box, change the Launch Configuration drop-down to the launch configuration you just created. Your screen should look similar to figure 11.29. This configuration is very important—it controls how many EC2 instances are part of the ECS cluster. We should have a number of instances equal to the number of workers we want in the Dask cluster, plus an additional instance to host the scheduler and one more instance to host the notebook server. With eight instances in the cluster, we'll be able to have six workers, a scheduler, and a notebook server. If you wanted 100 workers instead, we'd need 102 instances. Once you've completed configuring the Auto Scaling Group, click the Save button.

Because launch configurations are only run when an EC2 instance starts up, we'll need to terminate and relaunch the currently running EC2 instances for our configuration

Figure 11.27   Confirmation of key pairs

Figure 11.28   Auto Scaling Group Manager

Edit details - EC2ContainerService-dask-cluster-EcsInstanceAsg-   ×

1I91ZUNDAHBD8

Launch Instances Using ⓘ	○ Launch Template	
	◉ Launch Configuration	
Launch Configuration ⓘ	EC2ContainerService-dask-cluster-ECS-EFS2 ×	
Desired Capacity ⓘ	8	
Min ⓘ	0	
Max ⓘ	8	

Figure 11.29 Auto Scaling Group configuration

changes to take effect. To do this, navigate back to the EC2 Instances Manager. Then, select all the instances that are currently in the Running state, click the Actions button, select Instance State, then select Terminate. Your screen should look similar to figure 11.30.

When prompted if you're sure you want to terminate the instances, click Yes, Terminate. In a few seconds, you should see the instances change from the green Running to the amber Shutting Down state, and eventually the red Terminated state. After about 5–10 minutes, you should see eight new EC2 instances start up and change to the green Running state. After the instances have restarted, navigate back to the ECS Dashboard and ensure your ECS cluster now shows eight connected ECS container instances. If you see zero connected ECS container instances and have waited at least 15 minutes, double-check your launch configuration for an incorrect configuration. Be especially mindful that the IAM role must be set to ecsContainerInstance to avoid permissions issues that prevent the instances from associating with the cluster!

Once the EC2 instances have successfully rebooted, we now need to test the connection between the EC2 instances and EFS by uploading some data. To do this, navigate back to the EC2 Instances Manager, and copy the hostname or IP address of a running EC2 instance. Then, locate the arrays.tar file in the chapter 11 files. Open a Terminal window and type `scp -i dask-cluster-key.pem arrays.tar ec2-user@`**`<hostname>`**`:/home/ec2-user`. Fill in the name of your EC2 instance where <hostname> appears. This uses the SCP application to upload the arrays.tar file to the home directory on your EC2 instance. Your screen should look similar to figure 11.31.

Figure 11.30 Cycling out EC2 instances to apply new launch configurations

```
jesse@jesse-mbp:~/OneDrive/Data Science at Scale/Code/Chapter 11$ scp -i dask-cluster-key.pem arrays.tar ec2-user@ec2-54-204-192-32.compu
te-1.amazonaws.com:/home/ec2-user
arrays.tar                                                             100%   16MB  16.4MB/s   00:01
jesse@jesse-mbp:~/OneDrive/Data Science at Scale/Code/Chapter 11$
```

Figure 11.31 Using SCP to upload the data

After the data upload is complete, use SSH to connect to the EC2 instance. Once you've logged in to the EC2 instance, type `tar -xvf arrays.tar` to extract the data from the TAR file. Your screen should look similar to figure 11.32.

Next, type `rm arrays.tar` to delete the TAR file, then `sudo mv * /efs` to move the extracted data to the EFS volume you created. Verify the data has moved by typing `cd /efs`, then `ls`. You should see the two ZARR files displayed. Finally, verify that the data is accessible to all the other EC2 instances. To do this, go back to the EC2 Instance Manager, copy the hostname of a different running EC2 instance, connect to it using SSH, type `cd /efs`, then `ls`, and verify you can still see the two ZARR files. Whenever you need to store additional data that can be accessed by all your EC2 instances, you can follow the same pattern of uploading the data to one instance and moving it to the /efs folder.

11.1.6 Allocating space for Docker images in Elastic Container Repository

By this point, we're almost finished with building out the infrastructure for our cluster. The very last thing we need to do before we can deploy and launch our Dask cluster is allocate some space for the Docker images we're going to build in the next section. This will let us upload the complete images and launch them inside ECS containers. First, go back to the ECS Dashboard and click Repositories on the left menu. This will bring you to the Elastic Container Repository (ECR) Manager page. Click the Create Repository button in the upper-right corner of the screen to start the Create Repository wizard. We'll create a repository for the scheduler first. In the empty Name field, type `dask-scheduler`. Your screen should look like figure 11.33.

Click Create Repository. Once you've been returned to the ECR Manager page, repeat the process twice more. Create two repositories called dask-worker and dask-notebook. Once you've completed creating the repositories, we'll now build and deploy the images to the cluster.

11.1.7 Building and deploying images for scheduler, worker, and notebook

We'll start with building and deploying the scheduler image because the worker and notebook images need to be configured to point to the IP address of the scheduler for the cluster to work. Before we begin, ensure Docker is installed and currently running on your local machine. Also, ensure your AWS CLI is configured correctly using the security key you created in section 11.1.1. You can find instructions on configuring AWS CLI at https://docs.aws.amazon.com/cli/latest/userguide/cli-chap-configure.html.

Once you've verified everything has been configured, locate the scheduler folder in the chapter 11 files, and navigate to it in a Terminal window (or PowerShell if you're running Windows). In the ECR Manager page, select the repository for dask-scheduler and click the View Push Commands button. A pop-up will display similar to figure 11.34.

Figure 11.32   Extracting the uploaded data

Copy and run the commands from this dialog box, one after the other, in your Terminal or PowerShell window. You should see something similar to figure 11.35 while the build process runs. It may take several minutes to complete depending on the speed of your computer and internet connection.

ECR > Repositories > Create repository

Create repository

Repository configuration

Repository name

484113097927.dkr.ecr.us-east-1.amazonaws.com/ | dask-scheduler

A namespace can be included with your repository name (e.g. namespace/repo-name)

Cancel   **Create repository**

Figure 11.33   Creating an ECR repository

Push commands for dask-scheduler   ✕

macOS / Linux   Windows

Ensure you have installed the latest version of the AWS CLI and Docker. For more information, see the ECR documentation [↗].

1. Retrieve the login command to use to authenticate your Docker client to your registry.
   Use the AWS CLI:

   $(aws ecr get-login --no-include-email --region us-east-1)   ⎘

   Note: If you receive an "Unknown options: --no-include-email" error when using the AWS CLI, ensure that you have the latest version installed. Learn more [↗]

2. Build your Docker image using the following command. For information on building a Docker file from scratch see the instructions here [↗]. You can skip this step if your image is already built:

   docker build -t dask-scheduler .   ⎘

3. After the build completes, tag your image so you can push the image to this repository:

   docker tag dask-scheduler:latest 484113097927.dkr.ecr.us-east-1.amazonaws.com/dask-sche⎘l

4. Run the following command to push this image to your newly created AWS repository:

   docker push 484113097927.dkr.ecr.us-east-1.amazonaws.com/dask-scheduler:latest   ⎘

Close

Figure 11.34   Docker push commands for dask-scheduler

Figure 11.35   Building the dask-scheduler image

After the build completes, you can verify that the image was uploaded by clicking on the dask-scheduler repository. You should see a page similar to figure 11.36.

Now that the image has been uploaded to ECR, we need to tell ECS how to launch it in a container. This is done by creating an ECS task definition. Before we leave the ECR Manager page, copy the value in the Image URI column for the dask-scheduler image. We'll need this value in just a moment.

To create a task definition for the scheduler image, click Task Definitions on the left menu of the ECR Manager page. You will be brought to the ECS Task Definitions Manager page. Click the blue Create a New Task Definition button to start the Create Task Definition wizard. On the first page, select EC2 as the launch type, as shown in figure 11.37.

Click Next Step. On the next page, type `dask-scheduler` in the Task Definition Name field. Change the Network Mode drop-down to Host. Your screen should look similar to figure 11.38.

Leave the other settings as their defaults. Scroll down until you see the Volumes heading, and click Add Volume. You'll see a dialog box appear to add a volume. Type `efs-data` in the Name field and `/efs` in the Source Path field. Your screen should look like figure 11.39.

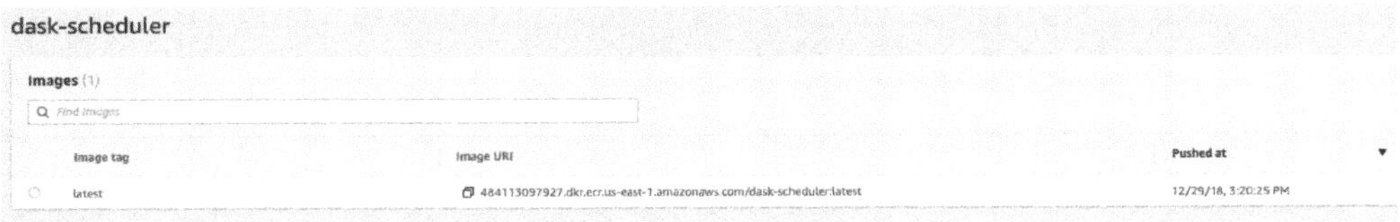

Figure 11.36   Verifying the image exists in ECR

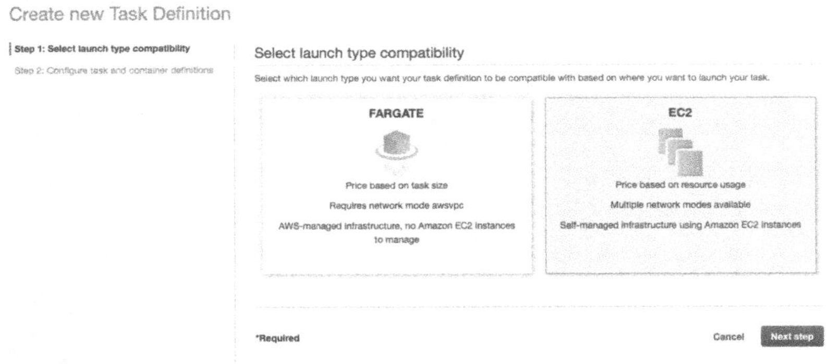

Figure 11.37   Selecting a launch type compatibility for the scheduler image

Configure task and container definitions

A task definition specifies which containers are included in your task and how they interact with each other. You can also specify data volumes for your containers to use. Learn more

Task Definition Name* dask-scheduler   ❶

Requires Compatibilities* EC2

Task Role   *Select a role...*   ▼   ⟳
            Optional IAM role that tasks can use to make API
            requests to authorized AWS services. Create an
            Amazon Elastic Container Service Task Role in the
            IAM Console ☐

Network Mode   <default>   ▼   ❶
            If you choose <default>, ECS will start your
            container using Docker's default networking mode,
            which is Bridge on Linux and NAT on Windows.
            <default> is the only supported mode on Windows.

Figure 11.38   Task definition configuration

Add volume   ✕

            Name   efs-data   ❶
                   Specify a volume driver

Source path   /efs   ❶

*Required   Cancel   **Add**

Figure 11.39   Volume configuration

Click the Add button to return to the task definition configuration page. Next, click the Add Container button under the Container Definitions heading. In the Container Name field, type `dask-scheduler`. Then, paste the image URI you copied from the ECR Manager page into the Image text box. Next, change the Memory Limits to a Soft limit of 700 MiB. Finally, add host and container port mappings for TCP port 8786 and 8787. Your screen should look similar to figure 11.40.

Figure 11.40   Container configurations for dask-scheduler

Scroll down to the Storage and Logging section and configure the Mount Points to match figure 11.41.

Check the box labeled Auto-configure CloudWatch Logs and leave the default settings. Your screen should look similar to figure 11.42.

Finally, click Add to finish adding the container to the task definition. Your screen should now look similar to figure 11.43.

Click Create to finish creating the task definition and observe that the task definition was created successfully. We now have a template that we can use to launch copies of our dask-scheduler image! Now all we have to do is launch it. To do this, we have to create an ECS *service* that binds to the task definition. First, navigate back to the ECS Task Definitions Manager page. Then, select the check box next to the dask-scheduler task definition, click the Actions button, and select Create Service. This will launch the Create Service wizard.

First, select EC2 for the Launch type. Next, type `dask-scheduler` into the Service Name field. Then, type `1` into the Number of Tasks field and select One Task Per Host from the Placement Templates drop-down. Your screen should look like figure 11.44.

Click the Next step button. On the next page, uncheck the check box next to Enable Service Discovery Integration. Leave the other settings as default. Click Next Step. Leave the settings as default and click Next Step. Finally, at the review screen, click Create Service. You will be taken to the Launch Status screen. Click the View Service button to be taken to the cluster status screen. Your screen should now look similar to figure 11.45.

Figure 11.41   Mount point configuration

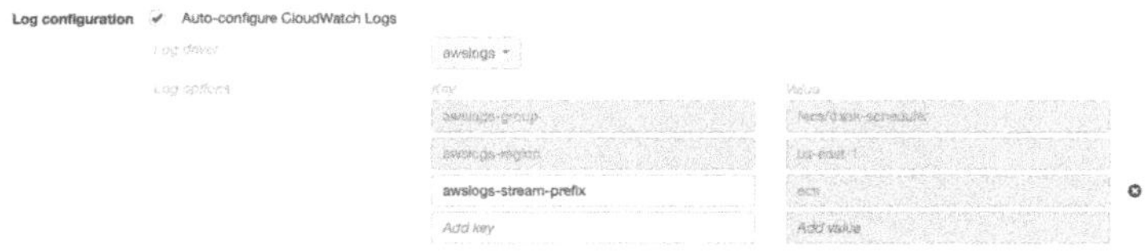

Figure 11.42   Logging settings

Figure 11.43   Complete container configuration

Figure 11.44   Service configuration for dask-scheduler

Figure 11.45   Status of dask-cluster

To get more information about the dask-scheduler service, click on the blue dask-scheduler link. This will bring you to the service status page. After a few minutes, you should notice that you have one running task, similar to figure 11.46.

If the service is sitting in a Pending state, wait a few more minutes and refresh the page. Sometimes it can take a few minutes for ECS to get set up with the image. Once the task is in a Running state, click the link under the Task column to pull up the task details. On the task detail page, you will see a link next to a field called EC2 Instance ID. Click the link to be taken to the EC2 Instance Manager. This is the EC2 instance where the dask-scheduler container is running! The public DNS name and public IP can be used to connect to the scheduler from outside AWS, such as when you want to log in to the monitoring dashboard. Copy down the public DNS name because we'll open the diagnostic dashboard after we've connected the workers to the cluster. An example of this information is shown in figure 11.47.

Now we're ready to deploy the images for dask-worker and dask-notebook! To do this, follow the exact same steps you followed to deploy and launch the dask-scheduler image, using the Dockerfiles in the worker and notebook folders, respectively. However, when creating the task definition and services for each, note a few exceptions in the configuration:

- **For the dask-worker image**
  - The Port mappings on the Add Container screen should be set to 8000 tcp instead of 8786 tcp and 8787 tcp.
  - The Number of Tasks field on the Step 1 screen of the Create Service wizard should be set to **6** instead of 1.
- **For the dask-notebook image**
  - The Network Mode drop-down box on the Step 2 screen of the Create Task Definition wizard should be set to Default instead of Host.
  - The Port mappings on the Add Container screen should be set to 8888 tcp instead of 8786 tcp and 8787 tcp.

Task status: (Running) Stopped

▼ *Filter in this page*		
Task	**Task Definition**	**Last status**
650cb303-dcd4-47c2-bfbc-6c746bf0d7af	dask-scheduler:3	RUNNING

Figure 11.46   Example of a running task

Public DNS (IPv4)	ec2-18-206-138-72.compute-1.amazonaws.com
IPv4 Public IP	18.206.138.72
IPv6 IPs	-
Private DNS	ip-10-0-1-240.ec2.internal (2)
Private IPs	10.0.1.240

Figure 11.47   Example IP and DNS information of an EC2 instance

Once you've verified that you have one running instance of the dask-scheduler service, one running instance of the dask-notebook service, and six running instances of the dask-worker service, we can connect to the cluster and begin running some jobs.

Service discovery: how the workers find the scheduler

One of the challenges posed by working in a cloud environment is that many aspects of infrastructure are transient. For example, when an EC2 instance starts up, it's not guaranteed to have the same IP address as it did the previous time it was running. This can make it tricky to avoid making our cluster's configuration fragile. If, for instance, we hard coded an IP address for our scheduler into the workers' configuration files, we would have to ensure that the scheduler's IP address always matched the configuration file. In the event the scheduler's IP address changed, the workers would no longer be able to talk to the scheduler without having their configuration files updated.

Service discovery solutions attempt to circumvent this issue by creating a well-known location, such as a database or a file on a shared filesystem and using that location to store information about which IP addresses and ports are hosting a service (kind of like a phone book). In our cluster, we're using a very simple form of service discovery to advertise the IP address of the scheduler. When the scheduler process starts up, it will write its hostname to a file called .scheduler in the shared EFS filesystem. When the worker and notebook images start up, they will read this shared file and configure themselves to talk to the scheduler at the location specified in the file. More sophisticated service discovery solutions are out there, such as Consul and Amazon's own ECS Service Discovery platform (which is, unfortunately, not available on AWS Free Tier), but for simplicity's sake, we've opted to use this file-based solution.

That said, make sure the dask-scheduler service always starts up before the dask-worker and dask-notebook services, since they depend on reading the location of dask-scheduler from the shared file.

11.1.8 Connecting to the cluster

The dask-notebook image contains a Jupyter Notebook server, which we'll use to interact with our Dask cluster. When Dask is running in cluster mode, it also offers some additional diagnostics tools that show how workloads are being distributed over the cluster. This is useful to see if a worker has gotten stuck, or to generally track the progress of a job. Before connecting to the notebook server, we'll take a look at the diagnostics page. To access the diagnostics page on your Dask cluster, open a web browser and type `http://<your scheduler hostname>:8787`, replacing <your scheduler hostname> with the public DNS value you copied down two pages ago. When the page loads, click Workers on the top menu. You should see a screen similar to figure 11.48.

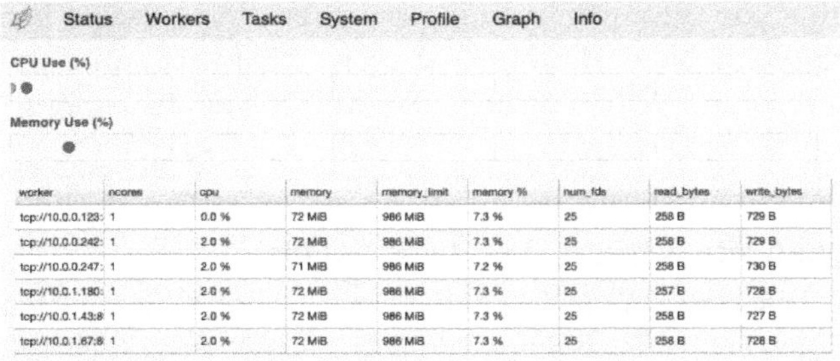

Figure 11.48   Dask cluster worker status

You should see six rows in the table. These correspond with each worker in the cluster. You can see each worker's current CPU usage, memory usage, and network activity. This page is useful to keep an eye on the overall health of the workers. Keep this window open because we'll come back to it later in the chapter.

Finally, we'll connect to the notebook server. To do this, look up the public DNS name of the dask-notebook container by following the steps you took to find the public DNS name for the dask-scheduler container. Once you've copied the public DNS name for the notebook server, open a web browser and type `http://<your notebook hostname>:8888` in the address bar, replacing <your notebook hostname> with the public DNS name you copied. Your screen should look similar to figure 11.49.

To look up the login token, go back to your web browser window where you're logged in to the AWS Console and go to the ECS Dashboard. Navigate to the task details for the currently running task in the dask-notebook service, then click the Logs tab. Your screen should look similar to figure 11.50.

We configured every task definition to send logs to AWS CloudWatch, so we're able to access the raw logs for any running container through the ECS Dashboard. If you ever need more insight into what's happening behind the scenes for a particular service, take a look at the logs. By default, Jupyter prints the login token in the logs when it starts up. Scroll down until you find the log entry lines that contain the login token. Copy this value and paste it into the Jupyter login window, then click Log In. Your screen should look similar to figure 11.51.

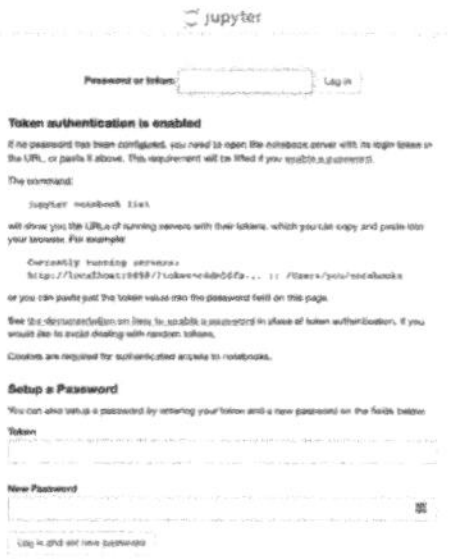

Figure 11.49   Jupyter login screen

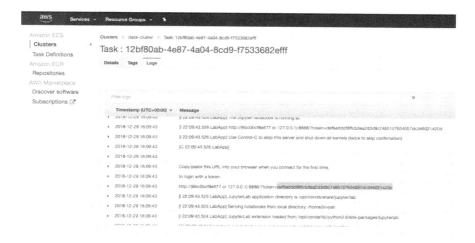

Figure 11.50   Task logging screen

Figure 11.51   The Jupyter Lab window

From here, we're ready to start running code on the cluster! In the next section, we'll have a look at how to upload notebooks to the notebook server and monitor the execution of jobs on the cluster.

11.2   *Running and monitoring Dask jobs on a cluster*

For this section, we'll return to the sentiment classifier problem we looked at in chapter 10 through the following scenario:

> *Using the Amazon Fine Foods dataset, build a sentiment classifier model using the Dask cluster in AWS and monitor the execution of the jobs.*

For the sake of brevity, the chapter 11 notebook is an abbreviated excerpt of the chapter 10 notebook. Rather than running the full process from raw data to a complete sentiment classifier model, the data you uploaded to EFS in the previous section contains the ZARR files that were generated in chapter 10. Therefore, the chapter 11 notebook is just a short example of building the classifier model from the preprocessed data, highlighting the minor differences necessary to run the code on the cluster. After walking through the chapter 11 notebook, you will be able to modify any of the notebooks from previous chapters to run on your cluster if you so desire. To begin, upload the chapter 11 notebook to your Jupyter Notebook server.

On the Jupyter Notebook server home screen, click the up-arrow icon in the file explorer pane, right under the Settings menu. The location of this button is shown in figure 11.52.

Navigate to the location of the chapter 11 notebook and click Upload. After a few seconds, you should see the notebook appear in the file explorer pane beneath the work folder. Double-click the notebook to open it in a new tab. As mentioned before, the code in this notebook is exactly the same as chapter 10. Only two differences allow the code to run on the cluster: using the Distributed Client interface, and a small change to the filesystem path where the ZARR files are stored.

The Distributed Client interface is the key to making the code run on the cluster rather than running locally on the notebook server.

Listing 11.2   Initializing the Distributed Client

```
from dask.distributed import Client, progress
client = Client()
client
```

Figure 11.52   Uploading a notebook to the Jupyter Notebook server

All we need to do in this case is simply initialize the Client. After this code executes, any compute-type Dask methods (such as `compute`, `head`, and so on) will be sent to the cluster rather than executed locally. We can, optionally, pass an IP address and port for the scheduler to the Client object, but in this case it's unnecessary. This is because the Dockerfile change that you made for the notebook server image in the previous section was adding an environment variable that holds the URI for the scheduler. In the absence of an explicitly passed scheduler URI in the `Client` constructor, it will read the value of the `DASK_SCHEDULER_ADDRESS` environment variable. After executing this code, you should see a result similar to figure 11.53.

This information shows that six workers are in the Dask cluster, just as we should expect! Now we can run any Dask code and it will execute on the cluster.

The second change made to the notebook for the cluster is in the second cell.

Listing 11.3   Changing the file paths for the data

```
from dask import array as da
feature_array = da.from_zarr('/data/sentiment_feature_array.zarr')
target_array = da.from_zarr('/data/sentiment_target_array.zarr')
```

As you can see, the data files being referenced are in the /data folder. This is because the mountpoint we set up in the task definitions in the last section exposes the /efs folder from the EC2 instances to the /data folder inside the containers. This means any data you copy to the /efs folder on one of the EC2 instances will instantly be available to your notebook server and workers in their /data folder. If you want to analyze other datasets on your cluster, use the steps you followed to upload the *arrays.tar* file to EFS using SCP in the previous section.

Lastly, before you execute the remaining cells in the notebook, go back to the Dask diagnostics window and click the Status link on the top menu. The Status page provides detailed information about the execution of Dask jobs. Once you have that page visible, execute the remaining cells in the notebook. This will kick off the process to build the sentiment classifier model on the cluster, and you will be able to see the details of that process on the diagnostics page. An example of the diagnostics page is shown in figure 11.54.

Figure 11.53   Client statistics for the cluster

Figure 11.54   An example of the Dask diagnostics page

Four sections of the Status page provide different information about the progression of the job through the cluster:

- Memory pressure
- Worker-level task queue
- Task stream
- Progress

Starting from the top-left, under Bytes stored, is the memory pressure information. The number of bytes stored lets us know how much data is being held in memory globally across the cluster. This number will generally fluctuate up and down as data processes. The graph shows the memory pressure for each worker. A blue bar signifies the worker has plenty of memory to spare, whereas a yellow bar signifies the worker is running out of memory and may have to spill data to disk. If you have jobs that run slowly or crash randomly, keep an eye on the memory pressure to ensure workers aren't running out of memory. If workers are consistently under a lot of memory pressure, it may be a good idea to repartition your dataset and increase the number of partitions. Smaller chunks of data will fit in memory easier and lowers the need to spill to disk.

Below the memory pressure graph is the worker-level task queue section. This shows a simple count of the number of tasks that are currently queued up to execute on each worker based on the scheduler's current execution plan. A blue bar indicates an acceptable number of tasks in queue, whereas a red bar indicates the worker is being starved for work. This typically happens when one worker has a dependency on some data that another worker is working on. Generally, tasks should be spread out evenly across workers. If one worker has a much higher number of tasks in queue than other workers, there may be something wrong with that worker that's causing it to process more slowly than other workers. It would be a good idea to check and see if another process outside of Dask is running on that worker or if it is having other performance issues.

To the right of the worker-level task queue section is the job progress section. This shows how many tasks are pending, how many have completed, and if any errors occurred. The progress bars will fill up over time as the job nears completion. Any errored tasks will be retried on another worker.

Finally, above the job progress section is the task stream section. This shows how long each task is taking to complete on each worker. The colors of the bars correlate to the color of the progress bars. For example, if a `pandas_read` task has a green progress bar, the duration of `pandas_read` tasks will show up in the task stream as green bars. This can be used to spot inefficiencies in slow jobs. If a certain type of operation is taking a long time, it may be possible to refactor your code to be more efficient. It can also be used to help spot performance issues with individual workers similar to the worker-level task queue. For example, if a worker is regularly taking 100 ms to complete a `pandas_read` task and other workers are only taking 50 ms per task, there may be something wrong with that particular worker causing it to slow down.

An alternative way to view the task stream is by viewing the underlying DAG (directed acyclic graphs). The diagnostic dashboard actually lets you view the underlying DAG in real-time as the job processes. To view the DAG, click the Graph link on the top menu. An example of the Graph page is shown in figure 11.55.

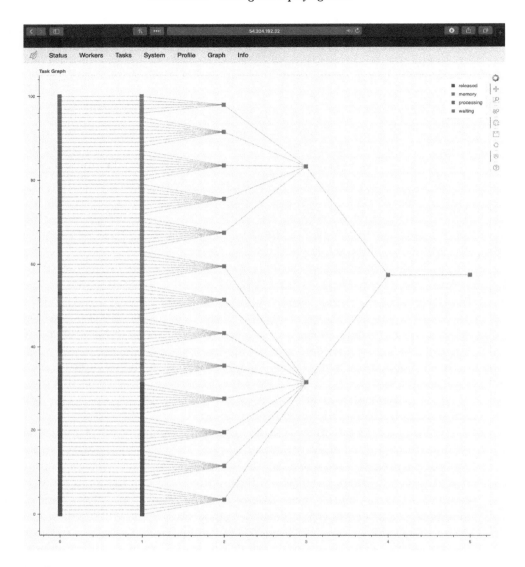

Figure 11.55   Real-time DAG view

The DAGs on this page are always read from left to right. Green blocks indicate a task that's currently processing. Gray blocks indicate tasks that are waiting for upstream dependencies, such as the blocks to the right side of the graph. Red blocks indicate tasks that have completed, and their result is being held in memory. All upstream dependencies of a downstream task will be held in memory until the downstream task has finished processing. At that point, the data from the upstream tasks will be released from memory, and the blocks will turn blue.

11.3 Cleaning up the Dask cluster on AWS

The last thing we'll cover is how to clean up the services in AWS. As mentioned earlier in the chapter, AWS uses usage-based billing. This means, for example, that whenever an EC2 instance is put into a Running state, AWS starts timing how long the EC2 instance has been up for and charges per minute of usage. The AWS Free Tier includes 750 hours of EC2 usage per month. With eight EC2 instances up in our cluster configuration, this uses eight hours of time per clock hour that the instances are up. This means that the cluster can be kept online for 93 hours, or just under four days, without incurring charges. Fortunately, you can easily turn the cluster on and off using the Auto Scaling Group we configured earlier in the chapter.

To shut down the EC2 instances, simply return to the EC2 Dashboard in AWS Console, click Auto Scaling Groups under the Auto Scaling heading in the left side menu. Then, select the auto scaling group for the ECS cluster (there should still only be one), and click Edit. In the Desired Capacity field, change the 8 to a 0 and click Save. Your screen should look similar to figure 11.56.

After a few minutes, the EC2 instances will begin shutting down. You can verify this by checking the EC2 Instances Manager and observing that the running EC2 instances are now either in a Shutting Down or Terminated state. To start the cluster back up later, you can simply change the Desired Capacity from 0 back to 8 (or whatever number of instances you'd like to bring up).

The other services to consider are EFS and ECR. Since these are both storage services, they are billed based on the size of storage being consumed. As long as you don't upload more than 5 GB total of data to the /efs folder, you will stay within the Free Tier limits for EFS.

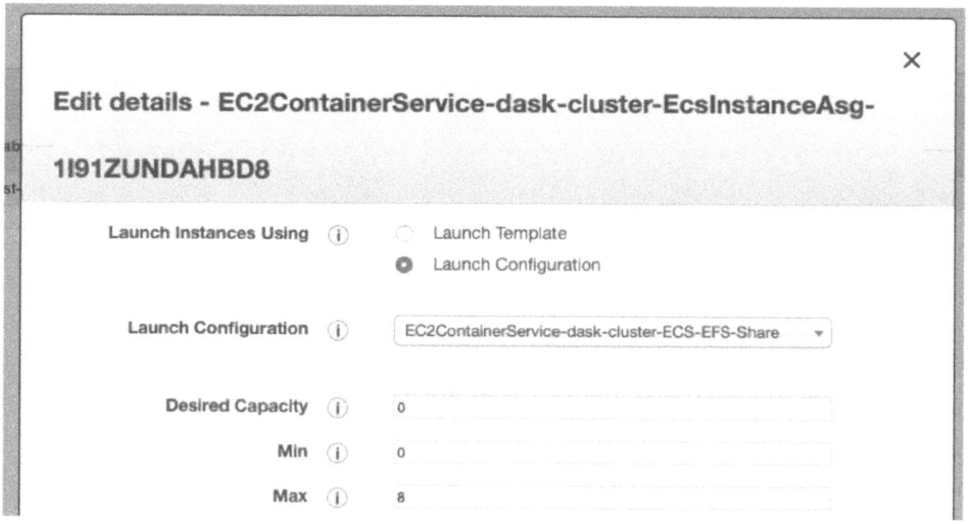

Figure 11.56   Shutting down the EC2 auto scaling group

Unfortunately, ECR is a bit more restrictive. The Free Tier limit for ECR is 500 MB per month. Storage on a per-month basis means an average of the storage used over a month is calculated, and if that average exceeds 500 MB, then there will be billable charges for usage. The total space consumed by the three Dask cluster images is about 2 GB, so if these images are left in ECR for more than about a week, you will exceed the ECR Free Tier limits. Based on ECR pricing of $0.10-per-GB/month for storage, it would cost $0.20 to store the images in ECR for the entire month. If you want to avoid all billable charges, you must delete the ECR repositories when you are finished with the exercise. You can do this from the ECR Repository Manager screen. However, this unfortunately means that if you wish to resume working with the cluster at a later time, you will have to re-deploy the images and re-create the ECS services.

Once you've shut down the EC2 instances and removed the ECR repositories, all usage-based billing will be stopped.

Summary

- A Dask cluster can be built in the cloud using Amazon AWS, Docker, and ECS, allowing you to easily scale the size of the cluster based on your workload's needs.
- Jobs are submitted to a Dask cluster using the distributed task scheduler client. The distributed task scheduler divides up and organizes the work across the entire cluster and ships the results back to the end user.
- The distributed task scheduler has a diagnostics page that runs on port 8787, allowing you to monitor the execution of jobs and identify problems with the cluster.
- EC2 Auto Scaling groups can be used to quickly boot up and shut down the cluster, allowing you to control resource costs and easily clean up when you're finished.

appendix
Software installation

To run the code notebooks and follow along with the examples in *Data Science with Python and Dask*, you should have the following software installed on your system:

- Python 2.7.14 or above or Python 3.6.5 or above (Python 3.6.5 or above is strongly recommended)
- The following Python packages:
  - IPython
  - Jupyter
  - Dask (version 1.0.0 or higher)
  - Dask ML
  - NLTK
  - Holoviews
  - Geoviews
  - Graphviz
  - Pandas
  - NumPy
  - Matplotlib
  - Seaborn
  - Bokeh
  - PyArrow
  - SQLAlchemy
  - Dill

The easiest way to install and maintain all necessary Python packages is to download the free Python distribution, Anaconda, available at www.anaconda.com/download. The Anaconda distribution is available for Windows, macOS, and most major Linux distributions. If you've installed Anaconda, all the required packages will be included with the installer except for graphviz and pyarrow. To install graphviz and pyarrow, follow the directions in section A.1. Otherwise, if you wish to install all packages from scratch, please follow the directions in section A.2.

A.1   Installing additional packages with Anaconda

If you've already installed the Anaconda distribution, you will need to install graphviz and pyarrow. If you've set up a virtual environment specifically for working with the examples, make sure you activate it before running the installation commands. Open a command prompt or terminal window and type the following commands.

> **Listing A.1 Installing graphviz and pyarrow**

```
conda install -c conda-forge pyarrow
conda install -c conda-forge dill
conda install graphviz
conda install python-graphviz
```

That's it! You're now all set to run the example notebooks.

A.2   Installing packages without Anaconda

If you prefer to install the packages without using a distribution like Anaconda, you can do so using pip. However, it is strongly recommended to use Anaconda because you may run into some compiler/runtime dependency issues when building packages from pip (for example, NumPy historically required a FORTRAN compiler to build). To get the appropriate packages, run the following commands in a command prompt or terminal window.

> **Listing A.2 Installing packages from source using pip**

```
pip install ipython jupyter dask graphviz python-graphviz pandas numpy
    matplotlib seaborn bokeh pyarrow sqlalchemy holoviews geoviews dask-ml
    nltk dill
```

Once installation is complete, you should be able to start a Jupyter Notebook server and run all the example notebooks.

A.3   Starting a Jupyter Notebook server

You can start a Jupyter Notebook server to run the accompanying code Notebooks by opening a terminal or Command Prompt and typing `jupyter notebook`, and then pressing Enter. Your default web browser should open after a few seconds and automatically navigate to the Jupyter home page. Make sure you leave the terminal window open while you work, because closing the window will cause the notebook server to terminate.

A.4 Configuring NLTK

For the examples in chapters 9 and 10, you will need to download some additional data for NLTK. To do this, run the following command in your terminal window.

Listing A.3 Downloading NLTK data

```
python -m nltk.downloader all
```

If you run into issues, try running the command with elevated privileges (either using sudo on a Unix/Linux/MacOS system or running Command Prompt as Administrator in Windows). After running this command, you are ready to use NLTK.

index